Nerys Purchon's
handbook of
natural healing

Nerys Purchon was born in Wales and grew up knowing the name and use of every root, seed, plant and berry growing near her home. Since migrating to Australia, Nerys has, among other things, run a herb-growing business, conducted courses on whole-food cookery and written six books.

Also by Nerys Purchon

Herbcraft
Bodycraft
Foodcraft
Aromatherapy
Jams and Preserves
Aromatherapy Secrets

Nerys Purchon's
handbook of
natural healing

A SUE HINES BOOK
ALLEN & UNWIN

Important Notice

The advice in this book is general and not specific to individuals
and particular circumstances. Before using herbs or treatments check
all cautions and restrictions. Neither the author nor the publishers
can be held responsible for any injury, damage or otherwise resulting
from the use of any treatments in this book. Do not try self-diagnosis
or attempt self-treatment for long periods of serious problems
without first consulting a qualified medical practitioner. Always
seek professional medical advice if symptoms persist.

2000/1178   0000078775
 # 3883269

First published in 1998
A Sue Hines Book
Allen & Unwin Pty Ltd
9 Atchison Street
St Leonards, NSW 2065 Australia
Phone: (61 2) 9901 4088
Fax: (61 2) 9906 2218
E-mail: frontdesk@allen-unwin.com.au
URL: http://www.allen-unwin.com.au

National Library of Australia
Cataloguing-in-Publication entry:

Purchon, Nerys.
Nerys Purchon's handbook of natural healing.
Bibliography.
ISBN 1 86448 645 7.
1. Naturopathy. I. Title. II. Title: Handbook of natural healing.
615.535

Designed by Ruth Grüner
Illustration of dandelion by Dhenu Jennifer Clary
Typeset by J & M Typesetting
Printed by Australian Print Group, Maryborough, Victoria

1 3 5 7 9 10 8 6 4 2

Front cover: Garry Moore

THIS BOOK IS FOR MY GRANDCHILDREN.
To Garrick the Leo, the handsome and special 'first grandchild'; Marney the funny, lovely and dramatic Sagittarian who complains bitterly that her name isn't in any of my books (you can stop agonising now Marney); Leon the Virgoan with a very big and very warm heart; Tammy the beautiful Taurean, the animal and Earth lover who reads my books and loves the essential oils; Amara the dainty Aquarian princess who likes order and beauty (and who also loves the essential oils); Luca another splendid Virgoan who has faith and always (may the gods bless him) maintains that 'Ma knows best' and to Rhiannon, a baby Scorpio and the youngest member of the clan. The privilege of being present at her birth was one of the highlights of my life.

Contents

Foreword

If you want to take responsibility for your health in your own hands, then this is the book for you. It reads, 'Treated with proper respect, the human body is wonderfully equipped to repel disease and invading organisms'. But you have to get personally involved—and this is a step that only you can take. Accept this responsibility and the process of healing is already more than half-accomplished.

Nerys Purchon's Handbook of Natural Healing makes it easy to find an appropriate treatment plan for what ails you. If the problem persists there are warnings to see your physician or other health professionals. The treatments make it possible to work hand-in-hand with your doctor—he or she might want to have this book as a reference! I firmly believe that allopathic and alternative medicines have much to offer each other, and already, this cooperation is beginning to happen. It can happen for you if you make a firm choice.

Wellness is also about preventative measures—eating well, sleeping and exercising sufficiently, managing stress and supplementing your diet when your lifestyle demands it.

This book encourages you to ask questions about yourself and provides answers through an abundance of interesting material. Readers will find many jewels in the form of tricks and tips that will enhance their lives and the lives of their families and friends.

Instilled into these pages is a lifetime of experience and wisdom that makes riveting reading even if you are not sick. I am sure that *Nerys Purchon's Handbook of Natural Healing* will become one of the great healing manuals to which you will constantly refer and that will be passed down from you to your children.

Satyen Schmitz, M.D.

Preface

I grew up in north Wales where all the remedies needed for health, healing and beautifying were readily available in the fields, streams and hedgerows. The air and soil were unpolluted and the water was pure. The vegetables we ate were grown in the garden without the use of pesticides, herbicides and other toxic chemicals. Meat and fish were caught in the wild where they had grown to maturity without being dosed with antibiotics or sprayed with chemicals. Houses were cleaned with simple carbolic soap, hot water and lots of 'elbow-grease'! Life was simple and wholesome.

North and west Wales have a particularly long tradition of herbal knowledge. In his book *Medical Herbalism* David Hoffman (see the bibliography) says, 'The origins of these mixtures lies in the medieval physicians of Myddfai from the courts of the princes of Wales. A deep and profound knowledge of herbs and the healing process was possessed by these people, well in advance of what was available in England and the rest of non-Islamic Europe at the time'. This knowledge was passed to the rural people after the invasion of Wales by the English and the destruction of the courts. The knowledge has been passed from generation to generation and still survives today. My passion for herbs has been handed down from my forebears and remains in my heart to this day.

These days we have many domestic labour-saving devices denied to our grandparents. Sophisticated cleaning materials, washing machines, vacuum cleaners and food processors, for example, give us more hours to pursue careers and hobbies, but in many ways our quality of life hasn't improved. Personal stress levels have certainly become much higher with an accelerated pace of life. People live longer without being healthier, in fact, many diseases once treatable by antibiotics are now resistant to these drugs, leaving us more vulnerable to disease than we have ever been. In the next century, antibiotic drugs may be useful and interesting treatments that were abused until they became valueless.

Treated with proper respect and care, the human body is naturally equipped to repel disease and invading organisms. We often deny the body its natural function, however, and destroy many of its natural defences by over-eating fat-laden food, by indiscriminate use of toxic chemicals, wearing artificial clothing materials, using antibiotics and other drugs.

Modern drugs have their place in medicine, but it is more appropriate instead to build up and enhance the natural defences of the body and enable it to heal itself and to use alternative and orthodox healing methods in conjunction with each other.

Ten years ago, alternative healing methods were generally viewed with some suspicion but now there are millions of people who will testify that these methods work, preferring to try a cup of peppermint tea rather than to take an aspirin to ease a headache or to try meditation rather than risk becoming addicted to substances like Valium to ease stress.

This book does not take the place of professional help. If you have a sudden and severe health problem or a long-term one, then consult a health professional and perhaps use natural remedies as a complementary treatment. Cancer patients, for instance, ideally need to be able to take advantage of any known means of treatment. Meditation, diet, aromatherapy and herbs are now recognised as valuable adjuncts to orthodox medical cancer treatments and sometimes have helped to alleviate unpleasant effects of the orthodox treatment.

We all need to learn to take more responsibility for our own health instead of handing that responsibility to others. We need to look at our lifestyle and decide to make changes, instead of taking medications to mask the underlying problem. Swallowing Valium won't *cure* stress. The source of the stress needs to be identified and adjusted. Indigestion won't be cured by swallowing antacid tablets. Eating habits need to be examined and possibly changed; if this doesn't work, then a visit to a health professional is indicated. Headaches won't be cured by popping an aspirin. Instead consider professional help to problems with eyesight, digestion, nerves or spinal maladjustment.

In this book you will find not only suggestions for the alleviation of a symptom but methods for helping the body to find a long-term solution. I would repeat that if a problem is very severe or long-term then self-help is not appropriate as some symptoms can mask more serious complaints.

If this all sounds very serious, the following pages also offer many fun ways of utilising herbs and essential oils to enhance your life and at the same time to save money. You will be able to throw out the cans and bottles of toxic insect repellents and killers, poisonous cleaning agents, hair sprays, artificial air fresheners and garden sprays. These all help lower our resistance to disease by undermining the strength of our immune systems rather than build health.

Using the recipes will profoundly change your life and in return for a modest outlay of money, the quality of your whole life and of those around you will be enriched and improved.

Acknowledgements

Once again I thank my husband Prakash who fills so many roles so willingly. He has been a patient researcher throughout the writing of this book and in addition has taken over all the 'domestics' in order to free me. Philippa Sandall (my sometime publisher and now friend, agent and editor) who always makes time to listen to my insecurities and who is unfailingly positive and humorous. Rebecca, my youngest daughter, a psychologist who gave her insight and expertise to the sections on grief and pain. Greta, our eldest daughter, for happily and efficiently keeping our business wheels so well oiled! Frances Sorenson, a homeopath and friend, who generously used her knowledge to edit the homeopathic sections in the book. Nirala, my dear friend, who is and always has been reliably there for anything I need. Last and certainly not least, I would like to acknowledge my debt (and the debt of all students who study essential oils) to Robert Tisserand. I have drawn heavily on his expertise for the last twenty years and the section in this book on safe usage of essential oils has been enriched by his painstaking research and that of Tony Balacs (see the bibliography).

Introductory Notes

Only the herbs and oils used in treatments are included and described in this book, listed and described under their common name. I have tried to only use herbs and oils that are readily available. If you can't get a herb or oil specified in a remedy, you may be able to use a substitute by carefully checking the lists of properties and choosing another herb or oil with the same properties.

Wherever possible I prefer to use herbal remedies in tincture or liquid-extract form rather than tablets. Tinctures or liquid extracts are very stable, contain no fillers, and the remedy begins to be absorbed in the mouth and is more quickly available to the body. Ask for tinctures or liquid extracts at your health-food shop—an increasing number of companies are offering herbal remedies in this form.

The cautions regarding buying herbs (see Herbalism & Herbs) are also applicable to essential oils. (See Aromatherapy & Essential Oils, Extraction of essential oils.) Since the art and practice of using essential oils has become so popular there are increasing numbers of unscrupulous people selling poor quality or even synthetic oils as 100 per cent pure essential oils—buyers beware.

All supplements should be taken before the main meal of the day unless otherwise indicated. A list of vitamins and minerals and foods which contain them is included under Vitamins and Minerals. If a health problem is only mild, increased consumption of these foods may be adequate to correct existing nutritional imbalances but if the problem is chronic, that is, of long-standing duration or is moderately severe, a course of supplements may be needed as a part of the treatment to effect a quicker response.

It should be noted that vitamins do not replace food and that a 'junk-food' diet containing a lot of unsaturated fats and sugar will not be enhanced by consuming lots of vitamins and minerals.

Homeopathic remedies (see Homeopathy) of low potencies 6–30^C are suitable for *acute* illnesses (those which come to a crisis and are relatively short lived) and home use. The number of doses taken daily depend on the severity of the complaint, for example, high fevers would require, say, Belladonna every 15 minutes until the symptoms lessen, then hourly until the fever is gone and the patient has recovered. If symptoms recur, commence the treatment again.

Never stop taking prescribed medication suddenly. Cut down on your doses slowly and only after discussion with your health professional. If you go to a doctor unsympathetic to your wish to try natural methods of healing, it may be wiser to find another doctor who is more supportive and open to using complementary healing methods.

Natural remedies usually take longer to work than pharmaceutical drugs (with the exception of first-aid remedies). If a problem is a long-standing one it may take six to eight weeks before a change is seen. Perservere and be patient—the gain will be worth the wait.

Homeopathic remedies taken as either drops or pillules should be placed under the tongue and held in the mouth for as long as possible before swallowing. Wherever possible, avoid taking remedies within half an hour of taking other medicine, cleaning teeth, using tobacco, drinking tea or coffee or eating food.

If you already have some of the remedies in your medicine box but they aren't the same potency as that described, don't rush out to buy more. Any potency from 6–30^C is suitable for home use. Single remedies aren't usually available in health-food shops but may be obtained from a homeopathic practitioner or by mail order from one of the suppliers listed (see Suppliers at the back of this book).

Note: If 1 teaspoon (5 ml) or 1 capsule is the recommended then taking 2 capsules will definitely *not* be better!

It's not suggested that you use *all* the remedies suggested at the same time. Each person is different and reacts differently to remedies. Try the ones that are suited to you and *give them a chance!*

Never lose sight of the fact that this is *your* body and that its ultimate wellness or dis-ease is largely dependent on you and how you treat it.

Constitutional medicine is prescribed on the basis of the temperament and character of the patient. Homeopathic remedies are prescribed with regard to both the constitution of the patient and the symptoms that are presented. Users of this book can cross-check remedies for individual problems with the profile entry for the particular remedy.

The remedies recommended in this book are 6^C or 30^C potency. *Potency* refers to the number of times the homeopathic remedy has been diluted and succussed (shaken) or triturated (ground). The process used is that of successive dilution. One part of the chosen material is mixed with 99 parts of water or water and alcohol and the mixture is then succussed. One part of this diluted mixture is again diluted in the same manner and the process may be repeated until the final desired dilution is achieved—this can be up to 100 000 times. If a remedy is labelled with an x it means that the dilution was one part chosen material to 9 parts water or alcohol and water, 6^x or 30^x would therefore be a lower potency than 6^C or 30^C.

In the case of serious, long-standing or complex complaints you will notice that I recommend a visit to a homeopathic practitioner who may prescribe higher potencies. For less serious conditions, the lower potencies of 6^C or 30^C are very effective and may be used with safety.

Remedies are sold in tablet or tincture form. If you purchase tablets, it's important not to touch them with your fingers. Shake the tablets into the lid of the container and tip them into your mouth without touching the container. Similarly, if using a tincture, don't allow the end of the glass dropper to come in contact with the tongue. Store the remedies in a cool place away from strong-smelling items such as essential oils.

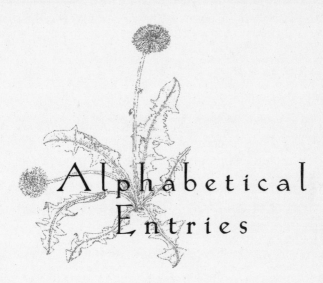

Alphabetical
Entries

Abrasions

A healthy body has a remarkable capacity for healing wounds such as abrasions and cuts, so often there is no need for any treatment other than an initial cleansing. Unless the wound is bleeding profusely or is in an area that will be exposed to dirt, it is best to leave the wound uncovered.

Young children are often accident-prone. Immediate treatment is needed when emergencies such as abrasions, minor burns, bruises and cuts occur. Herbal ice cubes (see Herbal ice cubes) provide an instant treatment rather than having to spend time making and cooling an infusion. For abrasions and cuts drop a herbal ice cube in a little boiled water and when it is melted use the liquid to swab the wound clean.

To treat minor burns and bruises, wrap the ice cube in clean cloth and apply to the injured area. If herbal ice cubes aren't available, use the Healing Blend (page 4).

ESSENTIAL OIL TREATMENT

ANTISEPTIC BLEND
2 drops lavender oil
2 drops tea-tree oil
1 drop lemon oil
1/2 cup (125 ml) boiled water

TO MAKE: *Add the oils to the water and stir well.*

TO USE: *Swab the wound gently with cotton wool dipped in the water.*
Leave the wound uncovered if possible. If a plaster is needed, use
1 drop of either lavender or tea-tree oil on the plaster or use healing
ointment (see Ointments).

HERBAL TREATMENT

HEALING BLEND

1 tablespoon (20 ml) distilled witch-hazel
1 cup (250 ml) cooled strong calendula tea or
1 teaspoon (5 ml) calendula tincture (see Tinctures)
TO MAKE: *Mix together and use to wash dirt from the abrasion.*
Smooth aloe vera gel or calendula ointment (see Ointments) over the
area and cover with a non-stick dry dressing if needed.

Abscesses

An abscess is a localised pus-filled cavity created by bacterial invasion. Frequent occurrences would indicate a compromised immune system (see Immune system) and steps should be taken to improve general health. See also Breasts and Bruises.

INTERNAL TREATMENT

✺ Drink 8 glasses (2 litres) filtered or bottled water a day.
✺ Eat a diet rich in fresh fruits and vegetables, wholegrain breads, cereals and other fibre foods.
✺ Avoid red meat—eat fish and free-range chicken instead.
✺ Drink 1 cup (250 ml) dandelion coffee (from health-food store) 3 times a day.

DAILY SUPPLEMENTS

✺ 1000 mg garlic oil capsules 3 times daily (or 2–3 teaspoons 'Long-life juice' 3 times daily).
✺ ½ teaspoon (2.5 ml) fluid extract of echinacea 3 times daily until the abscess has healed, then once a day for 3–4 weeks.

❀ 2000 mg vitamin C with bioflavonoids
3 times daily for 1 week, then once daily.

ESSENTIAL OIL TREATMENT

FOMENTATION BLEND

3 drops lavender oil

4 drops tea-tree oil

Small bowl hot water

TO MAKE: *Let the oils float over the surface of the water.*

TO USE: *Apply a fomentation (see Fomentations) every 2–3 hours.*

HERBAL TREATMENT

Make a hot poultice (see Poultices) from slippery elm powder, ground comfrey root or mashed potato, apply as hot as can be borne. Re-apply every 2–3 hours.

HOMEOPATHIC TREATMENT

All remedies at 6–30^c potency, take 4 times daily:

❀ Intense and painful nerve endings—Hypericum.

❀ Abscess suppurated and slow to heal, sensitive but cold to touch—Silica.

❀ Unhealthy skin, abscess hot, throbbing and sensitive to touch—Hepar sulph.

Acidity ❦ See Heartburn, Indigestion

Acidophillus

Acidophillus or *Lactobacilus acidophillus*, to give it its correct name, is a source of helpful intestinal bacteria, available in 'live' yoghurt or in capsule form. Antibiotics destroy beneficial intestinal flora and this often causes diarrhoea and thrush. The use of acidophillus during antibiotic treatment can help to avoid these problems. Taking acidophillus regularly can eliminate many digestive problems of the

Did you know that in an emergency, a cobweb applied to a cut will stop the bleeding and prevent sepsis (the presence of pus-forming bacteria in the body)?

gastro-intestinal tract from bad breath to constipation/diarrhoea and excessively bad smelling flatulence.

Acne

Acne is a distressing and common skin complaint occurring mainly on the face but can also occur on the shoulders, chest and back. The condition is most common in male adolescents but can continue or begin in adults.

Blocked and overly active sebaceous ducts (usually at puberty) can lead to blackheads, pimples, acne, whiteheads and pustules. Secondary infections can cause even more problems so it's vitally important, although *very* difficult, not to 'finger' the spots.

To a teenager it is a major calamity to have spots. Scrupulous cleansing of the skin is important, but over-enthusiastic cleansing with harsh products can do more harm than good as the sebaceous glands will produce even more oil to counteract the cleansing.

Wash the skin 2–3 times a day with good quality soap containing glycerine, pat dry and use one of the following treatments to tone and moisturise (see also Pimples, Skin care).

INTERNAL TREATMENT

It's important to maintain intestinal health by avoiding constipation. Juhlin and Michaelsson reported in their 1983 study that half the patients suffering from severe acne had increased blood levels of toxins absorbed from the intestines.[1]

- Eat a wholesome diet including lots of fresh, unprocessed wholegrain bread and cereals, and lots of fruit and vegetables.
- Eat fish and free-range chicken in preference to red meat. Avoid spicy and refined foods. Drink 6–8 glasses of filtered or bottled water a day.
- Drink up to 3 cups dandelion coffee a day to help the liver to detoxify (available from health-food stores).

Daily supplements

- 20 000 iu beta-carotene.
- 2 vitamin B complex tablets, 1 morning and evening.
- 1000 mg vitamin C with bioflavonoids.
- 20 mg zinc.
- 1500 mg borage (starflower) oil or evening primrose oil.
- ½ teaspoon (2.5 ml) fluid extract of echinacea 3 times daily.

Essential oil treatment

TONING LOTION

½ cup (125 ml) rosewater
20 drops lavender oil
5 drops geranium oil
3 drops lemon oil
1000 iu or 2 × 500 iu vitamin E capsules
TO MAKE: *Bottle, shake well, and leave for a few days to blend. Shake well before use.*
TO USE: *Sprinkle a few drops on a dampened cotton ball and use it to freshen the skin after cleansing and during the day.*

Have you heard that recent studies show that tea-tree essential oil heals acne better than major commercial preparations and causes less drying and flaking of skin?

NIGHT MOISTURISER

3 tablespoons (60 ml) coconut oil
15 drops lavender oil
5 drops geranium oil
2 capsules borage (starflower) oil or evening primrose oil
TO MAKE: *Melt the coconut oil in a screw-top jar placed in a pan of hot water, don't overheat.*

Take off the heat, mix in the oils until well blended. Screw the lid firmly. Gently shake the jar every few minutes until cool to blend the oils together. Store in the refrigerator in hot weather.
TO USE: *Smooth a little on the skin every night after cleansing.*

Herbal treatment

🌿 Milk thistle as directed.

HERBAL FACE WASH

3 teaspoons dried or 6 teaspoons freshly chopped lavender heads

5 teaspoons dried or 10 teaspoons fresh calendula petals

2 cups (500 ml) boiling water

1 tablespoon (20 ml) distilled witch-hazel

2 capsules borage (starflower) oil or evening primrose oil

TO MAKE: *Pour the boiling water over the herbs. Cover closely. Stand for half an hour. Strain through cheesecloth, squeezing the cloth to extract as much liquid as possible.*

Strain through coffee-filter paper.

Add the distilled witch-hazel and borage (starflower) oil or evening primrose oil. Bottle and shake well. The mixture will keep refrigerated for 4–5 days but may be frozen in ice-cube trays and used as needed. One or two melted cubes should be sufficient for one day.

TO USE: *Shake the bottle well, sprinkle a few drops on cotton wool balls. Wipe gently over the face and throat. Use several times a day.*

HOMEOPATHIC TREATMENT

Take 3 times daily:

❋ Many hot and tender pustules—Hepar. sulph. 12^c or 30^c.

❋ Slow healing and scarring—Silica 12^c or 30^c.

Aconite (*Aconitum napellus*) ❋ Homeopathic

Suited to those who are suddenly panicky, despairing and fearful or in sudden pain.

USE TO TREAT

Animal bites, anxiety, asthma, bereavement, bronchitis, colds, coughs, fever, fainting, great pain, grief, injury, insomnia, laryngitis, surgery, travel sickness.

Actaea rac (*Actaea racemosa*) ❋ Homeopathic

USE TO TREAT

Claustrophobia, headache, heavy periods, neuralgia, painful muscles (following sport or exercise), rheumatic pains in back and neck, shooting pains, tinnitus.

AIDS (Acquired Immunodeficiency Syndrome)

HIV is the Human Immunodeficiency Virus which damages the immune system to the point where it can no longer fight infection. It is generally accepted that HIV is responsible for AIDS but that not everyone with HIV will necessarily develop full-blown AIDS. J.E. Groopman (1985) found that in AIDS, roughly 70–90 per cent of those infected with the HIV remain asymptomatic during the first 3–5 years of infection. Some remain healthy carriers, while others progress to ARC (Aids Related Complex), AIDS or death.[1]

There is at present no known cure for AIDS but alternative therapies aim at strengthening the immune system, inhibiting viruses and treating opportunistic infections when they occur with herbs and oils known to have antiviral activity. Social and emotional support is also vital for sufferers of this disease.

Some of the early symptoms of HIV are weight loss, heavy night sweats, general debility and fatigue, swollen glands, thrush, cold sores and mouth ulcers. Do not assume though that these symptoms indicate HIV as there are many other diseases (such as glandular fever) that present some of the same symptoms.

AIDS sufferers need much emotional and physical support and need to be encouraged to exercise moderately and to use both meditation and visualisation (see Relaxation) to help the body to reduce susceptibility and improve both the recovery rate from secondary infections and improve the quality of life. The immune system (see Immune system) needs to be boosted and supported and every effort made to inhibit the virus.

The suggestions here should be used in collaboration with conventional treatment. They should be used alone as a complete treatment.

INTERNAL TREATMENT

❀ Optimal nutrition becomes vitally important when the immune function is suppressed and antibiotics are being taken. The diet should be high in complex carbohydrates and fibre, low in fat and moderate in protein such as lean meat and fish.

❀ Foods rich in vitamin C with bioflavonoids, vitamin E (d-alpha tocopherol), B6, B12, pantothenic acid, folate (folic acid), beta-carotene, zinc and iron should be included in the daily diet (see Vitamins and Minerals). Extra supplementation of some of these nutrients are advisable (see Daily supplements below), particularly if the appetite is poor or if there is nausea.

❀ It's sometimes easier to eat six small meals (rather than three larger ones) per day and to include high-kilojoule drinks or fruit or vegetable juices in the diet.

❀ If you don't feel confident to design a suitable diet it might be wise to obtain the advice of a trained dietician.

❀ Alcohol and the use of nicotine or other recreational drugs should be curtailed or stopped.

Daily supplements

❀ 1 vitamin B complex tablet.

❀ 25 000 iu beta-carotene.

❀ 2000 mg vitamin C with bioflavonoids 3 times daily.

❀ 400 iu vitamin E (d-alpha tocopherol).

❀ 15 mg zinc.

❀ Omega-3 essential fatty acids as directed.

❀ 1000–4000 mg borage (starflower) oil or evening primrose oil.

❀ Vitamin B12 as directed (studies show a deficiency in 50 per cent of HIV-infected patients).[2]

❀ 100–200 mg selenium (studies show a reduced cardiac selenium content in AIDS patients).[3]

Essential oil treatment

A weekly massage from an aromatherapist and a daily massage would be very helpful for both physical and emotional support of the immune system. If this isn't possible, the following oil blends can be used in the bath or for a massage.

Aromatherapy massage must always be done in consultation with the doctor in charge of the patient's overall treatment.

IMMUNE BOOSTER BLEND

5 tablespoons (100 ml) vegetable oil

30 drops bergamot oil

30 drops manuka or tea-tree oil

20 drops rosewood oil

10 drops thyme oil

TO MAKE: *Mix the oils in a small bottle, shake well to blend. Leave for a few days to synergise (see Synergy).*

TO USE: *Pour 1–2 teaspoons into a hot bowl (the oil will warm to a pleasant temperature for use) and use to massage.*

Pour 2 teaspoonfuls into a bath, agitate to disperse and soak in the bath for 10–15 minutes, massage any floating oil droplets into the skin. Pat dry with a soft towel.

The essential oils (without the addition of the vegetable oil) may be used as an air spray or in an oil burner.

SPIRIT LIFTER

Helps to raise drooping spirits and has antiviral properties. It can be used by anyone suffering from depression or low spirits.

5 tablespoons (100 ml) vegetable oil

30 drops bergamot oil

30 drops grapefruit oil

20 drops sandalwood oil

10 drops lavender oil

TO MAKE: *Mix the oils in a small bottle, shake well to blend. Leave for a few days to synergise.*

TO USE: *Pour 1–2 teaspoons into a hot bowl (the oil will warm to a pleasant temperature) and use to massage.*

Pour 2 teaspoonfuls into a bath, agitate to disperse and soak in the bath for 10–15 minutes, massage any floating oil droplets into the skin. Pat dry with a soft towel.

The essential oils (without the addition of the vegetable oil)
may be used as an air spray or in an oil burner.

HERBAL TREATMENT

❧ Unfortunately, echinacea, which is a T-cell stimulator, may be
inappropriate in the treatment of AIDS since laboratory research
indicates that most agents which stimulate T-cells also increase
replication of the HIV virus.[4] Research is ongoing in this area.
Instead use: Golden seal as directed (see Golden seal).

❧ Astragalus as directed (see Astragalus).

❧ 1000 mg garlic 3 times daily or 2–3 teaspoons 'Long-life juice' 3
times daily.

❧ ¼ teaspoon fluid extract of liquorice 3 times daily. While taking
liquorice for an extended period, it's very important to increase
the intake of potassium-rich foods (see Vitamins and Minerals).

HOMEOPATHIC TREATMENT

Consult a homeopathic practitioner.

Air fresheners ❦ See also Perfumes & Colognes, Pot-pourris and Sachets

ESSENTIAL OIL RECIPES

The following essential oil recipes are for use in a 300 ml spray
bottle. These blends may be also used with a diffuser by adding a few
drops to the water.

BASIC BLEND

4–5 tablespoons (80–100 ml) cider vinegar or vodka

50 drops essential oils (less for children) see suggestions below

1 cup (250 ml) water

TO MAKE: *Mix the vinegar or vodka with essential oils. Shake well
and leave for a few minutes to blend. Add water. Shake to mix.*

Add ingredients for the specific blend required.

*Shake well before use. Don't spray directly on polished furniture
or delicate fabrics.*

CHILDREN'S BEDROOM

15 drops lavender oil

5 drops mandarin oil

ADULTS' BEDROOM

10 drops geranium oil

20 drops lavender oil

20 drops ylang-ylang oil

LIVING ROOM

20 drops bergamot oil

10 drops lavender oil

10 drops lemon oil

10 drops grapefruit oil

SICK ROOM

20 drops tea-tree oil

10 drops eucalyptus oil

10 drops lavender oil

10 drops lemon oil

Did you know that the ancient Greeks and Romans used lavender oil to tame wild animals and that it can also be used to calm aggression in humans?

HERBAL AIR FRESHENERS

A bowl or vase full of mixed herbs will give a fresh, inviting fragrance to the living room. Most herbs last for a long time after cutting. Mix as many as possible of the heavily scented herbs—geranium, lavender, rosemary, lemon verbena—and, for colour contrast, some grey herbs such as wormwood and southernwood.

Herbal vinegars (see Bath vinegars) may be used as air fresheners by diluting 4–5 tablespoons (80–100 ml) in 1 cup (250 ml) of water and using in a spray.

HERBAL CHAFING DISHES

A centuries' old method of releasing the fragrance of herbs to the air. They were, and still are, used in sickrooms to sweeten and disinfect the air. The pans should not be left unattended nor should they be allowed to dry out entirely.

Choose a shallow pan or heatproof dish and add water, a couple of teaspoons of sugar to each 2 cups (500 ml) of water, heavily scented herbs and, if liked, a few pinches of spice. The pan needs to be placed on a heat source such as a stove, open fire, plate warmer or a candle with a suitable container. As the water evaporates the perfume becomes stronger.

Essential oils may be used in place of herbs. The following recipes are only suggestions and may be replaced with other herbs or oils.

SOOTHING CHAFING DISH

2 cups (500 ml) water

2 teaspoons sugar

20 heads lavender, rose or jasmine flowers (or a mixture)

10 drops geranium oil (or fresh leaves)

DISINFECTANT CHAFING DISH

2 cups (500 ml) water

2 teaspoons sugar

20 heads lavender flowers or eucalyptus leaves

10 drops eucalyptus oil (or fresh leaves)

10 drops lemon oil (or fresh lemon peel)

Alcohol

In the context of this book, alcohol is used for making tinctures, astringents and dissolving essential oils. Ethanol is a 95 per cent proof alcohol which, used at various dilutions, is very suitable for these purposes. In Australia and Britain it's not possible to buy this alcohol unless you have a licence. Isopropyl (rubbing alcohol) is readily available but isn't suitable for internal use (as in preparations such as tinctures) and I find it too smelly and harsh when used in external preparations. The acceptable alternative is to use very high-proof alcohols such as brandy and vodka. Vodka has the advantage of being tasteless and odourless and some brands are very high proof.

Allergens

Allergies are an immune-system response to a substance. Sometimes the response is inherited, for example, a reaction to emotional stress; an intolerance to certain foods, metals, chemicals. Rather than accept that one has allergies it is appropriate to attempt to find the cause(s) and to eliminate it (them). Stress management and/or elimination of foods such as milk and wheat are often enough to cure the problem.

If you are allergy prone or sensitive to substances that are used on your skin it's wise to do an allergy test before spreading a particular substance over a large part of your body.

TO DO A 'PATCH TEST'

Take a small amount of the substance (ground herb, essential oil etc.) that you want to test, make a paste by mixing the substance with some water and place a thick smear inside your elbow. If the substance to test is an essential oil, mix 1 drop of the essential oil with 10 drops of vegetable oil, mix well and smear inside your elbow. Cover the area with a sticking plaster and leave for 24 hours. If, after this time, there is no soreness, redness or itching you can safely use the oil or other substance.

Aloe vera (*Aloe vera*)

HERB PART USED

Gel inside leaves.

HERB ACTIONS

Emollient, purgative and vulnerary.

USE TO TREAT

Minor burns, itching from chickenpox, cuts and abrasions, insect bites, eczema, ringworm, nappy rash, sunburn. The juice and gel of the inside of the aloe leaf is softening to the skin and may be used in moisturising preparations. Taken internally it may help both types of arthritis and help to reduce the size of kidney stones. The part used is the pale green jelly inside the leaf but care must be taken to avoid the yellow juice between the inside of the leaf and the jelly as this is very bitter. In large amounts the gel, if taken internally, will cause griping pains. Stabilised aloe vera gel for internal use can be bought from health-food stores. This gel has been treated to remove intestinal irritants and is used to help heal peptic ulcers, arthritis and rheumatism. Follow the recommended instructions.

ESSENTIAL OIL ACTION
None.

Alteratives
Gradually produce a beneficial change in bodily functions.

HERBS
Burdock, golden seal, nettle and yellow dock (digestive system and skin); echinacea, golden seal (circulatory system, immune system and skin); chickweed, red clover and fumitory (skin); mullein and golden seal (respiratory system).

ESSENTIAL OILS
Make an infused oil (see Aromatherapy & Essential Oils, Extraction of Essential Oils) of the above herbs.

Altzheimer's disease
Altzheimer's disease is terribly distressing for both the sufferers and the carers that love them. It leads to progressive mental deterioration, loss of memory and an inability to carry out even the simplest tasks. Forgetfulness is different, it can affect *everyone* from the very young to the very old and is usually nothing more sinister than a lack of attention. As we get older we become more afraid that our simple forgetfulness is a sign of Alzheimer's disease or senile dementia. This fear can paralyse us and hamper efforts at improving our memories.

Let us do what we can to keep our brains in optimum condition. It is now known that in 50 per cent of dementia cases the condition can be reversed. It has been shown that many cases that are diagnosed as Altzheimer's are in fact dementia. A large number of these people have developed dementia as a result of the prescription drugs that they take or because of poor nutrition and hence a lack of vital vitamins and minerals.

There is an increasing body of evidence that shows a connection between high aluminium and silicon levels in the body and Altzheimer's disease.

The following suggestions are preventative measures and may be particularly useful for the elderly or those who have a poor diet.

The herb known as gingko biloba has been shown to improve the blood supply to the brain and to increase the rate at which information is transmitted to the brain.

INTERNAL TREATMENT

- Don't cook in aluminium pans.
- Eat lots of fresh fruit, vegetables, wholegrain bread, and cereals.
- Drink 6–8 glasses of filtered or bottled water a day.

DAILY SUPPLEMENTS

- Gingko biloba as directed.
- 1000 mg vitamin C with bioflavonoids twice daily.
- 10 000 iu beta-carotene.
- 400 iu vitamin E (d-alpha tocopherol).
- 15 mg zinc.
- 1000 mg calcium/magnesium citrate supplement.

ESSENTIAL OIL TREATMENT

MASSAGE BLEND
1 tablespoon (20 ml) vegetable oil
6 drops basil oil
6 drops rosemary oil
3 drops grapefruit oil
TO MAKE: *Mix together.*

TO USE: *For a whole body and foot massage or use 2 teaspoons (10 ml) of the blend in a bath.*

HERBAL TREATMENT
Gingko biloba (see above).

HOMEOPATHIC TREATMENT
Consult a homeopathic practitioner.

Amenorrhoea ❧ See Menstruation

Anaemia
Anaemia is the name given to a condition in which the blood is deficient in red blood cells or haemoglobin. People with anaemia are pale, feel weak, lethargic and breathless and tend to tire easily. The most common cause of anaemia is iron deficiency caused by bleeding, such as bleeding from piles and peptic ulcers and excessive menstrual bleeding. Other causes are folic acid and vitamin-B12 deficiencies. Members of the population most at risk are children under two years of age; teenagers; pregnant women, and those who are breastfeeding; the elderly and sometimes vegetarians.

If you suspect that you may be anaemic it's important to see a physician who will do the appropriate tests such a complete blood count and evaluate the cause and condition. The suggestions below are for home treatment after the tests have been done.

INTERNAL TREATMENT
❧ Eat iron and folic acid-rich foods at least once a day. Calves' liver being the most important source (consume no more than 120 g a day due to the high vitamin A content, and half the amount for pregnant women). Other foods recommended are green leafy vegetables, dried beans, kidney, heart, egg yolk, legumes, dried apricots and other dried fruits, shellfish, parsley.
❧ Eat salads containing several varieties of lettuce, young dandelion leaves, alfalfa, spinach and watercress daily.

Daily supplements

- 1000 mg vitamin C with bioflavonoids 3 times daily.
- Iron and folic acid as recommended by physician.
- 1 vitamin B complex tablet.

Essential oil treatment

None appropriate.

Herbal treatment

- Nettle, dandelion and watercress are very nutritive plants for those with anaemia. Nettle can be taken as a tea 3 times a day. Dandelion and watercress are a delicious addition to salads and sandwiches, try to eat them twice daily.
- Herbal bitters containing gentian will stimulate the flow of gastric juices and improve digestion and absorption of nutrients. Take as directed.

Homeopathic treatment

Consult a homeopathic practitioner.

Analgesics

Relieve or diminish pain (see Pain) by exerting a nerve-numbing effect.

Herbs

Meadowsweet, willow.

Essential oils

Basil, bergamot, black pepper, chamomile, eucalyptus, ginger, lavender, marjoram, peppermint, rosemary.

Anaphrodisiacs

Reduce sexual desire.

HERB

Marjoram.

ESSENTIAL OIL

Marjoram.

Angelica (*Angelica archangelica*) ❧ See also Dong quai

HERB PART USED

Root, medicinally; young stems, in cooking.

HERB ACTIONS

Antispasmodic, appetiser, carminative, diuretic, expectorant, stimulant, stomachic, tonic.

USE TO TREAT

Decoctions are used to treat flatulence, digestive and lung problems; and as a tonic and immune-system stimulant. It also has a culinary use as crystallised angelica.

ESSENTIAL OIL ACTION

This is a difficult oil to obtain. It may be used in baths and massage oils to treat arthritis, rheumatism and fluid retention.

Angina pectoris

Caused by insufficient oxygenated blood reaching the heart muscle due to clogged or hardening arteries. The problem may worsen with age as the arteries become thicker and harder. This is often accompanied by high blood pressure. Physical exertion, over-eating or emotional stress usually causes an angina attack. The symptoms are very similar to those of heart attack.

The pain may radiate down either arm, the jaw and across the chest or may be felt as a squeezing pain in the chest. The pain usually lasts for 1–15 minutes and may be worse when the patient is lying down. No pain of this type should be ignored, consult a doctor immediately.

Orthodox medicine uses drugs such as nitro-glycerine to dilate the arteries or will perform surgery. Both these approaches will temporarily alleviate symptoms but will not prevent the problem from worsening.

The suggestions below should form part of a comprehensive plan to restore a proper blood supply to the heart. This plan should be used in conjunction with medical treatment—it may enable you to take fewer drugs and eventually dispense with drugs entirely. Discuss the treatment with your doctor before beginning.

⚕ Exercise can be especially helpful for angina as it encourages the heart and muscles to work more efficiently. The heart then needs less oxygen to handle exercise which means you will be able to become more active without bringing on an angina attack. Listen to your body and gently build up an exercise programme that you can handle without causing pain. Walking and swimming are probably the two best forms of exercise.

⚕ Be a non-smoker in order to give your heart more of the life-giving oxygen that it needs.

⚕ Have your cholesterol levels checked regularly, eat a low-fat diet and, if necessary, lose weight.

⚕ See also recommendations for stress management, exercise etc. under Heart care and Atherosclerosis.

INTERNAL TREATMENT ⚕ See Atherosclerosis

DAILY SUPPLEMENTS

⚕ 300 mg carnitine (clinical trials have demonstrated that carnitine improves angina and heart disease).[1]

⚕ 20 mg Co-enzyme Q10 (in a double-blind, crossover trial Co-enzyme Q10 reduced the frequency of attacks by 53 per cent).[2]

HERBAL TREATMENT

❧ ½ teaspoon fluid extract of hawthorn (*Crataegus monogyna*)
   3 times a day or the equivalent in tablet form (see Hawthorn).
❧ 1 teaspoon fluid extract of gingko biloba 3 times daily.
Tablets containing both the above herbs are available in health-food shops.

HOMEOPATHIC TREATMENT

Arnica 30^c every 15 minutes during an attack, 4 times daily at other times.

Aniseed (*Pimpinella anisum*)

HERB PART USED
Seed.

HERB ACTIONS

Antiseptic, antispasmodic, carminative and expectorant, insect repellent.

USE TO TREAT

Colic, stomach cramps, nausea, griping and wind, and to ease the symptoms of whooping cough. Disguises the taste of unpleasant tasting herbs and is used to increase milk supply in nursing mothers. It is a good insect repellent in the garden. A tincture is more effective than a tea, as alcohol extracts more of the medicinal properties than water.

ESSENTIAL OIL ACTION

Rarely used as it has narcotic and toxic properties.

Anodynes
Relieve pain. See Analgesics.

Antibiotics
Combat infection in the body.

HERBS
Garlic, manuka, nasturtium, niaouli, tea-tree.

ESSENTIAL OILS
Garlic, manuka, niaouli, tea-tree.

Antidepressants
Help to lift the emotions from a depressed state (see Depression).

HERBS
Borage, lavender, oatstraw, rose, rosemary, vervain, ylang-ylang.

ESSENTIAL OILS
Bergamot, clary sage, geranium, grapefruit, jasmine, lavender, lemongrass, mandarin, melissa, neroli, orange, petitgrain, rose, rosemary, sandalwood, ylang-ylang.

Antiemetics
Help to reduce and control vomiting and nausea.

HERBS
Caraway, chamomile, fennel, ginger, marjoram, peppermint, raspberry and spearmint.

ESSENTIAL OILS
Aniseed, black pepper, chamomile, clove, fennel, ginger, peppermint and spearmint.

Antifungals
Inhibit fungus growth.

HERBS

Benzoin, geranium, golden seal, lavender, marjoram, myrrh, peppermint, tea-tree.

ESSENTIAL OILS

Benzoin, geranium, lavender, manuka, marjoram, myrrh, peppermint, tea-tree.

Anti-inflammatories

Reduce inflammation.

HERBS

Calendula, chamomile, comfrey, dandelion, devil's claw, liquorice, sage, thyme, violet.

ESSENTIAL OILS

Bergamot, chamomile, lavender, and myrrh.

Antiseptics

Help to control or destroy infection-causing bacteria.

HERBS

Most herbs have some antiseptic qualities but the following are particularly good: basil, calendula, eucalyptus, garlic, lavender, manuka, rosemary, tea-tree and thyme.

ESSENTIAL OILS

Most oils have some antiseptic qualities but the following are particularly good: basil, bergamot, eucalyptus, garlic, juniper, lavender, manuka, rosemary, tea-tree and thyme.

Antispasmodics

Prevent or relieve cramps and/or spasms in the intestines or uterus.

HERBS

Basil, catnep, chamomiles, coriander, dill, lavender, lemon balm, peppermint, spearmint, oregano, rosemary, thyme, valerian.

ESSENTIAL OILS

Basil, aniseed, chamomile, clary sage, dill, fennel, ginger, juniper, lavender, marjoram, melissa, myrrh, orange, oregano, peppermint, rosemary, spearmint.

Antisudorifics
Reduce sweating.

HERBS

Sage.

ESSENTIAL OILS

Clary sage, cypress.

Antivirals
Kill or inhibit the growth of viruses.

HERBS

Eucalyptus, garlic, hyssop, St John's wort, tea-tree.

ESSENTIAL OILS

Bergamot, eucalyptus, garlic, lavender, palmarosa, tea-tree.

Anxiety 🌿 See Stress

Aphrodisiacs
Increase sexual desire.

HERBS

Damiana, jasmine, ginseng, rose, ylang-ylang.

ESSENTIAL OILS

Black pepper, cedarwood, clary sage, jasmine, neroli, patchouli, rose, rosewood, sandalwood, vetivert, ylang-ylang.

Apis Mel. (*Apis mellifica*) ❀ Homeopathic

Suited to those who are sad, depressed and weepy, often with no apparent cause. There may be suspicion, jealousy and irritability for no apparent reason.

USE TO TREAT

Acute inflammation, arthritis, cystitis, burning and stinging pains, insect bites and stings, incontinence, listlessness, prostate problems, rheumatism, shingles, sore throat, swollen gums, urticaria (hives).

Argent. Nit. (*Argentum nitricum*) ❀ Homeopathic

Suited to those who worry about the future and its events, who are impulsive and irritable or nervous.

USE TO TREAT

Acidity, anxiety, colic, conjunctivitis, dizziness and vertigo, headache, impotence, indigestion, itching scalp, urinary incontinence.

Arnica (*Arnica montana*)

HERB PARTS USED

Flowers and roots.

HERB ACTIONS

Diaphoretic, diuretic, emollient, expectorant, stimulant, vulnerary.
Caution: *Arnica is toxic and must never be taken internally, unless in the homeopathic form (see below) which is too dilute to be dangerous.*

USE TO TREAT

Despite its inclusion in the list of actions described above, arnica is for external use only. Used as an ointment, infused oil or tincture on *unbroken* skin it is a wonderful remedy to promote the healing of sprains, bruises, skin irritation and sore muscles and joints. Used as a massage oil it will help to reduce pain and swelling. It can be very effective in treating RSI (see Repetitive Strain Injury).

ESSENTIAL OIL ACTION

None. Use infused oil as described above.

Arnica (Arnica montana) 🌺 Homeopathic

USE TO TREAT

Any injury, for example, bruises and burns. For exhaustion after sustained exercise; fainting, gout, insomnia due to exhaustion, when muscles ache all over, rheumatism, shock, sprains and strains.

Did you know that homeopathic Arnica is a wonderful remedy to take before and after surgery? It controls shock, soreness and bleeding.

Aromatherapy & Essential oils

The use of healing aromatic plants goes back thousands of years but in comparison, the use of the oils extracted from these plants is comparatively new.

Aromatherapy is a term used in the 1920s by René Maurice Gattefosse, a French chemist to describe a 'therapy using aromatics'. The word implies that the cure or treatment lies in the inhalation of the aroma of the plant and while this is true it is only part of the picture. Aromatherapy is now widely used in therapeutic massage and the oils are also used in medicine and the food, cosmetic and perfume industries.

Aromatherapy has been one of the fastest growing alternative therapies in recent years. There is a danger, however, in this popularity as the new enthusiast receives little or no information on the use of the oils from the packaging and sometimes none from the retailer.

Essential oils, which are very powerful in comparison to fixed oils (see following), are most commonly used in several ways including the following:

* **Mixed with oils, creams or lotions and applied to the skin either for massage or topically as an ointment:** When applied to the skin, the oil diffuses through the various dermal layers (with the larger oil molecules passing through more slowly than smaller ones) and is absorbed gradually into the bloodstream. As essential oils are highly volatile, the amount absorbed is influenced by whether the skin is covered or uncovered. Covering the skin as quickly as possible after application will considerably enhance absorption of the oil.

* **Floated on the surface of hot water and used as an inhalation:** The essential oils will evaporate due to the heat of the water and they will then be carried in the steam to the lungs and from there to the bloodstream. Inhalation (see Inhalations) is mainly used to treat problems of the respiratory system.

    Because the nose is close to the brain, inhaled essential oils can exert a profound effect on the limbic portion of the brain responsible for memory and emotion. Little research has been carried out on this effect but there is sufficiently strong anecdotal evidence to show that the oils are mood changing and have a valuable role in altering emotional states.

* **Added to a bath:** Adding oils to a bath (see Baths) has the advantages of both the above methods. The oils will be absorbed into the skin and also inhaled from the steam. The essential oils need to be mixed with either vegetable oil or full cream milk before adding to the bath. This will avoid 'hot spots' of oil which could cause local irritation, and also will assist the oils to be absorbed into the moist skin.

Apart from their therapeutic value, essential oils are very appealing because of the wide range of possible uses both on the body and around the home. Their antibacterial, antiviral and antifungal properties are immensely valuable in cleaning preparations, for pet care and for use in the garden.

Few people can resist the beguiling scents of essential oils and may begin to use them without having developed a proper regard for, or knowledge of, the uses and power of essential oils. Many people don't know the difference between say, olive and patchouli oil, other than that one is for cooking and the other has a strong smell. The major differences between pure essential oils and fixed oils follow.

PURE ESSENTIAL OILS

These are the end product of distillation (or other methods of extraction) of the aromatic substances or essences found in plants. They are volatile, evaporate on exposure to air and have a powerful aroma. They should not have had any of their components removed after extraction nor should any substance have been added: they should not have been adulterated or contaminated.

The aromatic substances are found in leaves (eucalyptus), petals (rose), bark (sandalwood), resins (myrrh), roots (valerian), bulbs (garlic), dried flower buds (clove), rinds (lemon), and seeds (fennel). The cost of the essential oils reflects the amount of oil in the plant, the high labour cost involved in collection of it and the difficulty of extraction.

FIXED OILS

These oils are usually non-volatile and don't evaporate. They are nutritive (containing nutritional value due to vitamin and mineral content) and occur plentifully in the seeds, kernels, beans etc. of plants. They are extracted by presses, chemicals or heat. Most fixed oils have little aroma. Examples of fixed oils are almond, apricot, avocado, olive, peanut, sesame and wheatgerm oils.

If you know the uses of a herb do not assume that its essential oil can always be used in the same way. The oil after distillation is very powerful and certain properties are very pronounced.

While the majority of essential oils (providing they are diluted) are safe for external use, there are a few that are dangerous and shouldn't be used at all. Unless the user is very knowledgeable about essential oils, their use should be restricted to treating common complaints and home/garden/office preparations. If a complaint is serious, oils may be used in conjunction with, and with approval from, a health professional. It is generally accepted that it is unwise to take essential oils internally unless being treated by a health professional who is very conversant with their uses.

PURCHASING ESSENTIAL OILS

When buying essential oils it is of paramount importance to buy the best quality available (see Suppliers). There are many synthetic oils being sold under various names such as 'Lavender. Pure Oil' which could turn out to be synthetic lavender in a vegetable oil base. Others may be called 'Fragrant Oil' or 'Perfume Oil'. Such oils are usually found in supermarkets or variety stores, for example, but sometimes health-food shops stock them.

Synthetic oils carry none of the therapeutic properties of pure essential oils and could possibly be harmful if applied over large areas of the body. Price can sometimes be an indication of quality. For example, jasmine, rose, lemon balm (melissa) and orange blossom (neroli) are plants which either contain only small amounts of the aromatic substances; or the oils are difficult and time consuming to extract, making the finished oils very expensive. Other oils such as lavender and rosemary contain a much larger amount of aromatics and consequently are relatively inexpensive. If the label on a 10 ml bottle says 'jasmine' and the price label says $5 then it's definitely *not* jasmine—you would need to pay around $150 for the same amount of the real thing!

Expensive oils have been made affordable by diluting them with vegetable oils such as almond or jojoba and labelling them appropriately, for instance: 'Chamomile 2.5% in jojoba'. This practice is perfectly acceptable and is a useful way in which to buy the oils.

Caution: *Some oils may not be what they seem to be, so buy carefully.*

* Tagetes (*Tagetes patula*) oil is often sold as calendula or marigold oil. True calendula oil is only produced in very small quantities and is difficult to obtain. Tagetes oil is distilled from French, African or Mexican marigolds. The two oils must not be confused as tagetes doesn't have the same therapeutic properties as calendula and is severely phototoxic (with an excessive reaction to sunlight).

- Thuja (*Thuja occidentalis*) is sometimes sold as white cedar oil or cedar-leaf oil. This oil is severely toxic due to its high alpha and beta thujone content, and deaths have been reported from its oral use. The oil named 'White cedar' should not be confused with Atlas cedar (*Cedrus Atlantica*) which is the correct aromatherapy oil to use.
- Verbena oil or lemon verbena (*Lippia citriodora*) is difficult to obtain, and the oil sold as lemon verbena is often a blend of citrus oils. However, since verbena oil is somewhat hazardous, the synthetic oil is probably safer than the natural oils.[1]
- Melissa oil is very costly, as huge amounts of plant materials are needed to produce a very small amount of oil. Most melissa oil offered is adulterated with other lemon-scented oils.
- Marjoram (Spanish) isn't marjoram at all but a species of thyme (*Thymus masticina*).

BABIES, CHILDREN AND ESSENTIAL OILS

There are some essential oils that aren't suitable to use for children. A list of these follows, with recommendations for safe percentages (see Blending essential oils). The skin on the body of a child is much thinner than that of an adult and as a result the oils penetrate far more quickly. In addition, body weight is also a factor to consider— children need a smaller percentage of essential oils in any preparation.

For safety of packaging with regard to children:

- Buy oils in bottles that have integral drop dispensers that are difficult to remove or which have safety (child-resistant) caps. There is no such thing as a 'child-*proof*' cap. Children are persistent and patient and will spend an extraordinary length of time to solve a problem that interests them. Children are also curious and impatient, they rarely smell the contents of a bottle and rarely sip; instead they up-end the bottle and gulp the contents. This has led to several recorded fatalities.
- Avoid buying oils in bottles that have wide, open necks with no drippers.

* Store the oils in a locked box in a locked cupboard.
* Always stay strictly within the guidelines of usage for children.
* Remember that 'natural' doesn't always mean safe.

Caution: *Most essential oils are too powerful to use on the skin of newborn babies and there are few that are safe to use before the baby is 2–3 months old.*

For amounts which can safely be used, see the chart.

AGE	OIL
2–3 MONTHS	Chamomile (*Anthemis nobilis & Matricaria chamomilla*) and lavender may be used after the infant is 48 hours old.
3–12 MONTHS	Add calendula, grapefruit, mandarin and tea-tree to the above list.
1–5 YEARS	Add geranium, lemon, palmarosa, spearmint and rose to the above lists.
5 YEARS–PUBERTY	All the oils considered safe for adults may be used but in smaller amounts.

BATHS: *Use age-appropriate oils chosen from the Essential oils list above.*

AGE	OIL
2–3 MONTHS	1 drop (total) of either essential oil mixed thoroughly with 1 tablespoon olive oil and agitated thoroughly into the bath water
3–12 MONTHS	2 drops (total) used as above
1–5 YEARS	3–5 drops (total) used as above
5 YEARS–PUBERTY	5–8 drops (total) used as above

MASSAGE: *Use age-appropriate oils chosen from the Essential oils list above.*

AGE	OIL
2–3 MONTHS	10 drops (total) mixed or single essential oils in 125 ml (½ cup) of mixed olive and almond oils. Shake well before use
3–12 MONTHS	10–16 drops (total) mixed or single essential oils diluted as above
1–5 YEARS	10–16 drops (total) mixed or single essential oils diluted as above
5 YEARS–PUBERTY	16–20 drops (total) mixed or single essential oils diluted as above

AIR SPRAYS: *Use age-appropriate oils chosen from the Essential oils list above.*

AGE	OIL
2–3 MONTHS	not recommended
3–12 MONTHS	not recommended
1–5 YEARS	quarter the adult quantities (see Percentage chart below)
5 YEARS–PUBERTY	as for 1–5 years above to adult quantities depending on age

Caution: *Essential oils must never be used internally and must always be correctly diluted before use. This is particularly important for babies and children as undiluted essential oils rubbed from the hands into the eyes could cause permanent damage to the eyesight.*

STORAGE OF ESSENTIAL OILS

Apart from the safety aspects outlined above, essential oils need to be stored very carefully. Not only do they lose their properties but also the properties can change because of oxidation and the oils may become skin sensitisers. In some cases the oxidation may have more serious consequences with the oils becoming carcinogenic or toxic. Certain oils rich in terpines are especially prone to oxidation. The most common of these are: bergamot (*Citrus bergamia*), dill (*Anethum graveolens*), Fennel (*Foeniculum vulgare*), grapefruit (*Citrus paradisi*), juniper (*Juniperus communis*), lemon (*Citrus limon*), lime (*Citrus aurantifolia*), mandarin (*Citrus noblis*), myrtle (*Myrtus communis*), neroli (*Citrus aurantium/amara*), orange (*Citrus aurantium/ sinensis*) (bitter and sweet), pine (*Pinus sylvestris*), tagetes (*Tagetes minuta, T. patula, T. erecta*).

Essential oils may also lose some or all of their therapeutic value when stored for a long time (especially when stored under adverse conditions).

The conditions that create swift degradation of the oils are light, heat and atmospheric oxygen. In order to preserve the oils for as long as possible and retard degradation follow the suggestions outlined below.

* The oil bottles should be as full as possible to exclude air.
* The oils should be kept either in the refrigerator (although some oils such as vetivert become very viscous when refrigerated) or some other cool place.
* Bottles should be dark coloured (e.g. amber or blue). Clear glass bottles allow too much light in, and light hastens oxidation.
* Certain oils rich in terpenes are especially prone to oxidation. The most commonly used of these are: bergamot, dill, fennel, grapefruit, juniper, lemon, lime, mandarin, myrtle, neroli, orange (bitter and sweet), pine, spruce, tagetes, tangelo. These oils need to be bought in small quantities and used within 6 months of purchase.
* Oils that are stored in the conditions outlined above will have a probable life span of 2 years.

HAZARDS

Essential oils should never be taken internally unless administered or prescribed by a health professional specialising in the uses and administration of essential oils. This is because there is a far greater risk of toxicity occurring when oils are taken internally as approximately ten times the concentration will reach the bloodstream. The other consideration is that many of the oils can irritate mucous membranes.

Problems can arise with external usage if oils are used continuously over a long period of time (using the same oils day after day in an oil burner, or massaging the same oils once a day over the whole body for several successive days). There can be a cumulative effect leading to mild chronic toxicity that can cause symptoms such as nausea, headaches, tiredness.

Most oils used externally and in the correct manner and dilution are perfectly safe but there are a few, however, which have special properties that can under certain conditions cause problems.

PHOTOTOXICITY

Certain chemicals when applied to the skin can cause an excessive reaction to sunlight (or sunlamps) for up to 12 hours (and possibly for much longer) after application. The combination of oil plus sunlight can result in burns that can range from mild to very severe depending on whether the oils are used undiluted or diluted. Even a mere 0.4 per cent of some oils can cause the phototoxic effect.

The following oils are all phototoxic and are listed in increasing order of strength.

* Not to be used at all: tagetes.
* No more than 0.5 per cent: bergamot, cumin, lemon, lemon verbena, lime (expressed).
* No more than 1.5 per cent orange (bitter).
* No more than 2 per cent: lemon.
* No more than 3 per cent: grapefruit, mandarin.
* Important to use fresh: see point 4 in Storage of essential oils.

SENSITISATION

This is a gradual build up of an allergic reaction and intolerance to a substance even when used in minuscule amounts. This sensitivity may be scarcely apparent on the first application but if the substance is used often the reaction usually worsens steadily.

Severe sensitisers: costus, elecampane, lemon verbena.

Moderate sensitisers: cassia, cinnamon bark, fennel, lemon verbena.

Mild sensitisers: citronella, lemongrass, may chang, melissa, myrrh, pine, ylang-ylang.

SKIN IRRITANTS

If you have sensitive skin or if you develop allergic reactions frequently you would be wise to use a patch test (see below) before applying any unfamiliar substance to your skin.

Severe reaction: Horseradish and mustard oils are examples of oils that produce such a severe reaction that they should never be used.

Moderate reaction: bay, cassia, cinnamon bark and leaf, clove, fennel, oregano, parsley, pine (if old and oxidised), rue, sage (Dalmatian), tagetes, thyme.

Patch testing essential oils: Wash the skin inside the elbow and dry well. Apply a drop only of the essential oil mixed with 10 drops vegetable oil and cover immediately with sticking plaster. Leave for 24 hours. If any redness, itching or other reaction is apparent, the oil should not be used again.

HIGH RISK OILS

Some oils are considered too dangerous to be used in aromatherapy because of the presence of various chemicals.

The following oils should *never* be used as they all contain high percentages of toxic, narcotic, abortifacient (capable of producing abortion) or carcinogenic chemicals.

Never use: almond, bitter (unrectified); aniseed; armoise (mugwort); arnica; birch (sweet); buchu; calamus; camphor (white, brown and yellow); cassia; cinnamon bark; elecampane; horseradish; mustard; oregano; pennyroyal; sage (Dalmatian); sassafras; savine; savory; tansy; tarragon; thuja and western red cedar; lemon verbena; wintergreen; wormseed; wormwood.

Use with caution: elemi, oak moss.

EPILEPSY

It is highly unlikely that *externally* applied oils would cause an epileptic seizure. If the oils are used for an extended period at more than 2 per cent concentration, however, problems are likely to arise. It is probably safest to avoid these oils. Those following are in addition to the above 'never to be used' list: fennel, hyssop, rosemary, sage (Spanish).

PREGNANCY

Certain emmenagogue (see Emmenagogues) oils should be avoided for the first four months of pregnancy. If there is any history of miscarriage it would be wiser to avoid the oils throughout the pregnancy.

Yet another effect of some of the oils is to strengthen contractions of the uterus (these oils are very useful during labour).

Even after four months of pregnancy, the oils shouldn't be used at more than 1–2 per cent strength for massage oils and 5 drops mixed in 1 tablespoon vegetable oil for baths.

Oils to avoid during pregnancy: any of the oils from the 'never to be used' list plus basil, birch, cedarwood, clary sage, cypress, geranium, hyssop, jasmine, juniper, marjoram, myrrh, nutmeg, peppermint, rosemary, tarragon, thyme.

Oils to avoid during the first four months of pregnancy: German and Roman chamomile, geranium, lavender, rose.

BLENDING ESSENTIAL OILS

Percentage guide

It's important to measure the essential oils carefully—if a recipe says 2 drops then 4 drops will *not* be better! Graduated droppers are available from pharmacies. The following list is a general guide to amounts of essential oil to use in a blend.

Essential oils will mix with fixed oils and with alcohol but not with water. There are dispersants (like Solubaliser from Sunspirit in Byron Bay) now available which enable essential oil and water to mix. Dispersants are very useful in air-spray blends, skin toners, toilet waters and other preparations that contain a lot of water.

PERCENTAGE CHART

MASSAGE OILS	2.0–2.5%
MASSAGE CREAMS	2.0–2.5%
COMPRESSES	10 drops to 100 ml water
FOMENTATIONS	as for compresses
OINTMENTS	3.0%
LOTIONS	1–1.5%
BATHS	10 drops maximum, depending on age, in 1 tablespoon vegetable oil
FOOTBATHS	4–6 drops, depending on age
ROOM SPRAYS	1 teaspoon in 300 ml water
INHALATIONS	2–5 drops, depending on age

MEASUREMENTS

20 drops = approx. 1 ml

100 drops = approx. 1 teaspoon or 5 ml

1 metric tablespoon = approx. 20 ml

BLENDING CHART

2 drops in 2 teaspoons = approx. 1%

4 drops in 2 teaspoons = approx. 2%

6 drops in 2 teaspoons = approx. 3%

20 drops in 100 ml = approx. 1%

40 drops in 100 ml = approx. 2%

60 drops in 100 ml = approx. 3%

Essential oils work well with other natural therapies (a few of the oils including camphor, eucalyptus and rosemary are contra-indicated for use with homeopathic remedies) and, in conjunction with good food, adequate sleep and enjoyable recreation, provide an important role in holistic health and healing.

EXTRACTION OF ESSENTIAL OILS

There are many ways in which the aromatic properties are extracted from the plant. The main method of extraction is by distillation. Some arguments maintain that this is the only method by which a true essential oil is obtained, and that other methods result in what are called 'essences' and 'absolutes'.

DISTILLATION

This method employs boiling water, steam or both. The plant material is either immersed in boiling water or placed on grids over boiling water where the steam passes through it. The essential oil cells break down and release the oils in the form of vapour. This vapour and the steam is passed along coils through containers of cold water where they separate again and are collected in a vat. Essential oil is lighter than the water; it floats and can easily be separated. The remaining water is called variously a flower water, herb water or hydrolat. It is delicately perfumed with the essential oil, making it useful as a toilet water, facial tonic or aftershave.

ENFLEURAGE

Enfleurage is a time-honoured and expensive way of recovering essences from delicate flowers such as jasmine, rose, tuberose and orange blossom. The lengthy and labour-intensive method accounts for the high price of these oils. For example, if using jasmine, the flowers must be collected at night. The following process can be done at home with time and patience!

Spread sheets of glass or enamel thinly with pure lard or hardened vegetable fat (not margarine). Sprinkle the fat with a single layer of heavily perfumed petals and press onto the fat. Place another sheet of glass or enamel on top and leave for 24 hours. Pick the petals off and replace with fresh ones.

Repeat this process daily 36 times! (This is the number of times that professionals exchange the flowers but you can stop when you have run out of patience or when the scent is to your liking.) At the end of this process pick the petals off and scrape the fat into a jar. At this stage it is known as a pomade or sachet and can be used as a perfume.

To produce an 'absolute', dilute the fat in a glass jar with vodka or a high-proof alcohol that has little or no smell, cover with a tight lid and leave in a dark, cool place for three weeks. Shake the container vigorously and often. After this time the oils will have separated from the fat and will be dissolved into the alcohol. Skim or strain the fat and bottle the perfumed alcohol.

The final stage (which I don't recommend!) is to evaporate the alcohol off in a double boiler over a very gentle heat. The theoretical result will be a small (*very* small) amount of essential oil and no alcohol. (When I tried, it didn't work and I wasted all that time, energy and most importantly, deliciously scented alcohol—genuine jasmine cologne.)

EXPRESSION

The oil in citrus fruits is contained in glands in the outer skin. Before suitable machines were devised, the fruit and white pith were scooped out and the outer skin was squeezed until the oil glands burst. The droplets were collected in sponges which were then squeezed to collect the oil. If you do this at home a cosmetic sponge or cottonwool balls may be used to collect the oil. If the quantity of oil is very small the oil-filled sponge or ball may be dropped in a little vodka or almond oil in a small jar covered tightly with a well fitting lid. Shake well and leave for 24 hours, shaking often. Remove the sponge or ball, squeeze well and decant the perfumed oil or alcohol into a small, dark bottle. Store in the refrigerator.

INFUSED OIL

Infusion is the most important method of extraction of essential oils for the home user. This extraction of essential oils from plants into fixed oils is technically known as a Phytol. The oil is not as strong as an essential oil but can often be better as it contains properties of the whole plant that are not necessarily found in the essential oil.

It is also a method of extracting properties from plants that don't yield an essential oil, and by so doing extending the range of valuable plants that we can use in aromatherapy. Calendula, comfrey, devil's claw, plantain and echinacea are some of the many herbs that can be used in this way.

Unlike for herb oil (see Herb oil) which is made and used in quite large quantities, I make only ½–1 cup (125–250 ml) of infused oil and store it in a dark bottle in the refrigerator. The reason for making a relatively small quantity is that I use the oils mainly in creams and for 'specific-problem' massage and would only make up a tablespoon (20 ml) of massage oil at a time. I make infused oils 'little and often' to ensure that they are always fresh.

TO MAKE: *Fill a screw-top jar with fresh leaves or petals or half fill with chopped root, seeds or dried leaves or petals. Top up the jar with warmed cold-pressed almond, grape-seed or other oil with little smell. Screw the lid on tightly and put the jar in a warm place as it is important that it not get cold. (I put the jar in a yoghurt maker that stays at a constant gentle temperature.)*

After 24 hours strain the oil, discard the plant material and replace with fresh material. Repeat the process four to six times.

Strain the finished oil through a sieve and then through cheesecloth or other fine cloth, squeezing to extract every precious drop of oil. Store the oil in the refrigerator in a jar or bottle that is as full as possible. Air, heat and light are the chief culprits for making oil rancid.

The oils may be used singly, mixed with a carrier oil or to essential oils in blends.

Arsen. alb. (*Arsenicum album*) ๆ Homeopathic
Suited to precise, particular, tidy and intelligent types of people.

USE TO TREAT

Anxiety, great restlessness and fear, asthma, burning stomach pain, catarrh, cramps in calf muscles, diarrhoea, food poisoning, hayfever, nausea and vomiting, psoriasis, sciatica, shingles, insomnia.

Arteriosclerosis

This is the term given to a thickening and hardening of the artery walls. This condition is usually found in conjunction with deposits of cholesterol on the artery wall and then becomes known as atherosclerosis. For more information and treatment, see Atherosclerosis.

Arthritis

Arthritis is not a single disease but a range of 150 or more separate conditions. Osteoarthritis and rheumatoid arthritis are the two most common forms of arthritis, both are characterised by pain, stiffness and inflammation.

See Pain for suggestions on dealing with pain. See also Bath vinegars.

OSTEOARTHRITIS

This is the more common form of arthritis. It occurs with ageing, affecting mainly the weight-bearing joints and the hands. The cartilage surrounding the bones becomes thin, rough and hardens causing friction. Degeneration of the joint and bony spurs develops and the joint becomes deformed and painful. Other symptoms may be muscle weakness, and cramp around the affected joint.

There is a tendency, because of joint pain, to avoid movement. There is a cliché that has much truth—'If you don't use it, you will lose it!' and this is particularly true of both types of arthritis. Try swimming or water aerobics in a heated pool as it is less painful and is a very good way of increasing movement and mobility.

The application of alternate heat and cold has a sometimes dramatic effect in lessening arthritic pain. The most convenient way of doing this is to buy 2 gel-filled packs from the pharmacy, these packs are made to be able to be heated or frozen. Keep one pack in the freezer and when needed, immerse the other in boiling water as directed on the packet. Wrap the packs in a thin piece of cloth (never apply directly to the flesh) and alternate 4–5 minutes hot, 4–5 minutes cold until relief is obtained. Conventional treatments using anti-inflammatory and pain-killing drugs seem to ease the discomfort but, far from helping the patient to recover, have been shown in many cases to worsen the problem.

It's important to maintain a correct body weight both to delay the onset of osteoarthritis and to prevent extra stress on the joints if the problem has already occurred.

Daily supplements

- 50 mg vitamin B6.
- 1 vitamin B complex tablet on alternate days.
- 1000 mg vitamin C with bioflavonoids.
- 500 iu vitamin E (d-alpha tocopherol).
- 2000–2500 iu borage (starflower) oil or evening primrose oil.
- 10 000 iu beta-carotene.
- 30 mg zinc taken on alternate weeks.

Essential oil treatment

MASSAGE & BATH OIL BLEND
1 teaspoon (5 ml) marjoram oil
60 drops juniper oil
20 drops chamomile oil
20 drops rosemary oil
TO MAKE: *Mix together in a tiny dark glass bottle. Label and store in a cool dark place.*
TO USE: *Add 10 drops to a warm bath, agitate the water to disperse the oil. Relax in the bath for 20 minutes.*

Add 12 drops to 1 tablespoon (20 ml) vegetable oil. Use for gentle massage.

Use for a fomentation. (See Fomentations.)

Herbal treatment

- 1 teaspoon (5 ml) celery-seed tincture 3 times daily in 2 tablespoons (40 ml) water.

Did you know that devil's claw has been used for years for its remarkable anti-inflammatory properties? It is said to reduce inflammation in the joints and may help arthritis, gout, neuralgia, fibrositis, lumbago and rheumatism.

Did you know that soaking in a warm bath containing one handful of Epsom salts can ease the stiffness and discomfort of arthritis?

- 1 ginger tablet 2–3 times daily with food. (Health-food stores and pharmacies sell tablets that contain zinax, the active ingredient in ginger which is harmless, causes no side effects and is very helpful in reducing arthritic pain.)
- *Capsaicin* cream (Zostrix), available from pharmacies and health-food stores, is made from chillies and is very successful in treating joint pain in arthritis. Rub it gently into the skin over the aching joint (don't use on broken skin).
- Gotu kola—take supplements as directed.
- Feverfew—take as directed.
- Devil's claw—take as directed; not to be used during pregnancy.
- 1000–4000 mg willow bark as needed for pain.

RHEUMATOID ARTHRITIS

This form of arthritis is less common and is an autoimmune reaction disorder affecting mostly women between 20 and 40 years of age. As well as the destruction of the cartilage there is a progressive destruction of the joints themselves. It begins with pain in the small joints of the hands and feet, progressing to the other joints.

The treatments that follow are suitable for both types of arthritis but I would advise rheumatoid arthritis sufferers to seek professional treatment as well as the natural therapies. Many of the herbal remedies will be found in combinations in health-food stores.

- I recommend sleeping in a sleeping bag. Many people find the constant warmth helps them to avoid much of the morning pain and stiffness.
- To relieve stiffness, add 1 cup of Epsom salts to a warm bath. Remain soaking in the bath for 15–30 minutes, massaging the limbs gently.
- Being overweight puts an extra load on joints and makes the symptoms worse.
- See also Pain and Relaxation.

Daily supplements

- ½ teaspoon (2.5 ml) echinacea fluid extract 3 times daily.
- 1000–1500 mg borage (starflower) oil or evening primrose oil.
- Siberian ginseng.
- 1000 mg vitamin C with bioflavonoids twice daily.
- 400 iu vitamin E (d-alpha tocopherol).
- 1 vitamin B complex tablet.
- 1000 mg calcium citrate.
- Bilberry extract (liquid if possible) as directed.

Essential oil treatment

BATH, MASSAGE & FOMENTATION BLEND

1 teaspoon (5 ml) rosemary oil

60 drops juniper oil

20 drops chamomile oil

20 drops ginger oil

TO MAKE: *Mix together in a tiny dark glass bottle. Label and store in a cool dark place.*

TO USE: *Add 10 drops to a warm bath, agitate water to disperse.*

Relax for 20 minutes.

Add 12 drops to 1 tablespoon (20 ml) grape-seed or almond oil. Use for gentle massage.

Use for a fomentation. (See Fomentations.)

Herbal treatment

TO MAKE: *Seed and chop 10 small hot chillies. Place in a jar and add 1 cup (250 ml) brandy. Soak for 1 week, shaking daily. Strain through coffee-filter paper and store in a small bottle in the refrigerator.*

TO USE: *Add 15 drops to a cup of caffeine-free tea two to three times daily. Continue until relief is obtained.*

- 1 cup (250 ml) of decoction of wild yam 3 times daily.
- Willow bark tincture or tablets as needed for pain.

INTERNAL TREATMENT — BOTH TYPES OF ARTHRITIS

The dietary suggestions apply to both types of arthritis and aim at reducing the amount of inflammatory acids in the body. The results may take a few weeks to be noticeable but the long-term relief will be worth the wait.

- Cut down or eliminate consumption of fried foods, salt, sugar and sugary food, red meat, milk and dairy foods and animal fat.
- Use soya milk or goat's milk as a substitute for cow's milk.
- Avoid coffee, vinegar and vinegar products.
- Sprinkle ½–1 tablespoon ground linseed daily on breakfast cereals or skim-milk yoghurt.
- Eat a diet rich in wholegrains (rice, breads, pasta, muesli), fresh fruits and vegetables but avoid citrus fruit, rhubarb, eggplant and tomatoes.
- Eat a serve of mackerel, herring, sardines or salmon daily.

HOMEOPATHIC TREATMENT — BOTH TYPES OF ARTHRITIS

All remedies are 30^c potency, take 3 times daily or as required for pain:

- Redness and swelling — Apis mel.
- No relief from pain, worse with warmth — Bryonia.
- Pains move from joint to joint. Patient feels better in the open air — Pulsatilla.
- Worse with rest and if air is damp, better with warmth and movement — Rhus. tox.
- Pain relieved by warmth — Ruta grav.

Asthma

A condition in which the small bronchial airways constrict, making it difficult for the person to exhale. This is potentially a very serious condition and the suggestions given below are an adjunct to, not a substitute for, professional treatment.

Asthma is often an allergic reaction to such things as dust mites, mould, cigarette smoke, car and other chemical fumes, animal fur or certain foods (see Allergens). The following items have been shown to trigger asthma attacks and so should be avoided: aspirin, tartrazine (Yellow No. 3) food colouring, monosodium glutamate, metabisulphite (found in many commercial dried fruits and dried fruit products). Being over-tired, very upset or other emotional factors can also trigger attacks.

INTERNAL TREATMENT

❧ Exclude milk and wheat products from the diet on a trial basis for one month. Reintroduce either milk or wheat to ascertain which (if any) is a problem.

❧ Eat a largely vegetarian diet with lots of fibre foods, fresh fruit and vegetables.

❧ Drink *lots* of filtered or bottled water, 6–8 glasses a day.

❧ Practice breathing exercises (see Breathing) to strengthen the lungs.

DAILY SUPPLEMENTS

❧ Take vitamin B12 as directed on container. Vitamin B12 provides much support in the treatment of childhood asthma.[1]

❧ Pyridoxine (vitamin B6) has been demonstrated to have profound benefits for many asthma sufferers. It takes at least a month before any improvement is seen and the benefits increase the longer the treatment is maintained. As isolated B vitamins should not be taken without the other vitamins in this group, take a vitamin B complex tablet daily.

❧ 500 mg vitamin C with bioflavonoids, 1000 mg during an attack.

Did you know that you can make smelling salts by dripping essential oils (such as lavender and chamomile for asthma or lavender, rosemary and peppermint for headaches) onto coarse sea salt and putting them into a box or bottle small enough to carry in your pocket?

ESSENTIAL OIL TREATMENT

INHALATION BLEND

20 drops lavender oil

20 drops chamomile oil

3 tablespoons (60 ml) vegetable oil

TO MAKE: *Mix together in a small bottle.*

TO USE: *During an attack allow the patient to sniff the bottle's contents. In between attacks, massage the chest twice daily with the blend.*

HERBAL TREATMENT

Weak chamomile tea sweetened with honey is often acceptable to children. If steeped for too long it can cause nausea. The tea has an anti-inflammatory and toning action on the bronchial system.

HOMEOPATHIC TREATMENT

While awaiting professional help, take the remedy every 15 minutes till settled, then 4 times daily:

* Anxious and restless, feels suffocated if lying down — Arsen. alb. 30^c.
* Attack occurs after long coughing spell and/or vomiting — Carbo. veg. 12^c.
* Wheezing and feeling of suffocation; cough with no mucus, the chest is full of phlegm but doesn't loosen with coughing — Ipecac. (*Ipecacuanha cephaelis*) 30^c.

Astragalus (*Astragalus membranaceus*)

HERB PART USED

Root.

HERB ACTIONS

Not to be used in cases of acute infection. It is indicated for chronic, long-term conditions and is the first line of defence for an immune-system weakened by chronic illness. It is an immune-system enhancer, increases interferon production, helps to prevent bone-marrow depression, eases side effects of both radiotherapy and chemotherapy.

USE TO TREAT

Helps to rebuild severe immune deficiency. Use to treat AIDS, hepatitis and cancer in conjunction with orthodox treatment.[1] Chronic bronchitis, long-term liver problems, sleeplessness and anxiety, Chronic Fatigue Syndrome, Ross River Virus, gastric discomfort.

ESSENTIAL OIL ACTION

None.

Astringents

Contract and tone tissues.

HERBS

Calendula, comfrey, nettle, plantain, sage, distilled witch-hazel, yellow dock.

ESSENTIAL OILS

Benzoin, cedarwood, cypress, frankincense, juniper, myrrh, rose, rosemary, sandalwood.

Astrology 🌿 See Planetary signs of herbs & oils

Atherosclerosis

This is a condition that develops over a period of years, where the arteries become harder and fatty deposits (Atheroma) line the walls of the arteries. The risks associated with atherosclerosis are the development of angina, and other forms of heart disease such as heart attacks and strokes may occur. Atherosclerosis may also affect the hearing.

There is evidence to show that atherosclerosis is a disease caused by the Western diet and lifestyle. There needs to be a total commitment to taking control of your life and health and making positive, health-enhancing changes.

Cigarette smoking, high blood pressure, high blood cholesterol, obesity, lack of exercise, stress and diabetes are all implicated as risk factors.

Controlled trials have demonstrated unequivocally that lowering cholesterol inhibits the progression of disease and in some cases assisted regression[1] (see Cholesterol). Diet, exercise and stress management are also most important to address (see Relaxation).

See also Angina and Heart care.

INTERNAL TREATMENT

Eat plenty of fruit and vegetables. All fruits and vegetables contain vitamins and minerals but in differing amounts. For instance orange fruits and vegetables are high in vitamin A. Choose from all the different colours when you shop to ensure getting the widest range of vitamins and minerals.

- Eat oily fish such as sardines, mackerel, trout, tuna and Atlantic salmon at least 3 times a week.
- Eat plenty of bread and wholegrain cereals.
- If you enjoy it, drink a glass of wine with your main meal.
- Eat free-range chicken and fish instead of red meat.
- Avoid the animal fat in meat, cheese, milk, butter; learn to enjoy soya milk, yoghurt and soya cheese instead.
- Cut down on products that contain sugar and fat such as cakes, biscuits, pastries and sweets (including chocolate).
- Sprinkle ½–1 tablespoon of ground linseeds (for their blood-thinning properties) on your breakfast cereal.
- Use only olive or canola oil for cooking.
- Avocados make a delicious and healthy spread instead of butter. They are a rich source of vitamin E and other vitamins, contain lots of potassium and folate (folic acid) and are high in monounsaturated fats. If you are overweight, restrict yourself to a thin scraping only as avocados contain many kilojoules.

DAILY SUPPLEMENTS

- ❧ 1 multi-vitamin-mineral capsule.
- ❧ 1000 mg vitamin C with bioflavonoids.
- ❧ 200 iu vitamin E (d-alpha tocopherol).
- ❧ 10 000 iu beta-carotene.
- ❧ 1 teaspoon fluid extract of gingko biloba 3 times daily.

ESSENTIAL OIL TREATMENT

MASSAGE OIL

½ cup (125 ml) grape-seed oil

2 tablespoons (40 ml) canola or olive oil

1 teaspoon (5 ml) wheatgerm oil

15 drops lemon oil

15 drops rosemary oil

10 drops juniper oil

5 drops black pepper oil

5 drops ginger oil

TO MAKE: *Mix together and leave for 24 hours to blend.*

HERBAL TREATMENT

- ❧ Hawthorn liquid extract or capsules as directed.
- ❧ 1000 mg garlic oil capsules or 2 teaspoons 'Long-life juice' 3 times daily.

HOMEOPATHIC TREATMENT

- ❧ Silicea and Calc. fluor.—both 12^x, take 4 times daily.
- ❧ Consult a homeopathic practitioner for a full treatment.

Athlete's foot ❧ See Foot care

Babies ❧ See also Pregnancy, Aromatherapy & Essential oils

Babies need special treatments and remedies—their tender and sensitive little bodies
can't tolerate any but the most gentle remedies. They can become very ill very quickly
but can also recover dramatically, which is
alarming and frustrating for parents. Never
take chances with your baby—if in doubt get
professional help.

Have you heard that
premature babies who are
massaged every day gain
weight 47 per cent faster
than babies who aren't
touched?

The only essential oils suitable for babies
aged between 48 hours and 3 months old are
chamomile and lavender, and these oils need to be diluted.

A drop of either oil in an oil burner or on a cloth tied to the cot in
the bedroom will calm fretfulness.

Massage your baby every day—you will both love it and it will
help to strengthen that special bonding. It also helps to ease the pain
of colic. Read also the cautions and percentage charts under
Aromatherapy & Essential oils.

ESSENTIAL OIL TREATMENT

BABY'S BOTTOM & BODY MASSAGE OIL

⅔ cup (170 ml) almond oil

⅓ cup (85 ml) olive oil

5 drops chamomile oil

6 drops mandarin oil

4 drops lavender oil

TO MAKE: *Mix together in a bottle, shake well.*

   Leave for 2 days before using.

TO USE: *Sprinkle on cotton wool and use to clean baby after a nappy change.*

   Use to massage the whole body after baby's bath.

   To lift cradle cap, the oil may be massaged gently onto the scalp, left on overnight and washed off in the morning. Repeat for as long as necessary.

HERBAL BABY OIL

The strongest oil of all may be made by adding 25 drops essential oil to 1 cup (250 ml) herb oil.

75 per cent almond oil

25 per cent olive oil

calendula petals

chamomile flowers

TO MAKE: *Fill a large jar with a mixture of the herbs. Cover with mixed oils, and a well fitting lid. Stand in a warm place for 2–3 days shaking often. Strain the mixture through cheesecloth or a sieve, squeezing the herbs well to extract as much oil as possible.*

   Put fresh herbs in the jar, cover with the herb oil, topping up with a little fresh oil if needed. Cover with the lid and repeat as before. These stages may be repeated once more if you wish and will produce a very strong and effective oil.

   Strain the finished oil through fine cloth to remove all plant material. Store in the refrigerator.

'BARE BOTTOM CREAM'

A

7 firmly packed, level tablespoons finely grated, beeswax

60 g anhydrous lanolin

½ cup (125 ml) calendula infused oil (see Aromatherapy & Essential Oils; Extraction of essential oils or buy from a health-food shop)

B

*2 teaspoons (10 ml) calendula tincture (see Tinctures or buy from a
health-food shop)*

10 drops lavender oil

TO MAKE: *Melt the ingredients for A together over a very low heat.
Don't overheat the mixture.*

*Add the ingredients for B and stir until no droplets of tincture or
oil can be seen.*

Pot in sterilised containers and cap immediately.

BABY POWDER

2 cups cornflour

2 tablespoons zinc oxide powder

10 drops lavender oil

5 drops chamomile oil

TO MAKE: *Mix the powders together very well. Add the oils, a drop
at a time, while stirring. Store in an airtight container.*

CRADLE CAP   🌿   See Baby's bottom oil

TEETHING

Teething usually begins around the age of six months and with many
babies may proceed without any problems. Some babies, however,
suffer a lot of pain and are miserable and fretful. They can also suffer
from diarrhoea, a runny nose and slight fever. Your baby needs to
have something hard to chew on such as a teething ring or a rusk.

INTERNAL TREATMENT

Drink plenty of either filtered or bottled water or diluted fruit juices.

ESSENTIAL OIL TREATMENT

1 drop chamomile oil in 1 teaspoon (5 ml) vegetable oil massaged
gently around the neck, jaw and cheeks. Pay special attention to the
area where the tooth is emerging and if the baby will allow it, apply
gentle pressure over this area.

HERBAL TREATMENT

- ✷ A weak chamomile tea given in teaspoon (5 ml) doses when needed (particularly at bedtime) will help the pain and fretfulness.
- ✷ Chill an eggcupful of chamomile tea in the refrigerator and when really cold, dip your finger (well scrubbed of course and with a very short nail) into the tea and use to gently massage the baby's sore gums. Use fresh tea each time.

HOMEOPATHIC TREATMENT

All 6–30ᶜ, give twice daily:
- ❋ Homeopathic Chamomilla 3 times a day.
- ❋ Calc. phos.

Bach Flower Remedies

Dr Edward Bach was born in England in 1886. He qualified as a doctor in 1912 but, even before qualifying, became concerned that even though drugs often relieved symptoms they did little to cure the underlying causes of disease. Dr Samuel Hahnemann, the founder of homeopathy, inspired Bach, and his principles became the basis of Dr Bach's system of healing, which was to 'treat the patient, not the disease'.

Being a nature lover and finding tranquillity when in the country-side, Dr Bach visited Wales and there by the mountain streams, he gathered the flowers with which he made his first 'Flower Remedies' that combine the spiritual essence of the flower with the emotional needs of the person. Over the next few years he spent much of his time in Wales, Norfolk and southern England collecting curative plants and developing the 38 remedies.

He died at the age of 50 but his work was carried on by his close friends, pupils and supporters Nora Weeks and Victor Bullen.

The following list is a *very* brief description of the remedies. For more information on the Remedies write to: Dr E. Bach Centre, Mount Vernon, Sotwell, Wallingford, Oxon, OX10 OPZ, England.

The remedies are available from most good health-food shops or from suppliers listed in the back of this book.

THE REMEDIES

BACH REMEDY	INDICATIONS
AGRIMONY	for those who hide their troubles from the world, putting on a cheerful face
ASPEN	for those suffering from vague, unknown fears and apprehension about impending disaster
BEECH	for those who are irritated by, and intolerant of, the ways, methods and lifestyles of other people
CENTAURY	for those so anxious to please others that they are exploited and neglect their own needs
CERATO	for those over-influenced by others through doubting their own judgement
CHERRY PLUM	for those who have uncontrollable fits of temper and fear loss of control and mental collapse
CHESTNUT BUD	for those who continually make the same mistakes and fail to learn from the past
CHICORY	for possessive people who manipulate and exert control over others or who are martyrs
CLEMATIS	for absent-minded daydreamers who lack concentration and tend to live in the future
CRAB APPLE	for those who have feelings of being unclean and who are ashamed of their bodies
ELM	for normally capable people who have become overwhelmed by burdens and responsibilities
GENTIAN	for those who become easily discouraged and despondent when set-backs occur
GORSE	for those who suffer extreme despair, hopelessness and defeatism
HEATHER	for self-absorbed people who want to talk about themselves but rarely listen to others

HOLLY	for those consumed with negative feelings of hate, envy, jealousy and revenge
HONEYSUCKLE	for those who dwell longingly and with nostalgia on the past; for homesickness
HORNBEAM	for procrastinators who feel too tired to face the day ahead
LARCH	for those who, though competent, make no effort to succeed through lack of confidence and certainty of failure
MIMULUS	for those who fear known things such as poverty, heights, pain, people; for the shy and timid
MUSTARD	for those who experience deep gloom, melancholy and sadness which has no cause and which can lift very suddenly
OAK	for battlers, who despite trials and tribulations never give up
OLIVE	for those suffering the complete loss of energy both mental and physical following a long illness or mental ordeal
PINE	for those dissatisfied with themselves and what they do; for those who take the blame for the faults of others
RED CHESTNUT	for those who are overly fearful and concerned for loved ones during illness, travel and other events
ROCK ROSE	for those experiencing extremes of panic, terror, fear and trauma
ROCK WATER	for the rigid minded and those who are overly strict with themselves, setting impossible ideals
SCLERANTHUS	for those who experience difficulty and uncertainty in making decisions, vacillating between choices
STAR OF BETHLEHEM	for those suffering mental and emotional trauma such as bereavement or accident

SWEET CHESTNUT	for those who have reached the absolute limits of despair or grief
VERVAIN	for those with strong wills and opinions who put too much effort and enthusiasm into their 'case', often becoming overbearing
VINE	for strong-willed people who like to take charge but can become arrogant, domineering and inflexible
WALNUT	regulates, stabilises and readjusts emotions during times of change such as puberty, menopause, divorce and moving home; helps protect from distracting influences
WATER VIOLET	for those who are capable and self-reliant, preferring to be alone, and while willing to advise, do not wish to interfere
WHITE CHESTNUT	for those who feel persistent intrusion of worries, the unwanted thoughts and mental arguments
WILD OAT	for those dissatisfied with their current lifestyle or work but unsure which path to follow
WILD ROSE	for those apathetically resigned to their 'lot' and unable to make the effort to change
WILLOW	for those who experience self pity and bitterness through perceived unjust and unfair treatment by others

RESCUE REMEDY

Rescue Remedy was devised by Dr Bach to calm and strengthen the emotions during trauma, anguish, bereavement or terror. It is made up of the following Flower Remedies:

ROCK ROSE	*Helianthemum nummularium* for terror, panic and fear
CLEMATIS	*Clematis vitalba* for unconsciousness, faintness and disorientation
IMPATIENS	*Impatiens glandulifera* for stress and agitation leading to muscle tension and pain
CHERRY PLUM	*Prunus cerasifera* for hysteria and fear of being 'out of control'
STAR OF BETHLEHEM	*Ornithogalum umbellatum* for shock and any mental and physical trauma

TO USE: *All the remedies are completely safe to use during pregnancy, childbirth, for young babies and for animals. They should be used in any situation where the previously described symptoms are apparent and may be used for humans and animals (birds seem to respond to them particularly well).*

Place 2 drops of the remedy or remedies in a cup of water and sip regularly.

For Rescue Remedy use 4 drops instead of 2, diluted in water as above or placed directly on the tongue as required. The remedies may also be applied to the inner wrists, behind the ears or rubbed onto the lips.

Bad breath

A dental check is indicated as bad teeth are a common source of bad breath.

Brush the tongue gently with toothpaste when brushing your teeth.

Stomach 'upsets' and insufficient gastric acids can cause bad breath.

INTERNAL TREATMENT

Eat 1–2 cups (250–500 ml) of 'live' yoghurt containing both acidophillus and bifidus cultures daily or, if preferred, take acidophillus tablets daily.

ESSENTIAL OIL MOUTHWASH

¼ cup (60 ml) sherry

2 tablespoons (40 ml) brandy

14 drops peppermint oil

4 drops oil of myrrh or ½ teaspoon (2.5 ml) tincture of myrrh

1 teaspoon (5 ml) glycerine

TO MAKE: *Mix together in a jar. Leave for 5–6 days to blend. Strain through coffee-filter paper. Store in a dark bottle.*

TO USE: *Add ½–1 teaspoon (2.5–5 ml) mouthwash to ½ glass warm water, rinse mouth several times with the mixture; spit out.*

HERBAL MOUTHWASH

1 cup (250 ml) brandy, sherry or cider vinegar

1 tablespoon crushed aniseed

1 tablespoon finely chopped peppermint leaves

4 cloves, bruised

½ teaspoon (2.5 ml) tincture of myrrh

TO MAKE: *Mix together in a jar with a well fitting lid. Leave for 1 week, shaking daily.*

Strain through a sieve and then through coffee-filter paper.

TO USE: *Add 2 teaspoons (10 ml) to 2 tablespoons (40 ml) warm water, rinse mouth, spit out.*

Have you heard that you can check if your breath smells by licking your forearm, waiting a few seconds and then smelling it? Better than waiting for your best friend to not tell you!

HOMEOPATHIC TREATMENT

Take four times daily:

火 Bitter taste on waking—Kali. phos. 12^x.

火 Metallic taste—Merc. sol. 6^c.

Basil (*Ocimum basilicum*)

HERB PARTS USED

Leaves and stems.

HERB ACTIONS

Antispasmodic, carminative, galactagogue, stomachic.

USE TO TREAT

Upset stomach, constipation, nausea, griping and wind, stomach cramps and vomiting. Eases chest infections. Used extensively in cooking and is a good companion to tomatoes in the garden.

ESSENTIAL OIL ACTION

Antidepressant, antiseptic, antispasmodic, expectorant, insect repellent.

USE TO TREAT

Muscle strain, rheumatism. Depression, headache, hysteria, mental fatigue. Bronchitis, whooping cough. Basil oil, included in a blend and massaged over the stomach, helps to ease digestive problems and painful periods.
Caution: *Avoid during pregnancy. Use 1 per cent only in blends and avoid long-term use.*

Baths

Bathing is an excellent way to treat many complaints; water cleanses, stimulates and promotes healing. Baths are also a simple and very useful way of gaining the benefits of essential oils and herbs.

Most water supplies in towns and cities are chlorinated, this can present a real risk of chlorine-gas poisoning if bathrooms aren't properly ventilated. Use a ceiling fan and leave the door or window open if the fan isn't very strong. Chlorine gas poisoning can cause mild to severe malaise.

TYPES OF BATHS

HOT BATHS

38–40°C (100–104°F); 8–10 minutes only. If the person having this type of bath is unwell, they should never be left alone while in the bath. Children, the frail or elderly or women who are pregnant shouldn't have very hot baths.

Use hot baths to reduce fevers and eliminate toxins by increasing perspiration and rate of breathing. Wrap the patient in warm towels and then in warm nightwear after the bath before returning to a pre-heated bed.

WARM BATHS

27–38°C (80–100°F); 20–30 minutes. Use to calm, relax and generally reduce stress.

COLD BATHS

21–27°C (69–80°F); 2–4 minutes only. Use to improve muscle tone and breathing, decrease fatigue, improve skin tone and thyroid function. Cold baths can help relieve constipation.

SITZ BATHS

A sitz bath is a hip bath used to tone or treat pelvic or abdominal ailments, relieve tissue congestion and improve the flow of blood and lymph to the area. It can also be used after childbirth to ease the discomfort of a sore perineum. The bath can be an ordinary bath containing only sufficient water to cover the hips or a bowl large and deep enough to sit in. The temperature of the water will vary depending on the complaint being treated.

FOOT BATHS

Hot or cold water as appropriate; 10–15 minutes. Choose a bowl (or bowls) with room for both feet. Use to ease the pain and swelling from sore and tired feet, to ease coughs and ward off influenza and colds and to ease headaches.

BATH BAGS

These bags are excellent for soothing sore, itchy, dry or sunburnt skin.

TO MAKE: *Mix equal quantities of bran and oats in a bowl. For each cupful add 15 drops single or mixed essential oils and/or ¼ cup dried, crumbled herbs (for suggestions see the following blends). Stir well to disperse the oils.*

Put ½ a cup of the mixture in a muslin bag and add to the bath as it is running. Squeeze to release the properties from the bran, oats, herbs and oils and use the bag as a washcloth.

Did you know that herbal tea-bags make good bath bags? Simply hang three or four under the hot tap as the water is running.

BATH SALTS

1 cup bicarbonate of soda

2 cups sea salt

1 cup Epsom salts

3 teaspoons (15 ml) essential oils (see recipes below)

TO MAKE: *Mix bicarbonate of soda, sea salt and Epsom salts together. Drip oils over while stirring well. Store in a tightly capped opaque container to avoid loss of perfume.*

TO USE: *Sprinkle 2–3 tablespoons in the bath, stir to dissolve.*

BATH OILS

CITRUS GROVE

Revives flagging minds and bodies.

1 teaspoon (5 ml) grapefruit oil

1 teaspoon (5 ml) bergamot oil

50 drops lemon oil

30 drops rosemary oil

20 drops sandalwood oil

AAAAH!

Sensual, warm and relaxing.

1 teaspoon (5 ml) ylang-ylang oil

1 teaspoon (5 ml) rose geranium oil

50 drops bergamot oil

50 drops sandalwood oil

SPIRITUAL BLISS

Helps us to find inner peace.

2 teaspoons (10 ml) sandalwood oil

½ teaspoon (2.5 ml) myrrh oil

30 drops frankincense oil

20 drops cinnamon

TO MAKE: *Mix together in a little bottle. Shake well.*

TO USE: *Mix 10 drops per bath for adults or 4–5 drops for children with 1 tablespoon (20 ml) full-cream milk or vegetable oil before adding to the bath. Agitate the water to disperse the oils.*

BATH VINEGARS

Vinegar is a therapeutic and refreshing addition to a bath. It restores the acid balance of the skin, eases the pain of sunburn and relieves dryness and itching of the skin. Most vinegars are suitable to use except malt vinegar, which is too harsh. White wine vinegar is the best for facial use; apple cider vinegar appears to have the most therapeutic value.

ESSENTIAL-OIL BATH VINEGARS

ARTHRITIS

2 cups (500 ml) vinegar

10 drops chamomile oil

10 drops rosemary oil

10 drops marjoram oil

5 drops black pepper oil

5 drops thyme oil

1 tablespoon (20 ml) glycerine

Did you know that dry-brush massaging gets rid of dead skin cells and stimulates the circulation and lymphatic system? Before showering or bathing, brush the whole body from the neck down using long, firm but gentle strokes. Avoid your tender bits but pay special attention to the groin and armpits.

CHILDREN (OVER 2 YEARS OLD)

2 cups (500 ml) vinegar

10 drops chamomile oil

5 drops lavender oil

5 drops mandarin oil

1 tablespoon (20 ml) glycerine

HEADACHES

2 cups (500 ml) vinegar

20 drops lavender oil

10 drops rosemary oil

5 drops chamomile oil

5 drops peppermint oil

1 tablespoon (20 ml) glycerine

MUSCLES, ACHING

2 cups (500 ml) vinegar

10 drops juniper oil

10 drops rosemary oil

10 drops lavender oil

5 drops eucalyptus oil

5 drops black pepper oil

1 tablespoon (20 ml) glycerine

STRESS

2 cups (500 ml) vinegar

20 drops lavender oil

10 drops clary sage oil

5 drops bergamot oil

5 drops sandalwood oil

1 tablespoon (20 ml) glycerine

SUNBURN & ITCHY SKIN

2 cups (500 ml) vinegar

40 drops lavender oil

1 tablespoon (20 ml) glycerine

HERBAL BATH VINEGARS

TO MAKE: *Substitute the essential oils in the above recipes with as many of the same herbs as you can obtain.*

Fill a jar with the mixed herbs, cover with warm vinegar then with an acid or vinegar-proof lid.

Stand in the hot sun or another warm place for 24 hours.

Strain the vinegar, add more fresh herbs and repeat the above process.

Repeat once more if very strong vinegar is desired.

TO USE: *Pour ½ cup (125 ml) in the bath after the bath has been drawn, mix well with the water. Stay in the bath for 15–20 minutes to obtain the full effect.*

Add 2 teaspoons (10 ml) to 1 cup (250 ml) water as a facial skin toner, aftershave or after-shower splash.

Use neat as a deodorant.

Beeswax 🌿 See Wax

Belladonna (*Atropa belladonna*) 🦎 Homeopathic

Suited to cheerful, energetic types of people.

USE TO TREAT

Acne, air sickness, boils, colic, cystitis, fever, headache, neuralgia (facial), insomnia, prostate problems, vertigo, whitlow.

Benzoin (*Styrax benzoin*)

HERB PART USED

The resin, which is collected from cuts made in the bark of the tree and allowed to harden is used. The ground resin makes an excellent tincture (see Tinctures) that has astringent, antiseptic, preservative and antifungal properties. Its preservative qualities make it suitable for use in creams and ointments. The ground resin can also be used as a fixative in pot-pourris and added to soap. If you buy tincture from a pharmacy be sure that you get *simple tincture of benzoin*. Compound tincture of benzoin (also known as Friar's balsam) contains 10 per cent benzoin, 90 per cent alcohol, 7.5 per cent storax, 2.5 per cent tolu balsam, and 2 per cent aloe. While this is a mixture of totally natural ingredients, it contains too little benzoin and too much alcohol and other ingredients to make it suitable for the healing processes described in this book. The dried gum is available through some of the stockists listed in the back of the book.

ESSENTIAL OIL ACTION

Anti-inflammatory, antifungal, antiseptic, antioxidant, fixative.

USE TO TREAT

Tissue inflammation, rheumatism and arthritis. Wounds, cracked sore skin. Bronchitis, colds, coughs and influenza. Eases nervous tension, depression and emotional 'burn-out'. Use as an antioxidant to help to preserve oils, as a fixative in perfumes and an additive to soaps, cosmetics and perfumes.

Bergamot (*Citrus bergamia*)

HERB PART USED
Rind of fruit.

ESSENTIAL OIL ACTION

Antibacterial, antidepressant, anti-inflammatory, antiseptic, deodorant, expectorant. Not to be confused with the bergamot herb, bergamot oil comes from tiny orange-like fruit. This oil gives Earl Grey tea its distinctive taste.

USE TO TREAT

Cystitis and urethritis, thrush, colds and flu, assists in avoiding infectious diseases. Acne, cold sores, psoriasis and scabies. Helps to promote new cell growth, heals wounds. Eases depression, tension and anxiety, and is emotionally uplifting. Fixative in perfumery and a major ingredient in traditional eau de cologne.

Caution: *Phototoxic—don't use before exposure to sun. Use only 0.5 per cent strength.*

Bicarbonate of soda

Otherwise known as baking soda or sodium bicarbonate. Mixed with salt it makes an excellent tooth cleaner for both humans and dogs (see Teeth and Pets)! A mildly abrasive powder for cleaning kitchen and bathroom sinks and other surfaces (see Herbal housekeeping). Mix to a paste with either vinegar or water and essential oils to make a pain soother when applied to bites and stings (see Bites & stings).

Bilberry (*Vaccinum myrtillus*)

HERB PART USED

Leaves and berries.

HERB ACTION

Antiseptic, astringent, antiallergenic, anti-inflammatory.

USE TO TREAT

A tea made from the leaves is used in the treatment of diabetes. The berries are effective in the treatment of many eye disorders such as chronic glaucoma (consult an eye specialist); poor night vision; tired, sore and inflamed eyes.

Birth 🌿 See Pregnancy

Bites & stings

Essential oils are the quickest and easiest way of treating bites and stings.

Carry a bottle of lavender and tea-tree oil in the car and if you are going swimming in the ocean add a spray bottle of vinegar to the kit.

BEE STINGS

- Scrape the sting out sideways, never pull with tweezers.
- Massage the affected skin with lavender oil and a paste of bicarbonate of soda and water. Repeat often. If an allergy is suspected, use the treatment on the way to the hospital.

DOG BITES

Wash the area around the bite immediately and thoroughly with tea-tree oil in water. Apply neat tea-tree oil and a dressing. Go to the nearest doctor or hospital outpatients section for further treatment.

JELLYFISH STINGS

- Some of the jellyfish in Australian waters are potentially lethal. The northern tropical waters are unsafe for swimming in from October to May—even paddling isn't recommended at this time.
- Carry a 2 litre bottle of vinegar and if you are stung flood the area of the sting for at least 30 seconds. Then apply lavender oil and, if available, apply ice to ease the pain.
- If you suspect that either the blue-ringed octopus or the box jellyfish has caused the sting, seek medical help *immediately* and carry out first-aid treatment on the way to hospital.

Did you know that if a mosquito bites you, the best remedy is spit and salt? Spit on the bite, sprinkle liberally with salt and rub hard!

MOSQUITO BITES

Ross River Virus and other debilitating viral diseases such as Barmah Forest Virus, Australian encephalitis and Dengue Fever carried by mosquitoes are rapidly on the increase in Australia. It's best to stay indoors at dusk and dawn or, failing this, to wear loose clothing and rub lots of insect repellent oil blend (see Ross River Virus) onto exposed flesh.

SNAKE BITES

Flood the wound with lavender oil. Bind the limb firmly but not too tightly. Keep the patient calm and still. Seek medical help immediately. Identify the snake if possible.

SPIDER BITES

Spray the area of the bite with vinegar and then cover with neat lavender oil. Try to identify the spider. If you suspect that it is a venomous variety go straight to hospital, dripping the puncture area with lavender oil until medical treatment begins.

WASP STINGS

Use vinegar and lavender oil as described for treatment of spider bites.

HOMEOPATHIC TREATMENT

Take every 15 minutes until settled, then 4 times daily for 1 week:
- Puncture wounds in general—Ledum and/or Hypericum 30^c.
- Animal bites—Aconite 6^c and or Echinacea 6^x.
- Red, painful and swollen—Apis mel. 30^c.
- Bee or wasp sting—Arnica 30^c.

Bitters

Bitters are remedies that stimulate the appetite and digestive juices and tone the digestive system (see also Indigestion). They can range from mildly bitter to 'Ugh' with the worst tasting ones perhaps having the most therapeutic effect. The most common bitters are gentian root, dandelion leaf, rue and wormwood. Gentian root is considered to be one of the best bitters and is the main ingredient in Angostura Bitters. If you suffer from poor appetite and digestion, you could take 1 teaspoon (5 ml) Angostura Bitters in mineral water before or during meals.

Black pepper (*Piper nigrum*)

HERB PART USED

Seed.

ESSENTIAL OIL ACTION

Antibacterial, antiseptic, antispasmodic, antiviral, aphrodisiac.

USE TO TREAT

Muscular aches and pains; for arthritis, rheumatism, neuralgia, muscle sprains, stiff joints and to dispel bruises; and as a pre-sport application on joints and muscles. Chills, colds, fever, flu. Massage the abdomen to ease colic, constipation and nausea. Boosts immune-system function and expels toxins. Strengthens the nervous system and brain.

Blisters

* Don't prick a blister or it may become infected.
* Dab gently as often as is practical with neat lavender oil.
* Cover with a non-stick dressing on which 2–3 drops of lavender or tea-tree oil have been placed.

Blood pressure

HYPERTENSION (HIGH BLOOD PRESSURE)

Persistently high blood pressure needs to be taken very seriously. The following suggestions should be followed only after consultation with your health professional.

Most cases of hypertension can be brought under control through changes in diet and lifestyle.[1] Increase carefully planned, non-stressful daily exercise such as gentle walking. Find ways to reduce the stress in your life. Read the Emotional & Nervous Problems, Stress and Relaxation sections.

INTERNAL TREATMENT

🌿 Population as well as clinical studies have repeatedly demonstrated that obesity is a major factor in hypertension.[2] Eat a low fat, high carbohydrate diet with lots of fruit, vegetables, wholegrain bread and cereals.

🌿 Eat fish and free-range chicken instead of red meat.

🌿 Eat oranges, bananas, garlic and onions every day.

🌿 Cut out or down on alcohol, coffee, cigarettes, caffeine, sugar and salt.

DAILY SUPPLEMENTS

🌿 1 multi-vitamin mineral supplement.

🌿 1000 mg choline.

🌿 Co-enzyme Q10 as directed.

🌿 1000 mg garlic or 2 teaspoons 'Long-life juice' 3 times daily.

ESSENTIAL OIL TREATMENT

MASSAGE BLEND

1/3 cup (80 ml) vegetable oil

40 drops marjoram oil

30 drops geranium oil

20 drops hyssop oil

10 drops lavender oil

TO MAKE: *Mix together in a 100 ml bottle. Leave for a few days to blend. Store in a dark cool place.*

TO USE: *Add 2 teaspoons (10 ml) to a warm bath, agitate the water well to distribute. Soak in the bath for at least 10 minutes. Massage a little of the blend into the skin after a shower.*

Have you heard of White-coat hypertension? It is a rise in blood pressure caused by anxiety when visiting a doctor and can result in the prescription of unnecessary medication, which can cause unpleasant effects such as dizziness and low blood pressure. Talk about this with your doctor if your blood pressure reading is high.

HERBAL TREATMENT

Herbs such as hawthorn berry and mistletoe are used to lower blood pressure. Check availability with your health-food store or they may be obtained through a naturopath or herbalist. Take as directed.

HOMÉOPATHIC TREATMENT

Consult a homeopathic practitioner.

HYPOTENSION (LOW BLOOD PRESSURE)

This condition is far less common than hypertension (high blood pressure) and is far less serious. It can cause lightheadedness, dizziness and fainting especially if you have been sitting or lying down for a long time as the blood collects in the lower part of the body. People with this condition often feel the cold and can tire quickly.

Regular exercise and massage are helpful for raising blood pressure. Essential oils such as rosemary, black pepper, peppermint and lemon can be used in inhalations, baths and massage oils. It would be wise to limit the use of lavender, marjoram, melissa and ylang-ylang oils, all of which are used to lower blood pressure.

Blue cohosh (*Caulophyllum thalictroides*)

HERB PART USED

Roots and rhizomes.

HERB ACTIONS

Antispasmodic, antirheumatic, diuretic, emmenagogue, uterine tonic.

USE TO TREAT

Eases and regulates painful menstruation, especially when delayed. Eases labour pains and helps to ensure an easy birth. Traditionally has been also used for asthma, colic and rheumatism.

ESSENTIAL OIL ACTION

None used.

Boils

Boils are large, sore pus-filled spots and are a staphylococcus infection. They are generally indicative that the sufferer is run-down, stressed or has a poor diet. The aim of treatment is bring the boil to a head and by doing so allow the pus to escape and the area to heal. At the same time to improve the diet, lower stress levels and strengthen the immune system in an attempt to avoid the infection from reoccurring.

Boils are very contagious and food shouldn't be prepared by the patient while the infection is present.

If a fever develops or red lines radiate out from the boil, medical help needs to be obtained.

Any clothes in contact with the area of the boil need to be washed separately and a few drops of tea-tree or lavender essential oil used in the washing and rinsing water (see also Skin care).

Internal treatment

* Drink 6–8 glasses of filtered or bottled water daily.
* Eliminate sugar and other refined carbohydrates from the diet.
* Eat plenty of fresh fruit and vegetables, wholegrain bread and cereals.

Daily supplements

* 1000 mg garlic oil capsules 3 times daily or 2–3 teaspoons 'Long-life juice' 3 times daily.
* ½ teaspoon (2.5 ml) fluid extract of echinacea 3 times daily.
* 1000 mg vitamin C with bioflavonoids 3 times daily.
* 1 vitamin B complex tablet.
* 30 mg zinc.
* 5000–10 000 iu beta-carotene.

Essential oil treatment

* Add 5 drops tea-tree essential oil and 5 drops lavender essential oil to 1 cup (250 ml) warm boiled water. Dip cotton wool into the mixture and use to wash the boil and surrounding area.
* Apply a fomentation (see Fomentations) twice a day using the above oils.
* Keep the boil covered with a non-stick dressing sprinkled with 2 drops of tea-tree essential oil.

HERBAL TREATMENT

❧ Use cotton wool and a very strong calendula tea or 2 teaspoons (10 ml) calendula tincture in ½ cup (125 ml) warm water (see Tinctures) to wash the area. Mix slippery elm powder with calendula tea and apply as a hot poultice (see Poultices) twice a day until the boil bursts.

or

❧ Apply fomentations (see Fomentations) of 2 tablespoons Epsom salts in 1 cup (250 ml) hot water. Repeat 3–4 hourly until the boil comes to a head and bursts then apply calendula ointment (see Ointments) and a non-stick dressing to the boil.

HOMEOPATHIC TREATMENT

Take 4–8 times daily until suppuration clears then 4 times daily as long as needed:

✳ Much redness and heat—Belladonna 30^c.

✳ Intolerably painful, the patient chilly, the boil hot—Hepar. sulph. 30^c and Echinacea 6^x.

✳ Small injuries suppurating, the patient is chilly, the boil is cold—Silica 12^c.

Borax

A mineral collected from the shores of alkaline lakes. Borax is mildly alkaline and softening and may be used to soften hard water for clothes washing and for shampoos. It is added to many cosmetic products to help emulsification.

It must not be used internally, on broken skin, or for babies. It may cause irritation on sensitive skin.

Breasts

ABSCESSES

Seek professional advice and also use the following treatments.

INTERNAL TREATMENT

As for abscesses (see Abscesses).

DAILY SUPPLEMENTS

- 1000 mg garlic oil capsules 3 times daily or 2–3 teaspoons 'Long-life juice' 3 times daily.
- ½ teaspoon (2.5 ml) fluid extract of echinacea 3 times daily until the abscess has healed, then once a day for 3–4 weeks.
- 2000 mg vitamin C with bioflavonoids 3 times daily for 1 week, then once daily.

ESSENTIAL OIL TREATMENT

FOMENTATION BLEND
5 drops geranium oil
5 drops chamomile oil
Small bowl of hot water
TO MAKE: *Add the oils to the water. Fold a piece of soft cloth in four and soak in the water.*
TO USE: *Apply fomentation (see Fomentations) to the breast every 2 hours. Cover cloth with a piece of plastic and keep in place with a brassiere.*

Did you know that even though chamomile oil is very expensive, it can be bought diluted and ready to use for a much more modest sum, or infused oil can be made at home?

BREAST OIL
20 drops geranium oil
20 drops chamomile oil
3 tablespoons (60 ml) vegetable oil
TO MAKE: *Mix together in a small bottle. Shake well.*
TO USE: *Massage breasts very gently 4 times daily.*

HERBAL TREATMENT

- Steam or iron a cabbage leaf until wilted. Cool until comfortable temperature. Place over breast, cover with a piece of plastic wrap and hold in place with a brassiere.

❧ Pour 2 cups (500 ml) boiling water over 5 chamomile tea bags or the equivalent of fresh chamomile. Cover and steep for 10 minutes. Remove bags and use the warm tea as a fomentation for 10 minutes 3 times daily. The above amount should be enough for 4 treatments. The mixture will keep for 3 days if refrigerated.

HOMEOPATHIC TREATMENT ❊ See Abscesses

FIBROCYSTIC BREAST DISEASE (LUMPY BREASTS)

Lumpy breasts are typified by nodules that can change in size and location. Sometimes there is soreness, swelling, pain and tenderness but these symptoms don't always occur.

Lumpy breasts are often a part of the symptoms of PMS as they appear to be caused by hormonal changes in the body. The lumps usually disappear at menopause unless you are on a hormone replacement programme.

See your doctor for a breast examination and if you are over forty years old, have a mammogram (see also Pregnancy).

INTERNAL TREATMENT

❧ Completely avoid tea, coffee, chocolate and cola drinks.

❧ Cut down on meat and increase fibre foods, fruit and vegetables.

❧ Eat lots of soya foods such as soya milk, tempeh and tofu.

DAILY SUPPLEMENTS

❧ 5000–10 000 iu beta-carotene.

❧ 1 vitamin B complex tablet twice daily.

❧ 1000 mg vitamin C with bioflavonoids.

❧ 500–1000 iu vitamin E (d-alpha tocopherol).

❧ 1000 mg garlic oil capsules 3 times daily or 2–3 teaspoons 'Long-life juice' 3 times daily.

❧ 3000 mg borage (starflower) oil or evening primrose oil.

ESSENTIAL OIL TREATMENT

Apply warm fomentations (see Fomentations) using 6–8 drops of mixed chamomile and lavender oil.

BREAST-MASSAGE BLEND

3 tablespoons (60 ml) vegetable oil

30 drops chamomile oil

10 drops lavender oil

10 drops geranium oil

TO MAKE: *Mix together.*

TO USE: *Massage both breasts twice daily.*

Did you know that sore and swollen breasts may be eased by applying cabbage leaves that have been chilled in the refrigerator?

HERBAL TREATMENT

Apply warm fomentations (see Fomentations) using a triple-strength chamomile and lavender tea.

HOMEOPATHIC TREATMENT

Consult a homeopathic practitioner.

Breathing (Diaphragm)

We all breathe, but if you take time now to watch your breath you will probably find that you are using merely the top few centimetres of your lungs and only when you sigh or yawn do you use much more of the lung capacity. We also tend to inhale more thoroughly than we exhale so we rarely get rid of as much carbon dioxide as our bodies would like to.

These days, in cities, the air is hardly worth breathing at all, but breathe we must, so make your home as 'breather friendly' as possible by using products that don't pollute the air (see Herbal housekeeping). Spend as many weekends as possible in the country and *breathe*!

Correct breathing improves many functions: the metabolism, the circulatory system, the brain and nervous system and all the organs depend on receiving oxygen via the lungs and blood and getting rid of carbon dioxide in the same way. It reduces stress. Watch your breathing when you are angry or upset—it becomes shallow and fast.

Slow down the breathing and the anger and/or stress begin to dissipate. (See Emotional & Nervous Problems; Stress.)

We need to *learn* to breathe properly and, in order to do this, we need to do some breathing exercises so that we can actually feel the difference between the half or quarter-capacity breathing we are doing now and the real thing. Try doing the following exercise either on its own or as a prelude to meditation (see Relaxation). Notice the difference in tranquillity and energy levels after you have been practising it for a short while. Some people report a calm but energetic feeling the first time they do the exercise.

❦ Sit in a comfortable upright chair and relax—particularly relax your abdomen.

❦ Imagine that there is an orange or red deflated balloon in your abdomen.

❦ Stay relaxed through the whole exercise, keeping shoulders down and relaxed.

❦ Breathe in *slowly* through your nostrils to the count of four, visualise the balloon filling and pushing your abdomen out.

❦ Hold the breath for a count of six, keeping the balloon full but stay relaxed.

❦ Now, *slowly* to a count of eight, let the air out of the balloon, through your mouth in an audible sigh 'whoo . . . oo . . . oo . . . oo . . . oo'. Allow your shoulders to relax and drop as you breathe out. See if you can let a little more air out of the balloon and then repeat the cycle four more times.

If you have problems visualising the balloon, just use the counting but keep your abdomen relaxed. Some people can breathe very slowly but it's important to adjust the rate of breathing until it is comfortable to you. As you practise, it will be easier to slow down.

Bronchitis

Bronchitis is an acute or chronic inflammation of the mucous lining of the bronchial tubes. Chronic bronchitis is a serious and potentially fatal condition that needs careful treatment. Smoking and drinking alcohol can make bronchitis worse and prevent its cure.

It's important to have bed rest when suffering from acute bronchitis otherwise serious complications like pleurisy and pneumonia can occur.

Postural drainage will help to drain the lungs of excess mucus and should be undertaken for 5–10 minutes 2–3 times a day. It is most helpful after an inhalation.

Lie across a bed with the top half of the body off the bed, support yourself with your forearms on the floor. If you have someone to help they can gently pat your back (padded with a towel) using the flat of a closed fist. Have a bowl or paper on the floor to collect any mucus.

INTERNAL TREATMENT

- Drink copious quantities of filtered or bottled water and fruit or vegetable juice.
- Cut out all dairy products from your diet to lessen mucus production.

DAILY SUPPLEMENTS

- 1000 mg garlic oil capsules 3 times daily or 2–3 teaspoons 'Long-life juice' 3 times daily.
- 5000–10 000 iu beta-carotene.
- 500 mg vitamin C every 2 hours for 2 days, 1000 mg daily for 1 week.
- ½ teaspoon (2.5 ml) echinacea fluid extract 3 times daily.
- 3 zinc lozenges daily during an attack.

ESSENTIAL OIL TREATMENT

A

3 drops benzoin oil

2 drops eucalyptus oil

1 drop thyme oil

TO MAKE: *Drop onto the surface of a bowl of boiling water and use as an inhalation (see Inhalations).*

B

6 drops thyme

12 drops lavender

1 tablespoon (20 ml) vegetable oil

TO MAKE: *Mix together and use to massage the chest and throat area three times daily and as needed at night.*

HERBAL TREATMENT

❧ Inhalation (see Inhalations) using crushed thyme in boiling water.

❧ Sip ½ cup (125 ml) very hot decoction (see Decoctions) of ginger root and/or mullein leaves sweetened with honey every 1–2 hours.

HOMEOPATHIC TREATMENT

Take 4–8 times daily:

❦ Rattling of mucus in bronchial tubes—Ipecac. and/or Aconite 30^c.

❦ Loss of voice or hoarseness—Phosphorus and/or Hepar sulph. 30^c.

Bruises

If you bruise easily it could indicate of a lack of vitamin C. Take 2000 mg 3 times a day for two weeks and 1000 mg a day from then on. Increase consumption of vitamin C-rich foods (see Vitamins and Minerals).

ESSENTIAL OIL TREATMENT

Sprinkle 3 drops of lavender oil on 1 cup (250 ml) of iced water. Use as a compress, re-apply frequently.

HERBAL TREATMENT

❧ 200 mg bromelain 3 times a day *between* meals. (This enzyme is absorbed from the gastro-intestinal tract and is able to promote the healing of tissue injury.)[1]

❧ Ice-cold compress of distilled witch-hazel, reapply frequently for 8–10 hours.

❧ Poultice with crushed comfrey root.

❧ Calendula ointment (see Ointments).

❧ Arnica ointment (if skin is not broken).

HOMEOPATHIC TREATMENT

Arnica 30^c, take 4 times daily; then take Ledum 30^c if bruise has blackened.

Buchu (*Agathosma betulina*)

HERB PART USED

Leaves.

HERB ACTIONS

Aromatic, carminative, diaphoretic, diuretic, stimulant, urinary antiseptic.

USE TO TREAT

Cystitis and urethritis, bladder inflammation, catarrh of the bladder

ESSENTIAL OIL ACTION

None used.

Burdock (*Arctium lappa*)

HERB PART USED

Root.

HERB ACTIONS

Alterative, aperient, diuretic, diaphoretic.

USE TO TREAT

Bacterial and fungal infections. Use a decoction of the root in conjunction with yellow dock root as a blood cleanser to help the liver and kidneys to detoxify the system and help to heal eczema, boils and rheumatic conditions. A tea made from the leaves can help long-standing indigestion. Use as a decoction and skin wash to aid in healing eczema and psoriasis.

ESSENTIAL OIL ACTION

None used.

Burns & scalds (Minor)

Moderate to severe burns need urgent medical attention. If there is clothing stuck to the burn, make no attempt to remove it.

Hold the burnt area under cold water or apply cold compresses for a full 10 minutes to reduce the heat in the area.

For minor burns over a small area, cool with water as described above then apply neat aloe vera gel (split open the leaf and apply the gel directly to the burn) and/or lavender oil or honey which should be dabbed on gently. Repeat at 10–15 minute intervals if needed.

To facilitate swift and scar-free healing, squeeze the oil from vitamin E capsules onto the burn area the day after applying the above first-aid treatment.

HOMEOPATHIC TREATMENT

For all burns and scalds—Cantharis 30ᶜ, take every 15 minutes until pain subsides, then 3 times daily for 2 days or more depending on severity.

Bursitis

Bursitis is the inflammation of a bursa, a small sac of moist fibrous tissue. Bursas are found sandwiched between tendons and ligaments and help to reduce friction. This condition often occurs in the kneecap (Housemaid's knee) and shoulder (Dustman's shoulder). The source of the problem needs to be removed before any inprovement is seen. Follow the treatment recommended for tendonitis (see Tendonitis, and Repetitive Strain Injury).

Bryonia (Bryonia alba)   ✳   Homeopathic

Suited to those who are easily angered and morose and who enjoy being alone.

USE TO TREAT

Arthritis, bronchitis, 'chestiness' (coughing and wheezing), colic, constipation, diarrhoea (after eating fruit), gall-bladder problems, influenza, rheumatism.

Calc. carb. (Calcarea carbonica) ✳ Homeopathic

Suited to plump, fair-haired, quiet, shy people who get depressed easily. They often have difficulty comprehending and making mental effort, are passive but often stubborn if asked to do something they don't want to do.

USE TO TREAT

Appetite (excessive), chilblains, cold hands, constipation, cracked skin in winter, itching skin, period pains, pre-menstrual symptoms, sleeplessness (especially in children), toothache, vertigo.

Calc. fluor. (Calcarea fluorica) ✳ Homeopathic

USE TO TREAT

Arthritis, catarrh, colds, cough, croup, piles, toothache, varicose veins, whitlow.

Calendula (Calendula officinalis)

HERB PART USED

Leaves and flowers.

HERB ACTIONS

Astringent and antiseptic. One of the most valuable healing herbs.

USE TO TREAT

Wounds, cuts, sores and abrasions. It is also good for sore nipples, ulcers, sprains and varicose veins. It helps to reduce inflammation and pain from stings and measles and chickenpox spots. Teas (see caution) will help to stimulate bile production.

Tincture of calendula is a most important addition to a first-aid box and very simple to make (see Tinctures).

Caution: *This herb is the true marigold/calendula and must never be confused with the African or French marigold which may have dangerous properties if used internally or as an essential oil.*

ESSENTIAL OIL ACTION

Rarely available. See caution. See also Aromatherapy & Essential oils.

Make an infused oil (see Aromatherapy & Essential oils, Extraction of essential oils) from the petals to extract the benefits.

USE TO TREAT

Rough, cracked skin. Skin problems in children such as grazes and nappy rash; for cracked nipples in nursing mothers; scars, varicose veins, chronic ulcers.

Cancer

It would be unethical and illegal to claim a treatment that can cure cancer, nevertheless, there are many alternative ways to support the immune system and alleviate unpleasant symptoms while still undergoing orthodox treatment. It's very important to tell your physician of the alternative treatments that you wish to use in conjunction with the treatment decided upon by her/him.

The word 'cancer' is treated with almost medieval fear, yet well over a third of people with cancer can expect to be cured and the remainder may experience years of remission of this disease. The intricate systems of the body constantly heal cuts, bruises, colds and other complaints naturally with no interventionist treatment. Mounting evidence shows that a positive attitude, certain foods, stress management including meditation and visualisation, and a generally healthy lifestyle may prevent the growth of tumours and in many cases cause cancer to go into remission.

The following suggestions may prove valuable for cancer patients.

* Learn to meditate and visualise. It's probably easier to join a group but, if this isn't possible, see Relaxation.
* Learn to control your stress with breathing, appropriate exercise such as gentle swimming or walking, eating a balanced diet, listening to music or enjoying a hobby and having fun.
* Don't keep your fears and problems to yourself. Your friends and family can be your greatest allies and it helps immensely to share your thoughts.
* Even though it may be very difficult, try to smile and laugh as much as possible. Smiling and laughing actually strengthen the immune system.
* Remain in control of your life. Make decisions on what you know and feel about yourself, don't let others (no matter how well meaning) over-persuade you.

See also Dry-brush massage; Stress; Relaxation; Breathing; Vitamins and Minerals; and Melanoma.

INTERNAL TREATMENT

* If the patient is feeling unwell and nauseous, skimmed-milk shakes or fruit and vegetable juices may be more acceptable and better tolerated than whole foods.
* Eat garlic and onions daily.
* Cut out or cut down on animal and other saturated fats.
* Eat fish in preference to meat.
* Avoid smoked meats and foods containing preservatives.
* Stop smoking and drinking alcohol.
* Eat plenty of fresh, organically grown fruit and vegetables for their antioxidant, beta-carotene and vitamin C content.
* Eat plenty of beans, nuts and wholegrains (in bread and cereals) for the fibre and mineral content.

❀ Drink 8 glasses of bottled or filtered water or diluted fruit juice daily. There are excellent fresh bottled juices available in supermarkets.

DAILY SUPPLEMENTS

※ Astragalus as recommended (see Astragalus).

※ 25 000 iu beta-carotene.

※ 500 iu vitamin E (d-alpha-tocopherol).

※ 2000 mg vitamin C with bioflavonoids 3 times daily for a month then 1000 mg 3 times daily.

※ 1000 mg garlic 3 times daily or 'Long-life juice' 2 teaspoons 3 times daily.

ESSENTIAL OIL TREATMENT

A professional massage is preferable, but a light, gentle massage with no deep kneading movements by a friend or family member can be relaxing and therapeutic. Discuss massage treatment with your physician before commencing treatment. Massage should not be used for patients with Hodgkins Disease or bone cancer.[1]

MASSAGE BLEND

10 drops tea-tree or eucalyptus oil

15 drops cedar oil

5 drops bergamot oil

2 tablespoons (40 ml) vegetable oil

TO MAKE: *Mix together in a small bottle.*

TO USE: *Massage as indicated above.*

HERBAL TREATMENT

Astragalus (see Astragalus) as recommended.

HOMEOPATHIC TREATMENT

Consult a homeopathic practitioner.

Candidiasis (*Candida albicans*)

Candida albicans, a harmless yeast present from birth, occasionally grows excessively and causes significant health problems.

This overgrowth is often attributed to overuse of antibiotics and other drugs. The drugs kill both friendly and unfriendly bacteria thus leaving the body vulnerable. There is a tendency for candidiasis to occur in patients suffering from cancer, AIDS and other such diseases that suppress the immune system. This is usually due to the use of long-term immunosuppressive drugs.

Candidiasis can also be caused by eating too much sugar and sugar-laden foods. The most common symptom is thrush, an infection of the mucous membranes caused by the *Candida albicans* fungus, which sometimes affects the mouth (especially in babies) but is more usually found in the vagina. Men can transmit thrush even though they may show no symptoms so it's important to treat both sexual partners.

Only wear cotton underwear and avoid wearing tight trousers, jeans, tights or pantyhose.

Candidiasis is a fashionable disease and is often diagnosed when the symptoms are vague and rather general. If the following treatment shows no sign of helping after 3–4 weeks consult a professional.

INTERNAL TREATMENT

- Follow a sugar-free diet. Avoid fruit and fruit juices (apples, pears and berries are acceptable).
- Eliminate yeasts and mould-bearing foods including yeasted breads and cakes, alcoholic beverages, cheese, most nuts and dried fruit from the diet.
- Cut out milk products except for 3 cups of 'live' yoghurt every day. Yoghurt can also be used as a douche to treat thrush.
- Eat lots of grains and vegetables, fish, poultry and meat.
- There are many good recipe books around. You will need the diet for at least 4–6 weeks before you see results. If there is no discernible improvement after this time, see your doctor.

Did you know that babies often contract thrush from the mother while in the birth canal?

DAILY SUPPLEMENTS

- ½ teaspoon (2.5 ml) fluid extract of echinacea 3 times daily.
- *Lactobacilus acidophillus* powder or capsules as directed.
- 1 multi vitamin-mineral tablet.
- 30 mg zinc.
- 1000 mg garlic oil capsules 3 times daily or 2–3 teaspoons 'Long-life juice' 3 times daily.

ESSENTIAL OIL TREATMENT

Not recommended.

HERBAL TREATMENT

- Add 1 teaspoon (5 ml) tincture of myrrh to 1 cup (250 ml) water. Mix and use as a douche (see Douches).
- If the vagina isn't too sore you can dip a tampon into yoghurt and insert it into the vagina. Replace every 2 hours.
- If the vaginal area is sore and inflamed the following suggestion will be very soothing and healing. Dissolve 4 tablespoons bicarbonate of soda in 4 litres warm water in a bowl big enough to sit in. Sit in the bowl, and holding the vagina open with one hand, 'swoosh' the water as far inside it as possible. Stay in the water for about 10 minutes.

HOMEOPATHIC TREATMENT

Take 4 times daily:
- Oral thrush—Merc. sol. and Borax 12^c.
- Painfully irritating—Nat. mur. 30^c.

Cantharis (*Cantharis vesicatoria*) ❧ Homeopathic

USE TO TREAT

Burns, cystitis, gnat bites, sunburn.

Caraway (*Carum carvi*)

HERB PART USED

Mainly seeds.

HERB ACTIONS

Antispasmodic, appetiser, carminative, emmenagogue, expectorant, stomachic.

USE TO TREAT

Flatulence and indigestion, colic, griping and wind. A delicious addition to cakes, biscuits and breads. To act as a digestive and prevent flatulence, sprinkle caraway over cabbage before cooking.

ESSENTIAL OIL ACTION

Antiseptic, astringent, carminative, diuretic, emmenagogue, expectorant, stimulant, stomachic, tonic.

USE TO TREAT

Bronchitis, coughs, laryngitis, colic, flatulence, gastric spasms, nervous indigestion, poor appetite.

Carbo veg. (*Carbo vegetabilis*) 🌿 Homeopathic

USE TO TREAT

Acidity and heartburn with flatulence, fainting, hoarseness and loss of voice, poor circulation, tinnitus with nausea and vertigo.

Carminatives

Help to expel gases from the intestines.

HERBS

Anise, bergamot, caraway, catnep, coriander, dill, fennel, ginger, peppermint, spearmint.

ESSENTIAL OILS

Angelica, aniseed, caraway, cardamon, coriander, dill, fennel, ginger, peppermint, spearmint.

Carnitine

This is a substance made in the body from lysine and methionine. It is sometimes known as vitamin B-T but is in fact not a vitamin. Carnitine is used in the body to transport and use fatty acids. Clinical trials have demonstrated that it may help in the treatment of angina and heart disease (see Angina and Heart care).

Carpal Tunnel Syndrome

A condition caused by compression of the nerve that enters the hand through a space (carpal tunnel) in the wrist. This causes pain and numbness in the first 3 fingers and the thumb and often spreads to affect the whole arm. There is often weakness and pins-and-needles in the fingers and thumb.

The cause of this condition is sometimes obscure. It is most common (for no apparent reason) in middle-aged and pregnant women. It is also found in arthritis sufferers (see Arthritis) and those who use a keyboard. I developed quite a severe case of this incapacitating complaint after working long hours on the computer keyboard. Here is the way in which I cured myself and learnt how not to be a 'repeat offender' (see also RSI and Tendonitis).

Part of the treatment is to buy a wrist and thumb brace to immobilise the affected area for much of the day.

Massage the wrist, thumb and forearm up to the elbow 4–6 times a day alternately with arnica oil and 3–4 drops chamomile oil in 1 teaspoon (5 ml) vegetable oil.

After the inflammation begins to recede and the pain lessens, do some gentle exercises: open both hands, with fingers open, and then close to make fists. Repeat 10–12 times.

Stretch the arms out and rotate the hands, with fingers open, from the wrists. Repeat 10 times, then 10 times in the opposite direction.

Continue with these exercises even when the problem has been resolved. Hopefully it won't recur.

DAILY SUPPLEMENTS

* 30 mg vitamin B6.
* 1 vitamin B complex tablet.

Catarrh

A small amount of thin watery mucus is necessary to keep the mucous membranes of the nose and throat lubricated and protected, but sometimes the membranes become irritated or infected, which leads to the production of copious amounts of thick mucus known as catarrh. The mucous membranes will often swell and this, combined with the mucus, results in runny and blocked noses, coughs and sometimes earaches.

Production of excessive mucus can be caused by infection; hayfever; and irritants such as tobacco smoke, chemical fumes, animal fur, pollens or food allergens.

INTERNAL TREATMENT

* Avoid mucus-forming refined sugar in drinks, biscuits, cakes and other foods; and dairy products such as milk and cheese.
* Eat garlic and onions and plenty of spicy foods such as horseradish, curries, black pepper and cayenne.
* Drink lots of fluids—at least 6–8 glasses daily of diluted fruit or vegetable juices, lemon water or bottled or filtered water.

DAILY SUPPLEMENTS

* 1000 mg vitamin C with bioflavonoids 3 times daily until the condition improves.
* 1000 mg garlic oil capsules 3 times daily or 2–3 teaspoons 'Long-life juice' 3 times daily.

ESSENTIAL OIL TREATMENT

CHEST MASSAGE BLEND

10 drops tea-tree or eucalyptus oil

15 drops rosemary or pine oil

5 drops peppermint oil

2 tablespoons (40 ml) vegetable oil

TO MAKE: *Mix together in a small bottle.*

TO USE: *Massage chest twice daily.*

  Use 2 drops of each essential oil in an inhalation (see Inhalations).

HERBAL TREATMENT

Drink a cup of mullein leaf tea 3 times daily, sweeten with honey if liked, or, even better, drink 15 drops of mullein leaf tincture in 2 tablespoons water 3 times daily.

HOMEOPATHIC TREATMENT

Take 4 times daily:

* Head cold with yellow-green discharge—Calc. fluor./Kali sulph. 12^c.
* Head cold with watering eyes and streaming nose—Euphrasia and/or Nat mur. 30^c.
* Thick yellow-green mucus—Pulsatilla 30^c or Kali sulph. 12^c.
* Stringy discharge—Kali. bich. 30^c.

Catnep (*Nepeta cataria*)

HERB PART USED

Leaves.

HERB ACTIONS

Anodyne, antispasmodic, aromatic, carminative, diaphoretic.

USE TO TREAT

Chickenpox, measles, fevers, hyperactivity, insomnia. An excellent remedy for children to calm and soothe colic and fevers. For adults it reduces fevers, is mildly relaxant, eases pain and relieves flatulence.

An infused oil (see Aromatherapy & Essential oils, Extraction of essential oils) would be useful for baths and massages for children.

Cats 🐾 See Pets

Cayenne (*Capsicum frutescens*)

HERB PART USED

Fruit.

HERB ACTIONS

Carminative, digestive, diaphoretic, rubefacient, stimulant, tonic.

USE TO TREAT

Colds, fevers, sinus congestion. Tonic for the digestive and circulatory system, and eases stomach pains and cramps, cold hands and feet and chilblains. Energy stimulant. Use as a tincture in liniments (for embrocations) to ease arthritis, rheumatism and lumbago.

ESSENTIAL OIL ACTION

Rarely used due to many adverse skin reactions.

Cedarwood (*Cedrus atlantica*)

HERB PART USED

The wood shavings make a pleasant scented base for pot-pourris and similar products.

HERB ACTIONS

Not generally used therapeutically.

ESSENTIAL OIL ACTION

Important to use only *Cedrus atlantica*. Antiseptic, aphrodisiac, astringent, deodorant, expectorant, insect repellent.

USE TO TREAT

Urinary tract, bronchial and vaginal infections. A 'masculine' aroma, use in deodorants for men. Stimulates new cell growth. Eases anxiety and stress.

Caution: *Not to be used in pregnancy.*

Celery (Apium graveolens)

HERB PART USED

Seed, whole plant.

HERB ACTIONS

Plant: Antirheumatic, appetiser, diuretic, emmenagogue, sedative.
Seeds: Antirheumatic, diuretic, carminative.

USE TO TREAT

Use celery juice to treat arthritis, rheumatism, gout, flatulence. Use a decoction of the seeds to treat bronchitis, arthritis, rheumatism and depression.

ESSENTIAL OIL ACTION

None.

Cervical dysplasia

This pre-cancerous condition of the uterine cervix is very treatable if diagnosed in its early stages, usually after a routine pap smear (see Pap smears). The condition is graded and the following treatment is for grades 1 and 2 (after consultation with a doctor). For grades 3 or 4 the treatment can be carried out alongside conventional treatment.

Factors which may be responsible for dysplasia include cigarette smoking, early-age sexual intercourse and/or multiple sexual partners, viruses, oral contraceptives and poor diet.

If diagnosed with cervical dysplasia stop smoking, use either condoms or a diaphragm as contraception and improve your diet.

Note: *After a month on the following treatment have a pap smear test.*

INTERNAL TREATMENT

- Eat beans, tofu, fish or chicken instead of red meat.
- Choose vegetables from all the different colour groups at the market and eat a variety for lunch and dinner every day.
- Eat fruit between meals instead of biscuits and cakes—cut out as much refined sugar as possible.
- Eat plenty of wholegrain bread and cereals with *a scraping only* of butter (not margarine) or a mixture of butter with either canola or olive oil.
- Drink 6–8 glasses of filtered or bottled water every day.

DAILY SUPPLEMENTS

- 1 vitamin B complex tablet.
- 4 mg folic acid daily for 1 month, 0.5 mg a day from then on.
- 100 000 iu beta-carotene daily for 1 month, 50 000 iu daily from then on.
- 1000 mg vitamin C with bioflavonoids 3 times daily.
- 15 mg zinc.

ESSENTIAL OIL TREATMENT

Douche (see Douches) using 2 drops of tea-tree oil in 2 cups (500 ml) warm water. Agitate the water really well just prior to douching.

HERBAL TREATMENT

Douche (see Douches) using a mixture of calendula and lavender teas with 1 teaspoon (5 ml) cider vinegar to 2 cups (500 ml) of herb tea.

HOMEOPATHIC TREATMENT

- 30^c, take orally and use a few drops mixed in water as a douche (see Douches).
- Calendula and/or echinacea and/or kreosotum.

Chamomile (*Anthemis nobilis* & *Matricaria chamomilla*)

There are two varieties: the German (*Matricaria chamomilla*), an annual, and the creeping perennial (*Anthemis nobilis*).

HERB PARTS USED

Flowers.

HERB ACTIONS

Analgesic, anti-inflammatory, antispasmodic, calmative, cholagogue, disinfectant, diuretic, emmenagogue, febrifuge, nervine. Both have similar properties but *Matricaria chamomilla* is less bitter when used as an tea. The teas are calming, soothing and anti-inflammatory.

USE TO TREAT

Headaches, nervousness, depression and insomnia. The tea works well to treat eczema; urticaria (hives); urinary tract infections; menstrual and menopausal problems; digestive problems caused by stress including heartburn, indigestion, colic, ulcers, colitis, irritable bowel syndrome and colic. The natural antihistamine properties of chamomiles ease the miseries of hayfever and allergic reactions.

ESSENTIAL OIL ACTION

Anti-inflammatory, antispasmodic, analgesic, calmative, cholagogue, disinfectant, diuretic, emmenagogue, febrifuge, nervine.

USE TO TREAT

The oil is used to treat the same problems as the herb. Chamomile is also valuable for its ability to ease dull aches and pains. It can be used for very young babies (see Babies). The oil is very expensive, but a very strong infused oil (see Aromatherapy & Essential oils, Extraction of essential oils) is a good substitute.

Chamomilla (*Matricaria chamomilla*) ✻ Homeopathic

Suited to cross and grumpy babies and children who don't want to be helped or bribed but need constant cuddling.

USE TO TREAT

Colic, flatulence, stress and also teething pain in infants.

Chaste tree (*Vitex agnus-castus*)

HERB PART USED

Fruit.

HERB ACTIONS

Tonic and regulator for reproductive organs.

USE TO TREAT

PMS, painful periods, menopause and other hormone-related problems.

ESSENTIAL OIL ACTION

None.

Chickenpox

A highly infectious viral disease with an incubation period of 10–21 days. It begins like a feverish cold before the rash appears. The red, spotty rash looks at first like insect bites and then develops into blisters that are often intensely itchy. Some children are covered from head to foot in the spots, others may have very few spots, while the rest are somewhere between these two extremes.

Trim the child's nails very short or put gloves or mittens on their hands as there is a risk of infection and/or scarring if the blisters are broken.

Caution: *Aspirin is thought to trigger Reye's Syndrome, a serious life-threatening disease if given to children suffering from chickenpox.*

INTERNAL TREATMENT

❋ Copious amounts of fluid—filtered or bottled water, diluted fruit juice.

❋ Vitamin C with bioflavonoids and echinacea fluid extract may be given as directed.

ESSENTIAL OIL TREATMENT

Children from 2 to 4 years: Follow the instructions for children over 4 years old but use only lavender and/or chamomile oil.

Children over 4 years old: Bathe frequently in lukewarm baths in which you have dispersed 2 drops tea-tree and 2 drops lavender oil.

Make a spray or lotion using the following oils:

5 drops lavender oil

5 drops tea-tree oil

5 drops chamomile oil

1 cup (250 ml) distilled witch-hazel

TO USE: *Pour in a spray bottle and spray the spots lightly or use as a lotion to dab on and cool the blisters.*

HERBAL TREATMENT

❧ Frequent baths using oat bath bags (tie a handful of rolled oats in muslin or thin cloth, drop in the bath and squeeze to release the milky liquid). Use the bag to *dab* the spots. (Be gentle as it's important not to break the blisters.)

❧ Feverish, fretful children will benefit from chamomile and/or catnep tea. Give 1 teaspoon (5 ml) doses to children under 4 years, 1 tablespoon (20 ml) doses to children over 4 years. Repeat 3 hourly.

❧ Compresses (see Compresses) and washes or sprays of chamomile tea will help to cool and reduce itching.

HOMEOPATHIC TREATMENT

30^c, take frequently (hourly if needed):

❋ To ease itching and pain use Rhus tox. and/or Hepar sulph.

Chickweed (*Stellaria media*)

Chickweed is one of the most important and effective herbs for treating skin complaints.

HERB PART USED

Whole herb.

HERBAL ACTIONS

Antirheumatic, carminative, demulcent, emollient, vulnerary.

USE TO TREAT

Skin irritations such as infantile and adult eczema, psoriasis, itching and irritation. (Chickweed ointments are available.)

ESSENTIAL OIL ACTION

None. An infused oil (see Aromatherapy & Essential oils, Extraction of essential oils) is useful for treating the problems mentioned.

Chilblains

Usually a winter affliction of people with poor circulation. If you have cold hands or feet don't warm them by a fire, instead immerse them in warm (not hot) water. Take frequent brisk walks to improve circulation.

DAILY SUPPLEMENTS

- ½ teaspoon (2.5 ml) fluid extract of echinacea 3 times daily during times of risk or infection.
- 500–1000 mg vitamin C with bioflavonoids.
- 5000–10 000 iu beta-carotene.
- 1 vitamin B complex tablet.
- Zinc lozenges as recommended.
- 500 iu vitamin E (d-alpha-tocopherol).

ESSENTIAL OIL TREATMENT

HAND & FOOT MASSAGE BLEND
6 drops marjoram oil
4 drops geranium oil
2 drops black pepper oil
1 tablespoon (20 ml) vegetable oil
TO MAKE: *Mix together.*
TO USE: *Massage the affected hands or feet. (Don't use essential oil treatments on broken skin.)*

HERBAL TREATMENT

Drink hot decoctions (see Decoctions) of fresh ginger root to improve circulation.

HOMEOPATHIC TREATMENT

Take 4 times daily:
* Itchy, swollen, stinging pain—Apis. mel. 30^c.
* Itching, burning, bluish red, swollen hands or feet, unbearable in heat of bed—Pulsatilla 30^c.
* For poor circulation and prevention of chilblain—Silicea 12^c.

Childhood complaints ❦ See Chickenpox, Measles, Mumps, Rubella, Whooping Cough

Cholagogues

Stimulate bile production and flow.

HERBS

Burdock, dandelion, garlic, milk thistle.

ESSENTIAL OILS

Chamomile, ginger, lavender, peppermint, spearmint, rosemary.

Cholesterol

Cholesterol is a fatty substance manufactured mainly in the liver and is one of the main fats found in blood. Cholesterol is bound to proteins called lipoproteins that transport cholesterol in our blood.

There is a misconception that all cholesterol is 'bad'. This is far from the truth. Cholesterol is needed to manufacture vitamin D on the surface of the skin, to help in the formation of cell membranes and to help to supply steroid hormones such as cortisone, testosterone, oestrogen and progesterone.

There are many types of cholesterol but two that need concern us are the LDL (low density lipoproteins) and the HDL (high density lipoproteins). HDL is a 'good' type of cholesterol. It is composed largely of lecithin and helps to clear cholesterol from the bloodstream. LDL is associated with heart ailments such as heart attack and stroke and the build-up of plaque on artery walls. This build-up results in the narrowing of the artery wall and leads to Atherosclerosis (see Atherosclerosis).

LDL is found in foods of animal origin particularly in egg yolk, liver, brains and fat in meat of all kinds (see also Heart care).

Circulation, poor

Poor circulation in the body extremities should never be ignored as it can lead to many more serious problems such as phlebitis or thrombosis, another less serious effect is chilblains (see Chilblains). Poor circulation affects mainly the elderly and the inactive but can also plague those who live in a cold climate.

INTERNAL TREATMENT

❧ Reduce the intake of nicotine and coffee as they constrict the small blood capillaries in the extremities.
❧ Try to use cayenne powder and ginger in cooking every day.

DAILY SUPPLEMENTS

❧ 500–1000 mg vitamin C with bioflavonoids.
❧ 5000–10 000 iu beta-carotene.

✣ 1 vitamin B complex tablet.

✣ 500 iu vitamin E (d-alpha tocopherol).

ESSENTIAL OIL TREATMENT

The following oil blend will cause the capillaries to widen, allowing a greater flow of blood to pass through.

MASSAGE BLEND

6 drops marjoram oil

4 drops rosemary oil

2 drops black pepper oil

1 tablespoon (20 ml) vegetable oil

TO MAKE: *Mix together.*

TO USE: *Massage the hands or feet fairly vigorously, squeezing and moving the fingers and toes to stimulate blood flow. Knead the palms of the hands and soles of the feet using the massage oil.*

HERBAL TREATMENT

✤ Drink hot decoctions (see Decoctions) of fresh ginger root to improve circulation.

✤ 750 mg gingko biloba capsules 3 times daily.

HOMEOPATHIC TREATMENT

Silicea 12^c, take 3 times daily.

Clary sage (*Salvia sclarea*)

HERB PART USED

Leaves and occasionally seed.

HERB ACTIONS

The leaves are little used these days as the seed oil seems to have the most powerful medicinal properties.

USE TO TREAT

Clary sage included in an ointment is useful to treat wounds. The leaves and seeds used as an eyewash and are also recommended for delayed or painful menstruation.

ESSENTIAL OIL ACTION

Antibacterial, antidepressant, antiseptic, antispasmodic, aphrodisiac, deodorant. Clary sage has many of the properties of sage without the risks of toxicity. It is a powerful relaxant.

USE TO TREAT

High blood pressure, stress, tension and the muscle tension that accompanies stress. Relieves asthma spasms, digestive cramps, colic pains. Can help scanty or missed periods. Can reduce excessive sweating and control excessive sebum production particularly on the scalp. Aphrodisiac.

Caution: *Not to be used in pregnancy. Be careful not to combine clary sage with alcohol—it can result in nightmares. In large amounts the odour of clary sage can be euphoric but can also lead to headaches.*

Cleaning (Cleaning agents) 🌱 See Herbal housekeeping

Cocculus 🌸 Homeopathic

USE TO TREAT

Travel and motion sickness.

Cocoa butter

Fat expressed from the cocoa bean of the cocoa plant (*Theobroma cacao*). This fat looks like beeswax, but has a very low melting point. When a block is rubbed on the skin it begins to melt immediately and, as it is has very emollient properties, it is a superb treatment for dry skin, and for rubbing on the stomach and breasts during pregnancy. Use it on its own or in creams and lotions to soften skin, particularly the delicate skin around the eyes, lips and throat.

Corns ❦ See Foot care

Chronic Fatigue Syndrome

Also known as ME (Myalgic encephalomyelitis) or post-viral syndrome, this debilitating and depressing complaint has only been recognised by the medical profession since the mid-1980s. Before then sufferers were often (and sometimes still are) treated unfairly as neurotic malingerers.

There is considerable confusion as to the cause of this ailment, as there are many reasons people can become chronically exhausted. An inefficiently working liver, undiagnosed allergies, mercury leaking from tooth fillings, candida or anaemia can all cause profound weariness but if accompanied by the symptoms described below it is probably a post-viral complaint which can last for years with the symptoms becoming less acute with time.

The problem seems to begin initially after a viral infection such as influenza or after profound emotional stress and shock when the sufferer becomes either physically and/or emotionally stressed—some authorities feel that chemical stress is also a cause. The end result of this stress is suppression of the immune system and the appearance of the syndrome.

The symptoms are many and varied but there is almost always a profound weariness and muscle fatigue, so complete that the patient becomes very depressed and extremely anxious, none of which helps to support and enhance the immune system. Other symptoms may be aching bones, joints and muscles, low grade fever, giddiness, headaches, depression and loss of concentration.

The treatment of Chronic Fatigue Syndrome is based largely on improving general health and that of the immune system.

Find a health professional such as a doctor practising complementary medicine or a herbalist, homeopath or naturopath experienced in the treatment of this problem, as careful detoxification is probably the first line of attack and involves processes unfamiliar to the average practitioner.

Lymphatic massage by an experienced aromatherapist or masseur is also an important detoxifying process.

Remember that, because depression has an adverse effect on the immune system, it's important to remain as positive as possible, even though this is often very difficult. Even when a cure seems to have been effected, the complaint can reoccur if high stress levels are allowed to develop.

Hot packs and hot showers or baths often help to ease the pain in the muscles (see also Glandular Fever, Immune system and Relaxation).

INTERNAL TREATMENT

- Eat a salad every day and lots of fruit and vegetables—as wide a variety as possible.
- Eat a low-fat, low- protein, high-fibre and complex-carbohydrate diet.
- Eat onions and garlic daily.
- Drink 6–8 glasses filtered or bottled water daily.

DAILY SUPPLEMENTS

- ½ teaspoon (2.5 ml) fluid extract of astragalus 3 times daily for one month.
- After the initial month, take ½ teaspoon echinacea liquid extract 3 times daily.
- 1000 mg vitamin C with bioflavonoids 2–3 times daily during the acute phase, 1000 mg daily afterwards.
- 5000–10 000 iu beta-carotene.
- 1 vitamin B complex tablet.
- 1000–2000 mg borage (starflower) oil or evening primrose oil.
- 1000 mg garlic oil capsules 3 times daily or 2–3 teaspoons 'Long-life juice' 3 times daily.
- Zinc lozenges as recommended for 1 week only during acute stage.

ESSENTIAL OIL TREATMENT

Make up a bottle of each of the essential oil blends and use at the appropriate times.

OIL FOR DEPRESSION

3 tablespoons (60 ml) vegetable oil

20 drops bergamot oil

10 drops grapefruit oil

10 drops ylang-ylang oil

TO MAKE: *Mix together in a small bottle.*

TO USE: *Massage oil or use 10 drops of the mixed essential oils in a warm bath or in an oil burner.*

OIL FOR EASING MUSCULAR PAIN

3 tablespoons (60 ml) vegetable oil

15 drops bergamot oil

15 drops marjoram oil

10 drops rosemary oil

5 drops black pepper oil

TO MAKE: *Mix together in a small bottle.*

TO USE: *Massage on sore muscles and joints or use 10 drops of the mixed essential oils in a warm bath.*

IMMUNO-STIMULANT & ANTI-VIRAL OIL

3 tablespoons (60 ml) vegetable oil

20 drops rosewood oil

5 drops thyme oil

10 drops tea-tree oil

10 drops lavender oil

TO MAKE: *Mix together in a small bottle.*

TO USE: *Massage the whole body or use 2 teaspoons (10 ml) of the blend in a warm bath.*

HERBAL TREATMENT

❧ Golden seal as directed.

❧ Skullcap for depression as directed.

- Siberian ginseng to strengthen the system when the worst stage is passed and the patient is convalescing.
- Drink chamomile tea instead of regular tea or coffee.

HOMEOPATHIC TREATMENT

Consult a homeopathic practitioner as the treatment is likely to be complex.

Cold sores 🌿 See Herpes

Colds & influenza

Influenza is *not* simply a bad cold. The symptoms can vary depending on the viral strain but can encompass fever, muscular pain (sometimes very severe), cough, headache and exhaustion. Bed rest is essential and with genuine influenza it's almost impossible to walk about. If influenza is neglected it can lead to severe complications, particularly in the very young or aged. If you get more than two colds a year your immune system may be depressed, see Immune system for treatment.

If you can be aware of the first subtle symptoms of colds or influenza, it's possible to alleviate some of the attendant miseries and prevent the symptoms worsening.

It shows a strong social conscience if you mix as little as possible with people when you have influenza or a cold, this will help to prevent the disease from spreading.

INTERNAL TREATMENT

- Free-range chicken soup (real chicken soup, not the stuff out of a packet) has been shown to get mucus moving 'up and out'.
- Drink copious amounts of liquid including diluted fruit juice, herbal teas

Did you know that colds are 'caught' mainly through touching something that an infected person has handled (such as money) and then putting your hand to your mouth or nose? Carry a small packet of tissues onto which you have sprinkled tea-tree oil and frequently wipe your fingers after handling money, shaking hands, etc.

(chamomile is good), filtered or bottled water, home-made lemonade.

❀ Use a saline nasal douche once or twice a day to clear mucus from the nose (see Douches).

DAILY SUPPLEMENTS

❀ Vitamin C with bioflavonoids: 2000 mg at onset of symptoms; 1000 mg every 2 hours for 3–4 days; 2000 mg 3 times a day daily thereafter until immunity is increased. The doses need to be lowered if the bowels become very loose.

❀ 1 teaspoon (5 ml) fluid extract of echinacea 3 times daily for 3 days, then ½ teaspoon (2.5 ml) 3 times daily until all symptoms have gone.

❀ 1000 mg garlic oil capsules 3 times daily or 2–3 teaspoons 'Long- life juice' 3 times daily.

❀ 1 vitamin B complex tablet.

ESSENTIAL OIL TREATMENT

MASSAGE BLEND
80 drops eucalyptus oil
60 drops tea-tree oil
40 drops lemon oil
20 drops thyme oil
TO MAKE: *Mix together in a small bottle.*
TO USE: *Add 10 drops to a hot bath. Agitate the water well to disperse the oils. Lie in the bath for 10–15 minutes breathing in the aroma.*

If you don't have a bath sprinkle 2–3 drops on a warm, wet flannel and rub over the whole body after showering.

Add 15 drops to 1 tablespoon (20 ml) vegetable oil and use to massage the whole body, in particular, the chest.

Sniff the contents of the bottle frequently to keep the head clear.

Make an air spray (see Air fresheners) using the mixed oils. Spray the house regularly to help prevent the infection from spreading.

HERBAL TREATMENT

- The age-old standby of hot herb teas of equal parts of elderflower, peppermint, yarrow and a pinch of cayenne cannot be beaten. Have a hot bath while sipping the hot tea. Go straight to bed with another mug of herb tea, and *sweat*.
- If you can't have a bath, a footbath is a good substitute. The following footbaths can help to ward off a cold or influenza as well as ease the symptoms. Mix 1 teaspoon chilli powder or 2 teaspoons mustard powder with a little water and stir thoroughly into a footbath of very hot water. Drink a herb tea (see above) while soaking the feet for 15 minutes. Go directly to bed after the treatment.
- Gargle with either a saline solution of ¼ teaspoon salt or 1–2 drops tea-tree oil in a glass of warm water.

HOMEOPATHIC TREATMENT

Take hourly until patient feels at ease, then 4–6 times daily:

- Sudden onset after exposure to draughts or cold winds — Aconite 30^c.
- Influenza-like symptoms — Gelsemium 30^c.
- Runny nose and sneezing — Nat. mur. 30^c.

Colic

ADULTS

Colic is usually caused by gas trapped in the intestines. Avoid fatty and indigestible foods and try to work out which foods cause the most problems.

INTERNAL TREATMENT

See Herbal treatment.

ESSENTIAL OIL TREATMENT

MASSAGE BLEND

8 drops chamomile oil

4 drops peppermint oil

1 tablespoon (20 ml) vegetable oil

TO MAKE: *Mix together in a small dish.*

TO USE: *Massage abdomen in a clockwise direction.*

HERBAL TREATMENT

✤ 2 capsules or 1 dropper of tincture of passionflower to act as an antispasmodic.

✤ Peppermint, chamomile, catnep, fennel or ginger tea sipped after a meal can either avert a colic attack or cure an existing attack.

✤ Chew fennel seeds after a meal, particularly if the food was fatty.

HOMEOPATHIC TREATMENT

Take as required during pain say, 15–30 minutes apart:

✺ Cutting pain—Colocynthis 30^c.

✺ Accompanied by flatulence—Argent. nit. 30^c.

✺ Easier when 'doubled-up'—Belladonna and/or Mag. phos. 30^c.

✺ Better when lying still—Bryonia 30^c.

✺ Accompanied with flatulence—Chamomilla 30^c.

BABIES

If a baby is being breast fed it's probably easiest if the mother drinks one of the teas suggested above, 3 times a day. The effects of the tea will reach the baby through the milk.

ESSENTIAL OIL TREATMENT

Massage the abdomen gently using Babies bottom and massage oil (see Babies) in a clockwise direction as foods, liquids and gases travel through the intestines clockwise.

HERBAL TREATMENT

COLIC MIXTURE

1 tablespoon aniseed

1 tablespoon fennel seed

1 tablespoon dill seed

TO MAKE: *Mix together, store in a screw-top jar.*

TO USE: *Make a tea and give ½–1 teaspoon (2.5–5 ml) doses 3 times a day.*

Colognes & Perfumes

Colognes and perfumes are easy and pleasurable to make at home. By making small amounts initially it's possible to tailor-make a perfume that is your distinctive signature. This will cost a fraction of what exclusive perfumes cost and will be free of the 'chemical' taint often found in commercial perfumes.

COLOGNES

Colognes and perfumes need several weeks to blend. Initially the perfume is 'raw', with all the individual scents being apparent.

HER COLOGNE

3 tablespoons (60 ml) vodka

3 teaspoons (15 ml) rosewater

25 drops glycerine

25 drops lavender oil

20 drops lemon oil

20 drops ylang-ylang oil

1 teaspoon (5 ml) bergamot oil

1 drop clove oil

TO MAKE: *Mix all together in a bottle (dark glass if possible). Shake well.*

> *Leave for several weeks to mature, shaking daily.*
>
> *Strain through coffee-filter paper before re-bottling.*

Did you know that drying flowers in the microwave will preserve the colour but destroy most of the perfume as the essential oils are driven off?

HIS COLOGNE

3 tablespoons (60 ml) vodka

3 teaspoons (15 ml) orange-flower water

25 drops glycerine

1 teaspoon (5 ml) sandalwood oil

25 drops bergamot oil

20 drops lemon oil

10 drops cedarwood oil

10 drops frankincense oil

1 drop clove oil

TO MAKE: *Mix all together in a bottle (dark glass if possible). Shake well.*

Leave for several weeks to mature, shaking daily.

Strain through coffee-filter paper before re-bottling.

HERBAL COLOGNE

This cologne isn't as strong as those made using essential oils but is very light and pleasant to use. A few drops of essential oil may be added if liked. This recipe can be enlarged or reduced as you wish.

1 cup heavily scented flower petals, for example, rose, jasmine, violet, either single or mixed

vodka to cover

½ teaspoon (2.5 ml) glycerine

20 drops essential oil (optional)

TO MAKE: *Put the petals in a jar with a well fitting, non-metal lid. Cover with vodka, add the glycerine and essential oils and put in a warm place. Leave for several days, shaking daily.*

Strain. Repeat using fresh petals until the liquid smells as strong as you desire. The final straining should be through coffee-filter paper.

PERFUMES

The following perfumes approximate the scent of the world's most famous and expensive perfumes. They are only made in small quantities as they are very strong and not cheap to make, but compared with the price of the commercial varieties are very inexpensive. They need several weeks to mature.

FRUITY FLORAL

40 drops orange oil

30 drops mandarin oil

10 drops neroli oil

10 drops jasmine oil

5 drops sandalwood oil

5 drops patchouli oil

2 teaspoons (10 ml) vodka

TO MAKE: *Mix all together in a little bottle (dark glass if possible). Shake well.*

Leave for several weeks to mature, shaking daily.

Strain through coffee-filter paper before re-bottling.

WOODY FLORAL

70 drops bergamot oil

10 drops ylang-ylang oil

5 drops rose oil

5 drops jasmine oil

4 drops sandalwood oil

8 drops vanilla essence

TO MAKE: *Mix all together in a little bottle (dark glass if possible). Shake well.*

Leave for several weeks to mature, shaking daily.

Strain through coffee-filter paper before re-bottling.

ESSENTIAL-OIL FLOWER WATER

Delicately perfumed waters are easy to make and can be used as toilet waters, skin tonics or after-bath/shower splashes. Use any blend that pleases you.

TO MAKE: *Add up to 80 drops of single or mixed essential oil to 1 cup (250 ml) distilled water. Leave to stand for one month, shaking daily. Strain through coffee-filter paper.*

HERBAL FLOWER WATER

Any heavily scented flowers such as lavender, jasmine or rose (or a mixture of flowers and citrus peels) can be used for this recipe.

2 cups finely chopped petals

distilled water to cover

vodka

5 drops essential oil (optional)

1 drop clove oil (optional)

TO MAKE: *Put the chopped petals and water in a pan, cover and heat gently to blood heat (about 37°C). Keep warm and re-heat to blood heat several times, don't overheat. Allow to cool.*

Repeat twice with fresh plant material, top up the water to cover. Strain through a sieve and then through coffee-filter paper.

Add ½ cup (125 ml) vodka to 1 cup (250 ml) flower water. Add essential oils. Bottle. Shake well before use.

TO USE: *The flower water can be used as a body splash after bathing or showering and also makes a refreshing facial skin toner.*

CREAM PERFUME

It's easiest to make this perfume in the jar in which it will be stored. Rub a little on pulse points where the perfume will be slowly released.

3 level teaspoons firmly packed, finely grated beeswax

3 tablespoons (60 ml) vegetable oil

1 teaspoon (5 ml) mixed essential oils (see suggestions for colognes and perfumes)

TO MAKE: *Melt the beeswax in a small jar in a pan of simmering water.*

Add the vegetable oil very slowly while stirring. Stop if the beeswax begins to harden. Stir and wait for the wax to remelt before continuing.

Cool slightly, slowly add the essential oils stirring very thoroughly.

Comfrey (Symphytum officinale)

HERB PART USED

Leaves and root.

HERB ACTIONS

Symphytine, one of the pyrrolizidine alkaloids present in comfrey was found to develop liver cancer in rats. There have been only 2 or 3 comfrey poisonings of humans reported and even these are doubtful. The fact remains that it is now illegal to sell comfrey for internal use. Comfrey is a valuable fertiliser plant (see Gardening).

USE TO TREAT

Bruises, fractures, cuts, eczema, tropical ulcers, burns, aching joints, fractures, sprains and strains.

ESSENTIAL OIL ACTION

No essential oil. An infused oil (see Aromatherapy & Essential oils, Extraction of essential oils) made from root and leaves is an essential in the medicine chest.

USE TO TREAT

Use for the same complaints as the herb.

Compresses

A compress is a method of applying very cold liquid to an area to reduce swelling, withdraw heat from an area, ease the pain of sprains and soothe abrasions.

ESSENTIAL OIL COMPRESS

TO MAKE: *Add 5–8 drops (depending on the age of the patient, see Aromatherapy & Essential oils) of the chosen essential oils to a small bowl of very cold water (add ice cubes if appropriate).*

Fold a piece of clean soft cloth in four and place on the surface of the water.

Squeeze out until still wet but not dripping.

TO USE: *Apply to the injured area, cover with plastic wrap. Fasten in place with a piece of towelling or strip of cloth.*

Leave until warm and renew. Repeat often for the first 3–4 hours.

HERBAL COMPRESS

Make a triple-strength tea of the chosen herb, cool in the freezer (see Herbal ice cubes) and follow instructions for essential oil compress.

Conjunctivitis   See Eyes & eyebaths

Constipation

It's more important to find the cause of constipation than to treat the symptom. Sometimes the cause is as simple as insufficient fluid intake, insufficient exercise or a low-fibre diet. Walking daily is sometimes all it takes to cure constipation. Meditation classes can be very helpful for constipation interspersed with diarrhoea that often afflicts nervously excitable people.

Drugs such as codeine can cause constipation.

INTERNAL TREATMENT

- Sprinkle 1 dessertspoon of either linseed or ground psyllium husks on cereal or stir into 1 glass of water. Drink and *follow with another glass of water*. This amount of seed can be varied to your requirements after you find what works best for you.
- Eat lots of fruit, vegetables and high-fibre foods.
- Substitute chamomile or lemon balm teas for ordinary tea.
- Drink at least 8 glasses of filtered water every day. The commonest reason for constipation is insufficient fluid intake.

HOMEOPATHIC TREATMENT

Take twice daily as required:
- With ineffectual trying—Nux vom. 30^c.
- Stool recedes when partly expelled —Silica 30^c.
- Large, difficult stool—Graphites 30^c.

Contagious diseases 🌿 See Epidemics

Cooking with herbs & spices

We often give our car better attention than we give our body. We give it the best oil and fuel, have it regularly maintained and try to keep it in top condition in order to get the longest life from the engine and the body. Our bodies are often given poor attention in comparison.

Throughout this book there are suggestions for the best foods to eat for optimal nutrition but we can also add herbs and spices to our food for their delicious flavour and the vitamins and minerals that make each meal extra healthy. Many of the culinary herbs and spices have therapeutic properties, for instance, caraway added to cabbage while cooking will act as a digestive and prevent flatulence; fennel seeds chewed after a meal will help to digest fat; ginger can prevent indigestion, relieve aches and pains and prevent excessive blood clotting.

Leafy herbs such as basil, oregano and marjoram are best added towards the end of cooking as their flavour can be lost and bitterness develop. Following are a few herb blends to try. Crumble dried herbs but don't powder them or they will lose flavour very quickly. Add a pinch at a time until the flavour is to your liking.

If freezing foods it's best to add herbs when reheating as the flavours can change and turn unpleasant during the freezing process.

HERB BLENDS

It's useful to have ready prepared mixtures of dried herbs to add to food. Keep a small jar available for immediate use but store the bulk in tightly sealed jars in a dark, cool cupboard in order to extend the life of the herbs. Even when stored in this way, the blends will have lost most of their scent and flavour after 12 months, so throw them on your garden and replace with freshly dried herbs.

FINES HERBES

2 parts parsley, 4 parts chives, 1 part celery tops, 1 part thyme.

SOUPS & STEWS

4 parts parsley, 2 parts bay leaves, 2 parts lemon thyme, 2 parts powdered garlic, 2 parts celery tops, ¼ part paprika.

MEAT DISHES

4 parts dried, ground onions; 2 parts parsley; 2 parts marjoram; 1 part thyme; 1 part celery tops; 1 part dried, ground garlic.

OMELETTE HERBS

3 parts parsley, 2 parts chives, 1 part dill weed, 1 part tarragon.

TOMATO DISHES

8 parts basil, 2 parts oregano, 2 parts marjoram, 1 part lemon thyme, 1 part powdered garlic.

CHICKEN RUB

Oil the chicken and rub some of the mixture over the chicken 1 hour before cooking: 1 part powdered garlic, 1 part thyme, 1 part each salt (optional) and pepper, 2 parts paprika, 1 part tarragon.

CHICKEN CASSEROLES

2 parts parsley; 2 parts dried, ground onion; 1 part tarragon; 2 parts celery tops; 1 part dried, ground garlic.

Have you heard that stripped, straight branches of bay, rosemary, lemon verbena and lavender make excellent gourmet kebab sticks?

HERB OILS FOR COOKING

The following recipe may be used for garlic, basil, thyme, tarragon or oregano; or a mixture of herbs may be used such as basil, garlic and oregano.

EXTRA-SPECIAL COOKING OIL

8 cloves of garlic each cut in 4 pieces or 1 cup chopped herbs (either single or mixed)

2 cups (500 ml) olive oil (virgin or light) or canola oil if you prefer

TO MAKE: *Mix all in a jar with a well fitting lid. Leave in a warm place for a few days, shake occasionally.*

Strain the oil through a sieve and then through cheesecloth.

Bottle and, if giving as a gift, add either fresh cloves of garlic or long sprigs of herb.

HOT CHILLI OIL

Only a very small amount of this oil is needed to give a hot 'zip' to your food. Mix with some plain oil for sautéing, stir frying, etc. Add a drop at a time to dips, dressings and marinades. The seeds are the hottest part of chillies so either leave them in or scrape them out depending on how hot you want the oil to be.

2 cups (500 ml) canola oil

½ cup (15 g) dried, chopped chillies

20 black peppercorns, bruised

6 cloves garlic, crushed

TO MAKE: *Warm the oil in a non-aluminium pan. Add the remaining ingredients and stand overnight stirring occasionally. Strain the oil through a double thickness of cheesecloth or a clean cotton teatowel. Pour into a sterilised bottle, add a few washed and dried chillies if liked.*

HERB VINEGARS

It's important to use good quality vinegar. Red and white wine vinegars are delicious, cider vinegar gives a robust and fruity flavour.

Vinegar strips the colour from herbs so if your herb vinegar is a gift, add fresh sprigs to the bottle just before giving.

TO MAKE: *The method is the same for all vinegars. Leave the herbs whole unless the recipes states otherwise. Heat the vinegar until very hot but not boiling and pour over the herbs in a wide-necked jar. Leave for 2–3 days, strain through a sieve and then through coffee-filter paper. If you want a very strongly flavoured vinegar, the process can be repeated once or even twice.*

OREGANO, BASIL & GARLIC VINEGAR

3 tablespoons basil, chopped coarsely

1 tablespoon oregano, chopped coarsely

4 cloves garlic quartered

2 cups (500 ml) vinegar

TO USE: *Include in salad dressings and sprinkle over sliced tomatoes with a little olive oil.*

MIXED HERB VINEGAR

5 stalks chives, chopped

5 stalks parsley, chopped

1 stalk dill weed, chopped

leaves from two sprigs thyme

8 oregano leaves

2 cups (500 ml) vinegar

GOURMET VINEGAR

2 spring onions, finely chopped

2 sprigs each rosemary and thyme

2 teaspoons chopped tarragon

2 garlic cloves, crushed

2 teaspoons grated horseradish root

grated zest and juice of 1 lemon

3 cups (750 ml) white wine vinegar

HERB SALTS

Read the labels very carefully on 'herb salts' that are sold in health-food and other shops. The contents are usually table salt with some ground herbs added. The whole point of using herb 'salt', however, is to cut down our consumption of ordinary salt. Try the vitamin and mineral-rich blend below as a salt substitute. You may like to experiment with a small amount at first, adapting until the flavour is to your liking.

REAL HERB SALT

¹/₂ teacup dried, ground celery tops

2 teaspoons dried, ground garlic

1 teaspoon dried, ground dill

4 cups dried, ground parsley

2 teaspoons dried, ground oregano or marjoram

2 teaspoons dried, ground lemon thyme

2 teaspoons dried, ground coriander leaf

¹/₂ teaspoon freshly ground black pepper

2 teaspoons paprika

TO MAKE: *Mix all ingredients and pass through a sieve. Regrind and sieve any particles that don't pass through the mesh. Keep enough of the mixture to use at the table or in cooking and store the remainder in an air and damp-proof container in the freezer.*

HERB BUTTERS

Herb butters add interest and extra flavour to foods and are very easy to make. The variety of flavours depends on the culinary herbs in your garden. The butters can be used on toast, vegetables, steak, chicken or fish. They keep for the same length of time as ordinary butters and are best stored in the refrigerator.

Other flavours such as garlic, grated lemon or orange peel, cayenne, mustard or pepper may be added. Sweet spice butters such as mixed spice, nutmeg or cinnamon are nice on toast, scones, teacakes and fruit loaves.

SAVOURY BUTTERS

TO MAKE: *To each 250 g softened (not melted) butter add 3 tablespoons chopped, fresh herbs and, if liked, salt, pepper, lemon juice or any of the extra flavourings mentioned above.*

Beat the butter until creamy. Mix the other ingredients in well. If using juice or other liquid add very slowly, beating until incorporated.

TO USE: *Pack in dishes or form into a roll in strong greaseproof paper. Refrigerate until firm, cut the roll into discs to serve.*

SWEET BUTTERS

To each 250 g softened (not melted) butter add 6–8 teaspoons of spices of your choice. Add sugar, honey, orange or lemon juice if liked. Make as savoury butter.

SUGARED FLOWERS

This is a method of preserving edible flowers to use as a garnish. Violets are traditionally the most popular flowers to treat in this way but carnations, rose petals, nasturtium flowers or any other non-poisonous flowers may be used. (Do not use a microwave oven for this process.)

TO MAKE: *Beat an egg white with a pinch of salt until broken down but not really frothy. Brush the flowers lightly with egg white using a fairly fine paint brush, don't use too much egg white or it will pick up too much sugar. Sprinkle with caster sugar and place on baking paper. Set the oven to its lowest temperature and put the tray of flowers on the floor or lowest shelf. Prop the door open slightly and leave for 20–30 minutes or until the flowers are crisp and dry.*

The flowers will store for a short time in an airtight tin between sheets of greaseproof paper.

Coughs

A cough is an indication that there is blockage (usually of mucus) in the airways. The following treatments aim at loosening, lessening and expelling mucus and strengthening the lungs. If coughs are frequent it would be wise to follow the regime for strengthening the immune system (see Immune system). If a cough is persistent and long-lasting, consult a health professional.

INTERNAL TREATMENT

- ❦ Cut out all dairy products as this will help to reduce the formation of mucus.
- ❦ Eat garlic and onions daily.

DAILY SUPPLEMENTS

- ჻ 1000 mg vitamin C with bioflavonoids 3 times daily until cough eases.
- ჻ 1000 mg garlic oil capsules 3 times daily or 2–3 teaspoons 'Long-life juice' 3 times daily.
- ჻ ½ teaspoon (2.5 ml) fluid extract of echinacea in 2 tablespoons (40 ml) water 3 times daily.

ESSENTIAL OIL TREATMENT

INHALATION BLEND

3 drops marjoram oil
2 drops benzoin oil
1 drop thyme oil
TO USE: *Use as an inhalation (see Inhalations).*

HERBAL TREATMENT

- ❧ Make an oxymel (see Oxymel) using marshmallow, thyme and coltsfoot or hyssop. Sip ½–1 teaspoon (2.5–5 ml) 3 times a day or as often as necessary.
- ❧ Prepare a footbath (see Baths) using water as hot as can be borne. Add 2 drops each peppermint, thyme and tea-tree essential oils. Agitate water to disperse the oils. Immerse the feet for 10–15 minutes, top up with more hot water if necessary.

HOMEOPATHIC TREATMENT

Take 2–4 times daily or as required:
- ❀ Rattling, choking with anxious wheezing—Hepar sulph. 30^c.
- ❀ Dry, painful cough—Bryonia 30^c.
- ❀ Spasmodic cough—Cuprum met. 6^c.
- ❀ Sudden violent attack—Drosera 30^c.
- ❀ Hoarseness and voice loss—Phosphorus 6^c.

Cradle cap ❦ See Babies

Cramps

Cramp is painful contraction of the muscles, usually in the feet or the calves of the legs. The causes can be lack of some of the B vitamins; inadequate calcium intake; poor circulation or salt deficiency from sweating, tiredness and stress.

Stretch the affected muscle by moving and stretching it either by walking or massage using the massage oil here. If the cramps happen at night, the legs and feet may not be quite warm enough. Try sleeping with your lower body in a sleeping bag.

DAILY SUPPLEMENTS

- ℘ 1 vitamin B complex tablet.
- ℘ 1000 mg calcium citrate taken at bedtime.
- ℘ 15 mg zinc.

Did you know that leg cramps can often be eased if you hold the big toe with your thumb on the nail and finger underneath and apply very firm pressure until the cramp eases?

ESSENTIAL OIL TREATMENT

MASSAGE OIL

3 tablespoons (60 ml) vegetable oil

15 drops lavender oil

10 drops rosemary oil

10 drops marjoram oil

TO MAKE: *Mix together in a small bottle. Shake well.*

TO USE: *Massage regularly onto the most affected area every night before bed and before sport or other activities that have induced cramp attacks. Massage the oil onto the affected muscle before and during an attack.*

HERBAL TREATMENT

- ❧ Cramp bark as directed.
- ❧ Ginger tea twice a day.

HOMEOPATHIC TREATMENT

Take 3 times daily:

* In calf muscles — Arsen. alb. and/or Mag. phos. 30^c.
* In fingers, legs and toes — Cuprum met. 30^c.
* Soles of feet — Colchicum 30^c.

Cramp bark (*Viburnum opulus*)

HERB PART USED

Bark.

HERB ACTIONS

Antispasmodic, sedative, astringent.

USE TO TREAT

Muscle tension and spasm. Relaxes the uterus relieving painful period cramps. May be used to try to avert threatened miscarriage. Helps to control excessive menstrual bleeding.

ESSENTIAL OIL ACTION

None.

Cuprum met. (*Cuprum metallicum*) ❧ Homeopathic

USE TO TREAT

Cramp in fingers, legs or feet, nausea with stomach pain.

Cuts & wounds

If a cut is very deep and needs stitches, cover the wound with a firm dressing onto which you have dripped distilled witch-hazel and take the patient to the nearest hospital or surgery.

ESSENTIAL OIL TREATMENT

Add 1 drop each of lemon, lavender and geranium oil to ½ cup (125 ml) boiled water. Use to bathe the wound. If bleeding persists, apply a firm sterile pad of gauze or non-stick dressing onto which you have dripped 2 drops of tea-tree oil. Bandage the dressing in place.

HERBAL TREATMENT

Wash the area with distilled witch-hazel.

HOMEOPATHIC TREATMENT

Take several times daily. May also be used in water to bathe the wound:

* Very painful wounds and those involving nerve endings — Hypericum 12^c or 30^c.
* Calendula 12^c or 30^c.
* Ledum 30^c.

Cypress (*Cupressus sempervirens*)

ESSENTIAL OIL ACTION

Antiseptic, antispasmodic, astringent, deodorant, detoxifying, insect repellent.

USE TO TREAT

Asthma, bronchitis, colds, coughs, whooping cough. Nervous tension, anxiety and stress. Excessive perspiration (good for sweaty feet), incontinence, heavy menstruation. Muscle cramps, tired muscles, rheumatism. Piles, varicose veins.

Cystitis

Cystitis is an inflammation of the bladder caused by bacterial infection of the urinary tract. The cause is often not apparent. As many as 21 per cent of women will suffer one or more cystitis attacks a year.

The symptoms are burning or scalding when passing urine, wanting to pass urine frequently, a persistent dull ache above the pubic bone, urine which smells or contains blood or pus. If the attack is accompanied by fever and low back pain the infection may be in the kidneys as well as the bladder and urethra, and professional help is needed.

- 🌿 Always empty the bladder within 10 minutes of having sex, and wash the genital area thoroughly.
- 🌿 Drinks containing caffeine are an irritant to the bladder.
- 🌿 Always wipe from front to back after a bowel action.
- 🌿 Wear cotton underpants and loose trousers or skirts.
- 🌿 Go to the toilet often, never wait until your bladder is over-full.
- 🌿 Avoid using scented products such as soaps, spermicidal jellies or tampons.

People with cystitis often feel depressed, anxious, embarrassed and very tired. Don't try to carry the load alone, find someone to confide in, a friend or relative who has had the problem or a counsellor at a woman's health-care clinic.

INTERNAL TREATMENT

- 🌺 Drink 3 litres of fluid a day.
- 🌺 20 000 mg cranberry capsules (cranberry sauce or unsweetened juice may be used) during an attack.

DAILY SUPPLEMENTS

- 🌿 500 g vitamin C with bioflavonoids four times daily.
- 🌿 30 g zinc daily.
- 🌿 1000 mg garlic oil capsules 3 times daily or 2–3 teaspoons 'Long-life juice' 3 times daily.
- 🌿 Golden seal capsules or tincture as directed.
- 🌿 ½ teaspoon (2.5 ml) fluid extract of echinacea in 2 tablespoons (40 ml) water every 2 hours during an attack, 20 drops twice daily for 2 months after an attack to help prevent a re-occurrence.

ESSENTIAL OIL TREATMENT

MASSAGE *&* FOMENTATION BLEND
1 tablespoon (20 ml) vegetable oil
6 drops sandalwood oil

6 drops marjoram oil

4 drops lavender oil

TO MAKE: *Mix the oils together.*

TO USE: *Massage over the bladder or use the essential oils as a fomentation (see Fomentations) over the bladder.*

HERBAL TREATMENT

❧ Substitute regular tea with dandelion leaf tea and chamomile tea.

❧ 1 cup (250 ml) of fresh corn silk tea or decoction of marshmallow root drunk 3 times a day.

HOMEOPATHIC TREATMENT

All 6–30^c, take 4 times daily or more often if symptoms are severe:

❧ Stinging pain after urinating—Apis mel.

❧ With fever—Belladonna.

❧ Frequent urination with pain, burning pains—Cantharis.

❧ Pink staining in urine—Lycopodium.

❧ Burning, mucous in urine—Berberis.

d

Damiana (*Turnera aphrodisiaca*)

HERB PART USED

Leaves and stalks.

HERB ACTIONS

Antidepressant, laxative, stimulant, tonic, urinary antiseptic.

USE TO TREAT

The nervous and hormonal systems especially in men where it strengthens and tones. Use where there are feelings of sexual inadequacy causing depression.

ESSENTIAL OIL ACTION

None.

Dandelion (*Taraxacum officinale*)

HERB PART USED

Root and leaf.

Did you know that in Chinese herbal medicine, decoctions are made fresh each morning in special ceramic pots kept for this purpose only?

HERB ACTIONS

Anti-inflammatory, anticongestive, stimulant; tonic both through its action on the liver and gallbladder (mainly root) and the number of vitamins and minerals it contains (14 000 iu vitamin A per 100 g compared to 11 000 iu for carrots). The leaf is a safe and powerful diuretic. It is a source of the vital potassium that is normally stripped from the body by other diuretics. Loss of potassium can intensify cardiovascular problems. Research has found that dandelion contains more vitamins, iron and other minerals, protein and other nutrients than any other herb. It has a long history of use in the treatment of anaemia, presumably due to its high nutritive content.[1]

USE TO TREAT

Gallstones, jaundice, cirrhosis, indigestion, constipation, rheumatism and gout.

The white latex that oozes from the cut flower stem is traditionally the best way of getting rid of warts. Apply several times a day to the wart only and not the surrounding skin which it can irritate.

The flower petals and young green leaves are delicious in salads and sandwiches.

ESSENTIAL OIL ACTION

None.

Dandruff ❧ See Hair care

Decoctions

A liquid made by simmering coarser plant materials such as roots and barks in water to extract their properties. Decoctions have the same uses as teas but are made in a different way.

A crock-pot is useful for making decoctions as the properties are gently drawn from the herbs over a few hours. The decoction can then be strained and frozen in small amounts for use as needed. Make a 4–5 day supply at one time as the process is quite time consuming.

TO MAKE: *Chop the material as finely as possible, place in a non-aluminium pan.*

To each cup (250 ml) of cold water add the equivalent of 2 teaspoons fresh or 1 teaspoon dried herb. Cover the pan and bring slowly to a boil. Simmer for 10–30 minutes depending on the coarseness of the material.

Strain, measure, and make up to the original amount of fluid with fresh boiling water.

Store in a covered container in the refrigerator for 4–5 days. For dosages, see Teas.

Decongestants

Release mucus from the nose, throat and lungs.

HERBS

Golden seal, mullein, peppermint, pine, garlic, eucalyptus, tea-tree.

ESSENTIAL OILS

Clove, eucalyptus, garlic, lavender, peppermint, pine.

Deodorants

Reduce odour.

HERBS

Geranium, lavender, rosemary, sage, witch-hazel.

ESSENTIAL OILS

Bergamot, clary sage, cypress, eucalyptus, geranium, lavender, lemongrass, patchouli, petitgrain, rosewood.

ESSENTIAL OIL DEODORANTS

DEODORANT SPLASH
1/3 cup (80 ml) distilled witch-hazel
1 teaspoon (5 ml) glycerine

Have you heard that bad underarm smells may be caused by an orange-coloured fungus that grows on underarm hair? Shave the armpits and apply a solution of 1 teaspoon (5 ml) tincture of myrrh in ½ cup (125 ml) water.

20 drops bergamot or petitgrain oil
20 drops lavender oil
10 drops rosewood oil
15 drops cypress oil
TO MAKE: *Mix together in a bottle. Shake well to mix. Shake well before use.*

DEODORANT POWDER
½ *cup bicarbonate of soda*
¼ *cup cornflour*
30 *drops bergamot or petitgrain oil*
20 *drops lavender or rosewood oil*
15 *drops cypress oil*
TO MAKE: *Drip the oils slowly onto the mixed powders, stirring constantly to prevent lumping.*
Apply using cotton wool balls.

HERBAL DEODORANT POWDER
¾ *cup bicarbonate of soda*
¼ *cup cornflour*
2 *tablespoons dried, powdered lavender flowers*
2 *tablespoons dried, powdered rosemary leaves*
1 *tablespoon dried, powdered sage leaves*
TO MAKE: *Mix together and pass through a fine sieve. Store in an air-tight container.*

Depression 🌿 See Emotional & Nervous problems and Pregnancy, Post-natal depression

Depuratives
Agents used to purify the blood.

HERBS

Borage, burdock, dandelion, echinacea, fumitory, nettle, red clover, watercress, yellow dock.

ESSENTIAL OILS

Fennel, garlic, juniper, rose.

Dermatitis ❦ See Eczema

Devil's claw (*Harpagophytum procumbens*)

HERB PART USED

Root.

HERB ACTIONS

Anti-inflammatory and analgesic properties. Reputed to reduce serum cholesterol and uric acid levels. Reduces inflammation in the joints.

USE TO TREAT

Rheumatism, gout, lumbago, fibrositis, myalgia, tendonitis, rheumatoid arthritis and osteoarthritis.

ESSENTIAL OIL ACTION

None.

Diarrhoea

The given treatment is for acute (as opposed to chronic) diarrhoea. Mild or short-term diarrhoea can be nature's way of ridding the body of infection or contaminated or unfamiliar food. This cleansing action is beneficial and shouldn't be discouraged in the short-term (i.e. 24 hours). If the diarrhoea persists, seek professional help.

INTERNAL TREATMENT

One of the dangers of diarrhoea is dehydration, so take plenty of liquids; filtered, bottled or mineral water or diluted fruit juices are ideal. Electrolytes are electrically charged particles in blood plasma containing sodium, potassium, chloride, bicarbonate and a small amount of other substances. Electrolytes are lost during the loss of body fluid when vomiting, diarrhoea, heavy sweating or bleeding. Lethargy and dehydration accompany this loss.

ELECTROLYTE DRINK

This will replace lost electrolytes and rehydrate the body. Use for one day only.

1 cup (250 ml) apple juice

1 cup (250 ml) mineral water

3 teaspoons honey

1/2 teaspoon salt

1/2 teaspoon bicarbonate of soda

ESSENTIAL OIL TREATMENT

MASSAGE OIL

6 drops chamomile oil

4 drops eucalyptus oil

2 drops ginger oil

1 tablespoon (20 ml) vegetable oil

TO USE: *Massage on the abdomen.*

HERBAL TREATMENT

Chamomile and lavender tea 3 times daily.

HOMEOPATHIC TREATMENT

All 30ᶜ, take every hour until symptoms subside:

❋ Excitement and worry about forthcoming events—Argent. nit.

❋ Mild food poisoning—Arsen. alb.

Digestives ❦ See also Bitters

Aid digestion and ease indigestion.

HERBS

Angelica, caraway, cumin, dill, gentian, ginger, marjoram, parsley, peppermint, spearmint, rosemary.

ESSENTIAL OILS

Aniseed, black pepper, caraway, cardamon, chamomiles, dill, marjoram, rosemary.

Dill (*Anethum graveolens*)

HERB PART USED

Seeds and leaves.

HERB ACTIONS

A well-known cooking and pickling spice.

USE TO TREAT

Indigestion; sweetens the breath and is widely used to ease colic in babies (see Colic).

ESSENTIAL OIL ACTION

Fresh or dried plant preferable.

Diuretics

Increase flow of urine.

HERBS

Buchu, dandelion, parsley, watercress.

ESSENTIAL OILS

Chamomiles, cedarwood, fennel, geranium, juniper, parsley.

Diverticulitis

A condition in which pouches (diverticuli) form in the wall of the colon. The pouches often become inflamed, creating the condition known as diverticulitis. Symptoms include lower-abdominal pain and/or discomfort and cramping, flatulence, constipation and/or diarrhoea.

This problem seems to be caused mainly by eating a diet lacking in natural fibre, lack of exercise, cigarette smoking and/or stress. Give up smoking, take up some form of exercise, meditate (see Relaxation) or find some other way of dealing with stress (see Emotional & Nervous problems, Stress), and breathe! See Breathing.

INTERNAL TREATMENT

🌿 Take extra fibre in the form of ground psyllium or linseed. Sprinkle 1 dessertspoonful over cereal, yoghurt or other food and follow with a glass of water or stir 1 dessertspoonful into a glass of water or fruit juice, drink and *follow with another glass of water*.

🌿 Cook all fruit and vegetables, as raw fruit and vegetables may cause more irritation until the problem is cured.

DAILY SUPPLEMENTS

1–2 capsules enteric-coated peppermint oil (0.2 ml available from pharmacies) take between meals.

ESSENTIAL OIL TREATMENT

MASSAGE OIL BLEND
1 tablespoon (20 ml) vegetable oil
4 drops chamomile oil
4 drops peppermint oil
5 drops rosemary oil
2 drops marjoram oil
TO MAKE: *Mix together. Warm very slightly before use.*
TO USE: *Twice a day, massage the abdomen with the warm oil in a clockwise direction. If preferred, the essential oils can be used as a fomentation (see Fomentations for the number of drops of oil).*

HOMEOPATHIC TREATMENT

Consult a homeopathic practitioner.

Dogs 🪱 See Pets

Dong quai (*Angelica sinensis*)

Herb part used
Root.

Herb actions
Possesses oestrogenic activity. Relaxes and stimulates the uterus.

Use to treat
Mainly women's ailments. PMT, abdominal cramps and uterine pain, irregular or difficult periods and period headaches. Menopausal symptoms such as rheumatism, hot flushes and flashes, vaginal spasms. Helps to improve liver function when impaired by hepatitis or cirrhosis. A general tonic for women who are feeling run-down.
Caution: *Not to be taken during pregnancy.*

Douches

Vaginal douches
Unnecessary douching can result in an upset acid–alkaline balance in the vagina and can destroy the natural and necessary secretions. Douches should be used only when there is a local infection. Fresh secretions are only unpleasant if there is an infection or if washing is neglected.

Douche 3 times a day for up to a week. If the infection hasn't cleared in this time get professional help as untreated, undiagnosed vaginal infections can lead to, or be indicative of, serious problems. I prefer to use herbs for douching; essential oils are concentrated and might damage the delicate lining of the vagina. The only exception I would make is tea-tree, where you can add 2 drops to 2 cups (500 ml) warm water in the douche bag.

TO MAKE: *Prepare a herbal tea or decoction or use ingredients as suggested in remedies (such as thrush, see Candidiasis) in this book. Store, covered, in the refrigerator for no more than 24 hours.*

Heat or cool tea to blood heat. Pour into the douche bag (available from pharmacies).

Sit on the toilet seat, lean back and insert the nozzle of the douche into the vagina. Allow the liquid to bathe the inside of the vagina.

SALINE NASAL DOUCHES

This is a yoga practice that is very effective for clearing the nostrils and the back of the throat of pollens, dust and mucus. It is also very effective as a preventative method when there are epidemics of colds and flu. Over the years I have recommended this procedure to many people and most who have tried it (particularly hayfever sufferers) end up doing it regularly for the sheer pleasure of having a clear nose and easy breathing.

Try this if you are suffering from hayfever, colds, influenza, sore throat or have excessive mucus in the nostrils or throat.

TO MAKE & USE: *Add 1/4 teaspoon salt to 1 brimming glass of lukewarm filtered water (the water should feel the same temperature as your finger). Mix to dissolve.*

Bend over the washbasin, hold the head sideways, hold the glass to the lower nostril and gently sniff up the water using each nostril in turn. You will find the position where the saline goes up one nostril and down the other. Sniff the saline 2–3 times up each nostril and then blow your nose to clear the nasal passages. Don't swallow the saline or it might make you nauseous.

Drosera (*Drosera rotundifolia*) ❀ Homeopathic

USE TO TREAT

Coughs, laryngitis, vertigo, whooping cough.

Dysmenorrhoea ❀ See Menstruation

Earache

Earaches must never be treated lightly as any infection can spread to the middle and inner ear. Never poke around in the ear. The following suggestions are to be used to treat simple earache caused by draughts or mild infections. If earache persists seek the help of a professional.

DAILY SUPPLEMENTS

1000 mg garlic oil capsules: adults 3 times daily; children over 5 years of age, 1 per day *or* 2–3 teaspoons 'Long-life juice' 3 times daily; children over 5 years, 1 teaspoon twice daily.

Did you know that the smallest object you can safely put in your ear is your elbow?

ESSENTIAL OIL TREATMENT

Squeeze 2 drops chamomile and 1 drop tea-tree oil or the contents of 1 garlic perle and 1 teaspoon (5 ml) of vegetable oil into a warmed spoon. Drip the oil into the ear and plug with cotton wool.

HERBAL TREATMENT

- Apply a hot fomentation (see Fomentations) of chamomile tea.
- One of grandmother's remedies which works *really* well is the cooked onion! Cut an onion in half and wrap one half in foil. Bake or grill until soft. Open the foil but leave under the onion

as a holder. Hold the onion to the sore ear where the steam, heat and fumes will enter the ear (the onion is not touching until cool enough not to burn the skin). Keep the ear warm after the treatment by using a hot water bottle or by wrapping a scarf around the head.

HOMEOPATHIC TREATMENT

All 30^c, take 6–8 times daily until condition improves:
* Redness, acute throbbing and hot—Belladonna.
* With discharge—Graphites.
* Relief from warmth—Mag. phos.
* Pain worse from warmth—Chamomilla.

Echinacea (Echinacea angustifolia & E. purpurea)

HERB PART USED

Root, fresh if possible.

HERB ACTIONS

Alterative, antibacterial, antiviral, powerful immune-system stimulant and enhancer for use in acute conditions.

USE TO TREAT

Echinacea is recommended for acute conditions temporarily affecting the immune system, but not at first for chronic illnesses. For chronic, deep-seated illnesses begin a course of treatment with astragalus (see Astragalus) and then to follow up with echinacea. Echinacea is traditionally used as a blood purifier, analgesic, antibiotic and antiseptic remedy. It improves a low white blood-cell count, and is particularly effective against influenza and herpes. Use with yarrow for cystitis. Use externally to heal septic sores and wounds.

ESSENTIAL OIL ACTION

None.

Eczema 🌿 See also Skin care

This is an inflammatory condition of the skin that can be difficult to treat unless the cause is found and treated. Search for the causes from any of the following: allergies, low stomach acid, stress.

Use products such as Tarsol instead of soap.

INTERNAL TREATMENT

3 cups of dandelion coffee daily instead of regular tea

DAILY SUPPLEMENTS

- 5000–10 000 iu beta-carotene.
- 500 iu vitamin E (d-alpha tocopherol).
- 500–1000 mg vitamin C with bioflavonoids.
- 50 mg zinc.

Did you know that swimming in the ocean can often have a beneficial effect on eczema and psoriasis?

ESSENTIAL OIL TREATMENT

HEALING OIL

1 tablespoon (20 ml) aloe vera gel or olive oil (try alternately to see which works best)

2 capsules borage (starflower) oil or evening primrose oil (pricked and squeezed into the other oils)

2 drops lavender oil

2 drops chamomile oil

1 drop melissa oil

TO MAKE: *Mix all together.*

TO USE: *Smooth gently onto affected area.*

Compresses (see Compresses) using 3–4 drops only of either chamomile or lavender oil are very soothing.

HERBAL TREATMENT

🌿 Compresses (see Compresses) using calendula and chickweed or burdock root help to heal and to reduce irritation.

❧ Comfrey or calendula ointment (see Ointments) on weeping, inflamed lesions.

HOMEOPATHIC TREATMENT

All 30ᶜ, take 2–3 times daily:
- ❀ Skin cracked and weeping—Graphites.
- ❀ Skin sensitive to touch—Hepar sulph.
- ❀ At edges of hair—Nat. mur.

Elderflower (*Sambucus nigra*)

HERB PART USED

Flowers, berries, bark and root.

HERB ACTIONS

The bark and roots have been used as diuretics, emetics and purgatives but the action seems to be too violent to be safe for internal use.

The leaves used externally are emollient and vulnerary; used internally they are expectorant, purgative, diuretic and diaphoretic.

The flowers are diaphoretic and anticatarrhal.

The berries are laxative, diuretic and diaphoretic.

USE TO TREAT

The flowers mixed with peppermint and yarrow make the classic herb tea used to treat colds and influenza, hayfever, sinus congestion and rheumatism; a soothing gargle for hoarseness and sore throat. An eyewash (see Eyes & Eyewashes) using the flowers can be used to treat conjunctivitis and styes. The US herbalist John Lust recommends 2 tablespoons (20 ml) twice a day of the *cooked* elderberry juice to treat neuralgia, sciatica or lumbago.

ESSENTIAL OIL ACTION

None.

Emmenagogues
Encourage and regulate menstrual flow.

HERBS
Feverfew, pennyroyal, rosemary.

ESSENTIAL OILS
Basil, chamomiles, clary sage.

Emotional & Nervous problems ❦ See also Stress
and Relaxation

ANXIETY & NERVOUS TENSION
INTERNAL TREATMENT

- Medications for anxiety can lead to depression and can be addictive. One of the best cures for anxiety is breathing (see Breathing).
- If insomnia is a problem try taking a milk drink 30 minutes before retiring for the night.
- Relaxation can be extremely helpful (see Relaxation).

DAILY SUPPLEMENTS

- 1 vitamin B complex tablet.
- 1 or 2 valerian capsules ½ hour before bed; don't use valerian continuously for more than 3 weeks, have a break of one week before re-commencing.
- Passionflower, dosage as directed; alternate with valerian.

ESSENTIAL OIL TREATMENT

'TENSION-TAMER' OIL BLEND
1 teaspoon (5 ml) lavender oil
60 drops ylang-ylang oil
20 drops clary sage oil
20 drops sandalwood oil

TO MAKE: *Mix together in a tiny dark glass bottle.*

Label and store in a cool dark place.

TO USE: *Add 10 drops to a warm bath, agitate to disperse. Relax in the bath for 20 minutes.*

Add 12 drops to 1 tablespoon (20 ml) vegetable oil. Use for massage.

Add 20 drops to 2 tablespoons (40 ml) vodka in a 100 ml spray bottle, mix and add water. Shake well before spraying the room.

Use a few drops on water in an oil burner.

HERBAL TREATMENT

- Drink chamomile tea in place of regular tea.
- Enjoy relaxing baths using bath bags (a mixture of lavender and lemon balm is appropriate) and essential oils (see Baths).

HOMEOPATHIC TREATMENT

All 30^c, take as often as required:

- Trembling, nervous, apprehensive — Arsen. album.
- Anxiety with mental confusion — Aconite.
- Wanting to be left alone; face looks sleepy and exhausted — Gelsemium.
- Rescue Remedy.

GRIEF

Grief is a natural and important part of the acceptance and letting go of loss. Comfort needs to found in the release of tears, the company of family and friends and sometimes the assistance of those trained to help one to deal with unresolved feelings.

Some people remain 'stuck' in grief. It may be too painful to face the overwhelming emotions that may need to be processed before moving on. There are three phases of resolving grief after the death of a loved one.

- **Acknowledgement of the loss:** Behaviour such as refusing to attend the funeral or visit the grave of a family member who has died, or keeping the deceased's clothing and room undisturbed for years or months after the death may indicate a denial of the death. To acknowledge the loss, it is important to say goodbye and acknowledge the death. Most importantly, the grieving person should be encouraged to visit the burial site, deal with the possessions and perhaps light a candle to commemorate the death as soon as possible after the death has occurred.

Did you know that many scientific studies show that ginseng improves intellectual performance, competence, concentration, and is also an excellent stress reducer and tonic?

* **Feel the feelings:** Understandably, acknowledging the death will release a flood of feelings such as anger, fear and pain. It is important to acknowledge that one of the strongest feelings when a loved one dies is anger, a feeling largely unrecognised or disapproved of by society. Subsequently the angry person feels guilty, which in turn encourages denial. It's alright to be angry and express your anger.

* **Resolving the loss:** This phase of grieving involves reinvesting the emotional energy in a new direction. You may have a change in goals or new relationships. Essentially you are readjusting to a life where the loved one is missing, and this phase involves integrating the loss and making it part of your identity. In this way the loss has meaning in your life. A good way to express and explore your new identity is to begin a diary focusing on your feelings, perhaps writing about things you liked and disliked about the person that you have lost. Creating a 'picture' of them in your diary in both words and illustrations is a way of preserving them.

The following essential oils will help to provide spiritual solace and lighten melancholy.

ESSENTIAL OIL TREATMENT

GENTLE-TOUCH BLENDS

6 drops cypress oil

4 drops marjoram oil

2 drops clary sage oil

1 tablespoon (20 ml) vegetable oil

or

6 drops frankincense oil

4 drops orange oil

2 drops cypress oil

1 tablespoon (20 ml) vegetable oil

TO MAKE: *Mix the essential oils together in a little bottle. Leave for 1–2 days to blend.*

TO USE: *Massage a few drops on pulse points such as the throat and the inside of wrists.*

Carry the bottle and sniff the contents occasionally.

Add 1 teaspoon (5 ml) to a warm bath just before getting in, agitate the water to disperse the oil.

HOMEOPATHIC TREATMENT

All 6ᶜ–30ᶜ, take as often as required:

※ When death was sudden and shock severe—Aconite.

※ Becoming ill after loss or trauma, keeping a 'stiff upper lip' in front of others—Nat. mur.

※ Prolonged mourning, no respite from grief—Ignatia.

※ Bach Remedies: Walnut and Rescue Remedy.

DEPRESSION

Depression can be diagnosed if you have several of the following symptoms: insomnia, poor appetite with weight loss or increased appetite with weight gain, lack of interest in daily routine and hobbies, feelings of guilt or worthlessness, lack of power to concentrate, thoughts of suicide, fatigue and lack of energy.

It's important to trace the source of depression as, if it continues, it can lead to many physical complaints. Exercise such as brisk walking or swimming (even though you don't feel like doing it) is very helpful. Ask someone to come with you for company and see if after 2–3 weeks you don't feel considerably better.

A trained therapist may be needed if the depression is profound or of long duration, but the following treatments will also help.

INTERNAL TREATMENT

Drink herb tea or tea containing no caffeine. Avoid coffee.

DAILY SUPPLEMENTS

- ॐ 2 vitamin B complex tablets: 1 with lunch, 1 with dinner.
- ॐ 1000 mg vitamin C with bioflavonoids 3 times daily.
- ॐ 10 mg folic acid.
- ॐ 1000 mg magnesium.

ESSENTIAL OIL TREATMENT

These essential oil blends will certainly help to raise the spirits.

DEPRESSION COMING AFTER LONG-TERM STRESS
1 tablespoon (20 ml) vegetable oil
6 drops bergamot oil
4 drops orange oil
2 drops chamomile oil
TO MAKE: *Mix the essential oils together in a little bottle. Leave for 1–2 days to blend.*
TO USE: *Massage a few drops on pulse points such as the throat and the inside of wrists.*

Carry the bottle and sniff the contents occasionally.

Add 1 teaspoon (5 ml) to a warm bath just before getting in, agitate the water to disperse the oil. Soak for as long as you like!

DEPRESSION CAUSED BY LOSS OF INTEREST IN LIFE
1 tablespoon (20 ml) vegetable oil
6 drops ylang-ylang oil
4 drops orange oil

2 *drops rosemary oil*

TO MAKE: *Mix the essential oils together in a little bottle. Leave for 1–2 days to blend.*

TO USE: *Massage a few drops on pulse points such as the throat and the inside of wrists.*

Carry the bottle and sniff the contents occasionally.

Add 1 teaspoon (5 ml) to a warm bath just before getting in, agitate the water to disperse.

See also the Spirit lifter blend in AIDS.

HERBAL TREATMENT

Skullcap and St John's Wort as directed.

HOMEOPATHIC TREATMENT

All 6^c–30^c, take 2–4 times daily depending on severity:

* Confused and despondent—Actaea rac.
* Emotional people and bereavement—Ignatia.
* Women in particular who are easily depressed—Sepia.

Emphysema

This is a progressive and incurable disease caused by heavy smoking and breathing heavily polluted atmospheres. Emphysema occurs when the tiny air sacs in the lungs become inflamed, then swell and burst, forming larger scarred sacs. The result is lung stiffness and a less efficient exchange of oxygen and carbon dioxide. More effort is needed to breathe and this in turn puts a strain on the heart. Eventually this strain can result in heart failure.

There is no definitive treatment which will reverse the disease but there are treatments that help to prevent the condition from worsening and maximise the remaining lung capacity. The first step is to *stop smoking* or, if the environment in which you work or live causes the emphysema, make a change. Breathing exercises (see Breathing), whistling and graded exercise such as gentle walking, swimming or cycling may help to develop more lung efficiency.

Acupuncture has been found to increase the oxygen to the lungs and promote easier breathing.

Medical help must be sought immediately if there is any sign of respiratory failure such as blue lips or extreme shortness of breath.

INTERNAL TREATMENT

𐫱 Eat plentiful amounts of fruit and vegetables containing vitamin C, beta-carotene, vitamin E and vitamin B (see Vitamins and Minerals). These are the anti-oxidant vitamins that neutralise free radicals which cause damage to living cells.

𐫱 Avoid cow's milk and milk products. Choose goat's milk or soya milk instead.

DAILY SUPPLEMENTS

𐫱 2000 mg vitamin C with bioflavonoids 3 times daily.

𐫱 400 iu vitamin E (d-alpha-tocopherol).

𐫱 10 000–20 000 iu beta-carotene.

𐫱 1 vitamin B complex tablet.

ESSENTIAL OIL TREATMENT

Use thyme, eucalyptus and basil in an oil burner.

MASSAGE BLEND

2 tablespoons (40 ml) vegetable oil

15 drops cedarwood oil

15 drops eucalyptus oil

10 drops peppermint oil

TO MAKE: *Mix together in a small bottle.*

TO USE: *Massage the chest and upper back twice a day.*

HERBAL TREATMENT

Make a mixture of 1 part liquorice extract to 3 parts tincture of mullein. Take 1–2 droppers in 2 tablespoons water or soya milk 3 times daily (see Mullein and Liquorice).

HOMEOPATHIC TREATMENT

All 6^c–30^c, take regularly especially when uncomfortable:

* Worse in cold air—Hepar. sulph.
* Noisy wheezing with no mucus—Antim. tart.
* Consult a homeopath for a full treatment.

Emulsifying wax ❧ See Wax

Endometriosis

Endometriosis is a very painful condition affecting about 10 per cent of all women for which no cause has yet been found. It is conjectured that hormonal imbalances, stress, an under-active immune system and inflammations could contribute or be the culprits but this is still supposition.

The cells which normally line the uterus (endometrial cells) travel up the fallopian tubes and from there spill into the pelvic and abdominal cavity. They then proliferate causing many different and unpleasant symptoms. These may include: heavy and painful periods, internal bleeding, painful sexual intercourse, painful ovulation, painful bowel movement, constipation/diarrhoea, infertility and more. Endometriosis has earned the title of 'The Career Woman's Disease' as it appears that childbearing lessens your chances of developing the complaint.

SITZ BATH TREATMENT

This treatment involves the use of two baths (baby baths or similar) big enough to sit in with the pelvis and abdomen immersed in the water. It will stimulate the flow of blood to the pelvic area and relieve congestion.

Pour hot water in one bath and cold in the other. Sit for 10 minutes in the hot bath, 5 minutes in the cold. Repeat once more (for half an hour altogether) topping up the hot water if necessary. This treatment should be carried out daily.

INTERNAL TREATMENT

🌿 Internal treatment concentrates on reducing inflammation by eating a low-fat and low-salt diet and avoiding processed and junk foods.

🌿 Eat plenty of raw, fresh, fruits and vegetables.

🌿 Eat plenty of fibre foods such as muesli, oat and rice bran, lentils, rice, kidney beans and chickpeas.

🌿 Several times a week eat avocado; tinned fish including sardines, mackerel, tuna or salmon; fresh fish; raw nuts and seeds (linseed, pumpkin, sesame and sunflower).

🌿 Eat chicken and red meat once or twice a week only.

🌿 Drink dandelion coffee in place of ordinary tea or coffee.

Did you know that a good way of ensuring a balanced intake of vitamins and minerals is to put fruit and vegetables of all the different colours in your shopping trolley?

DAILY SUPPLEMENTS

🌿 1000 mg calcium/magnesium citrate.

🌿 2000 mg borage (starflower) oil or evening primrose oil.

🌿 400 iu vitamin E (d-alpha tocopherol).

🌿 10 000 iu beta-carotene.

🌿 1000 mg vitamin C with bioflavonoids.

ESSENTIAL OIL TREATMENT

MASSAGE BLEND

2 tablespoons (40 ml) vegetable oil

15 drops geranium oil

10 drops cypress oil

10 drops clary sage oil

5 drops nutmeg oil

TO MAKE: *Mix together in a small bottle.*

TO USE: *Massage the abdomen and lower back twice a day.*

HERBAL TREATMENT

- ❧ Chaste tree as directed.
- ❧ Pau d'arco tea or tincture 3 times a day for one month. Stop for a week and repeat the cycle.
- ❧ 1000 mg celery seed extract.
- ❧ 1–3 cups chamomile tea.

HOMEOPATHIC TREATMENT

Treatment is likely to be complex. Consult a homeopathic practitioner.

Epidemics

By keeping your immune system at optimum strength you are creating an environment in which your body will be able to repel invaders. To do this the stress levels, nutritional factors and daily surroundings need to be carefully monitored to ensure that balance is being maintained. The suggestions to be found under Immune system should be followed during times of risk.

During outbreaks of influenza, gastro-enteritis and other diseases it's wise to protect yourself at work, when out shopping or at other times when you will come in contact with many people. The easiest way to do this is to carry essential oils (see following recipe) in your pocket or handbag to sniff frequently and to wipe your fingers on after handling money or shaking hands. It has now been established that these are the prime ways of catching someone else's disease. (It's good to learn to do this hand-wiping very discreetly or you may fail to win friends and influence people!)

Spray the air in your home or place of work with the Sick room blend suggested in Air sprays.

ANTI-INFECTION HAND WIPES

HAND-WIPE BLEND

3 tablespoons (60 ml) vodka
20 drops lavender oil
10 drops geranium oil

20 drops tea-tree oil

10 drops lemon oil

TO MAKE: *Spray small sheets of cloth (environmentally sound) or kitchen paper towel (stronger and cheaper than tissues) with the following blend. Cut to fit a small tin. Re-spray as often as necessary to keep the oils fresh.*

TO USE: *See above.*

Essential oils 🌿 See Aromatherapy & Essential oils

Eucalyptus (*Eucalyptus globulus*)

HERB PART USED

Leaves.

HERB ACTIONS

Antiseptic, antiviral, antibiotic, antifungal, decongestant, deodorant, disinfectant, expectorant, insect repellent. One of the most powerful herbs for treating wounds.

USE TO TREAT

Bronchitis, bronchial congestion, coughs, sinusitis.

ESSENTIAL OIL ACTION

As above and use also in baths and massage oils to ease rheumatism and sore muscles. Use as a stain remover on clothing.

Caution: *Use with care and at dilutions of 1 per cent only. Don't use for an extended period of time.*

Euphrasia (*Euphrasia officinalis*) 🌸 Homeopathic

USE TO TREAT

Colds with watering eyes and runny nose, conjunctivitis, eyes sensitive to bright light, hayfever.

Evening primrose (*Oenothera biennis*)

HERB PART USED

All parts are useful but the oil is extracted from the seeds.

HERB ACTIONS

The seed oil contains the acid GLA (gamma-linolenic acid) which seems to be responsible for many of the herb's healing properties and is an effective anti-inflammatory agent with none of the side-effects of anti-inflammatory drugs.[1]

USE TO TREAT

Arthritis, autoimmune disorders, hangovers, hyperactivity, multiple sclerosis, PMS, prostate problems, menopausal symptoms, fibrocystic breast disease, eczema, acne, psoriasis. The anticoagulant properties may help to reduce high blood pressure and coronary artery disease and prevent heart attack. It is necessary to persist with the treatment for at least 6 weeks before seeing improvement in the condition.

Expectorants

Help to remove excess mucus from bronchial passages.

HERBS

Angelica, aniseed, caraway, eucalyptus, mullein, oregano, peppermint, rosemary, tea-tree, thyme.

ESSENTIAL OILS

Eucalyptus, frankincense, lavender, peppermint, rosemary, tea-tree.

Eyebright (*Euphrasia rostkoviana*)

HERB PART USED

Leaves and flowers.

Herb actions

Anticatarrhal, astringent, anti-inflammatory, tonic.

Use to treat

Most eye ailments (see Eyes & eyebaths). Use internally to treat catarrh, sinusitis, coughs, sore throat and hay fever.

Essential oil action

None.

Eyes & eyebaths

Severe or long-standing eye problems should always be referred to an eye specialist but the following treatments act as support to orthodox treatments.

Like your skin, your eyes can also be damaged by radiation from the sun. The short-term damage can cause painful inflammation, excessive blinking and tears, a feeling that there is grit in your eyes, difficulty in looking at bright lights, and swelling of the eyes. Long-term damage can cause very serious eye problems that may include cataracts, a condition similar to snow blindness, cloudiness of the cornea, cancer of the membrane covering the white part of the eye and skin cancer of the eyelids.

This damage is easily prevented by wearing good sunglasses with a maximum eye protection factor (EPF) that conform to a general Australian Standard (AS 1067) and a wide-brimmed hat when outside in the sun or in areas where there is a lot of glare.

The skin around the eyes is thin, has few or no oil glands and is very delicate. Rough treatment can stretch this fine skin and all treatments need to be gentle.

Studies have shown that bilberry (*Vaccinium myrtillus*) fruit can provide a rich source of flavonoid molecules that are helpful for easing poor night vision and eyestrain.

CONJUNCTIVITIS

The symptoms of conjunctivitis are a yellow discharge, sore, red and itchy eyes, and inflamed eyelids. It isn't a serious problem except in newborn babies when medical attention should be sought.

DAILY SUPPLEMENTS

* 6000 mg vitamin C with bioflavonoids taken in 3 doses through the day.
* ½ teaspoon fluid extract of echinacea in 2 tablespoons water 3 times daily for 2 weeks.

ESSENTIAL OIL TREATMENT

Not appropriate.

HERBAL TREATMENT

* Use the eyewash described below with one of the herbs listed under Herbal treatment below.
* Golden seal tea, well strained through coffee-filter paper, is a premium treatment for eye infections and irritations.

EYEWASHES

Everything used on eyes must be scrupulously clean—sterile in fact. It's best to buy two eyebaths from the pharmacy as, if both eyes are to be treated, there will be less chance of transferring infection from one eye to the other (particularly important for complaints such as conjunctivitis). Immerse the eyebaths in boiling water before and after use and store in a bag or box.

Made-up eyewash should be stored in the refrigerator in a sterilised screw-top jar. The mixture must be used within two days.

TO USE: *Fill the eyebath three quarters full with warm herb tea or decoction (see suggestions in Herbal treatment) that has been filtered through coffee-filter paper. (The mixture is best used cold if there is inflammation or swelling.) Hold the eyebath firmly over the eye, tilt the head back and blink rapidly several times.*

Use the treatment several times a day until relief is obtained.

EYE EXERCISES

If you spend most of your day at a computer or reading it's important to exercise your eyes at regular intervals—every half to one hour.

1 Cup your palms over your eyes and 'look black' for a count of 10.
2 Shrug your shoulders slowly up and down 5 times. As 1.
3 Look up and down 5 times. As 1.
4 Look from side to side 5 times. As 1.
5 Look from corner to corner and then the opposite corner to corner 5 times each. As 1.

These exercises take less than 2 minutes and can save a great deal of long-term discomfort.

In addition to these exercises it's good to look up often from your work to a point as far away as possible—this lengthens and shortens the muscles and prevents strain.

HERBAL TREATMENT

⚜ A tea (see Teas) of any of the following herbs may be used as an eyewash for soothing sore, tired and 'gritty' eyes: calendula, chamomile, chickweed, eyebright, fennel. Make and use as described above.

⚜ The tannin in ordinary tea is good for soothing sore and tired eyes. Put used tea-bags in the fridge and then place them, deliciously cold and wonderfully soothing, on your eyes for 5 minutes. Chamomile tea-bags may be used in the same way.

⚜ Slices of cold cucumber or potato help to reduce under-eye puffiness caused by eyestrain.

HOMEOPATHIC TREATMENT

Take 4–5 times daily:

⚜ Eyes sore and inflamed—Euphrasia 12^c.
⚜ Swollen eyelids and conjunctivitis—Apis mel 30^c.
⚜ Eyes itchy with a discharge—Pulsatilla 30^c.
⚜ Injury to socket and soft tissue around the eye—Arnica 30^c.

APRICOT EYE CREAM

Use this cream to moisturise and retard the appearance of wrinkles on the thin, delicate skin around the eyes.

A

1 tablespoon anhydrous lanolin

2 teaspoons (10 ml) apricot oil

2 teaspoons (10 ml) wheatgerm oil

1 teaspoon (5 ml) olive oil

B

3 teaspoons (15 ml) hot distilled water

C

3 drops geranium oil

TO MAKE: *Melt A very gently until just liquid but not hot. Slowly add B to A stirring constantly until no water droplets can be seen. Add C, mix until blended. Spoon into a sterile jar, and cap immediately.*

TO USE: *After a bath or shower, gently pat a tiny amount of the cream around the eyes using the middle finger only. Avoid getting the cream into the eyes. Leave for 20 minutes and gently wipe off any surplus with a tissue.*

Fainting

Fainting is caused by a sudden lack of blood to the brain and can be caused by standing up suddenly from a prone or crouching position (particularly if one suffers from low blood pressure or anaemia), or by physical or emotional shock or weakness.

The person who feels faint should sit on a chair with their head between the knees. If they have already fainted they should be left prone with the legs raised to encourage a flow of blood back to the brain.

INTERNAL TREATMENT

A drink of water or cup of peppermint tea is a good restorative.

ESSENTIAL OIL TREATMENT

* Hold a bottle of any of the following oils: lavender, marjoram or rosemary under the nose or sprinkle a few drops on a tissue or handkerchief for the patient to sniff.
* Massage 2–3 drops of lavender on the temples (keep away from the eyes).

HOMEOPATHIC TREATMENT

All 6^c–30^c, take every few minutes until faintness has passed:
* All symptoms of shock—Rescue Remedy, rub on wrists or inside bottom lip.

❧ Accident and injury—Arnica.

❧ From a hot, airless atmosphere—Pulsatilla.

False unicorn root (*Chamaelirium luteum*)

HERB PART USED

Roots and rhizomes.

HERB ACTIONS

Diuretic, emetic, uterine tonic. Tones and strengthens the reproductive system. Normalises hormonal balance due to its oestrogen-like activity.

USE TO TREAT

Ovarian pain, threatened miscarriage and morning sickness.

ESSENTIAL OIL ACTION

None used.

Febrifuges

Cool and reduce fever.

HERBS

Catnep, elderflower, ginger, hyssop, lemon balm, meadowsweet, peppermint, rosemary, yarrow and willow bark.

ESSENTIAL OILS

Bergamot, eucalyptus, lavender and peppermint.

Fennel (*Foeniculum vulgare*)

HERB PART USED

Seeds, root, leaves.

HERB ACTIONS

Antispasmodic, aromatic, carminative, diuretic, expectorant, galact-agogue, stimulant, stomachic and for urinary tract infections. The seeds are the most used part of the plant, although the leaves make attractive garnishes and are delicious added to salads, fish dishes, sauces and soups.

USE TO TREAT

Colic, nausea, hiccoughs and to aid digestion particularly when fatty food is eaten. Fennel seeds were once eaten during church services to allay hunger pangs. Use to ease urinary tract problems and for diuretic properties. Use in eyewashes (see Eyes & eyebaths) for tired, sore eyes. Fennel has oestrogen-like properties which can help regulate the menstrual cycle, particularly late or scanty periods. It helps to regulate hormonal problems during menopause.

ESSENTIAL OIL ACTION

Antiseptic, antispasmodic, detoxifying, diuretic, for urinary tract infections.

USE TO TREAT

Use in baths and massage oils to counteract the effects of too much alcohol. A valuable addition to massage oil for cellulite, menstrual cramps and scanty periods. Helpful to menopausal women as it contains oestrogen-like properties.

Caution: *The oil shouldn't be used for young children or those with epilepsy. Never use at more than 1 per cent strength.*

Ferr phos. (*Ferrum phosphoricum*) 🜍 Homeopathic

Suited to pale people of delicate physique and those who are solitary in disposition, hate noise and sometimes feel inadequate.

USE TO TREAT

Fever, dizziness, nosebleeds and inflammation of all areas.

Fever

Many bacteria and viruses cannot withstand high temperatures and fever is the way that the body reacts to defend itself against infection. A temperature of 39–40°C can be very beneficial and shorten the duration of the complaint. If the temperature becomes higher or is allowed to continue for more than 2 days the patient may begin to feel weak and their temperature will need to be reduced by encouraging sweating and/or cool baths or sponge baths.

Allopathic medicine seeks to reduce temperature artificially which may alleviate the symptoms temporarily but does nothing to accelerate the healing process, in fact this suppression may result in prolonged infection and illness (see also Babies, Teething).

INTERNAL TREATMENT

- Give copious quantities of fluids—filtered or bottled water, herb tea, or dilute fruit juices.
- The patient often has a diminished appetite during a fever but if hungry, a light diet of fish, chicken or tofu with steamed vegetables and rice is appropriate.
- *Real* chicken soup (not from a packet or can) has been shown to have properties that loosen mucus.

DAILY SUPPLEMENTS

See Colds and Influenza.

ESSENTIAL OIL TREATMENT

To promote sweating use 10 drops of mixed lavender and tea-tree oil in a warm bath or, if the patient feels too unwell, put 3–4 drops in a bowl of warm water and use to give a bed bath.

Using 3–4 drops of the same oils in a cool compress (see Compresses) on the forehead is very soothing as fever is often accompanied by headache.

To reduce fever, add 2 drops lavender, 1 drop peppermint and 1 drop eucalyptus oil to a small bowl of cool (not cold) water and use to sponge the body and head. Repeat at hourly intervals until the body temperature is reduced.

Fever may also be reduced by giving a warm eucalyptus footbath (see Baths) using 6 drops of eucalyptus oil mixed thoroughly into the water. Soak the feet for 10–15 minutes.

HERBAL TREATMENT

See Colds and Influenza.

HOMEOPATHIC TREATMENT

Take often until the worst symptoms are over, then 4 times daily:

- ⚘ Sudden fever, anxious, restless with dry cough—Aconite 12^c.
- ⚘ Hot skin, red face, racing pulse—Belladonna 30^c.
- ⚘ First stages—Ferr. phos. 30^c.

Feverfew (*Chrysanthemum parthenium*)

HERB PART USED

Leaf.

HERB ACTIONS

Anti-inflammatory, carminative, emmenagogue, uterine stimulant, tonic, vasodilator. Feverfew is particularly beneficial in treating migraines and may ease arthritis and pre-menstrual symptoms.[1]
Caution: *Not to be used during pregnancy. Some people report problems such as mouth ulcers and digestive upsets after eating the raw leaf—this can be overcome by taking capsules.*

ESSENTIAL OIL ACTION

None.

Fibrositis

Use the treatment outlined in Rheumatism.

First-aid

Everyone has been, or will at some time, be faced with an injury to either themselves or a member of their family. It's important to know what to do in these situations as early intervention can reduce pain and trauma and even save a life.

To be an effective helper you need to take either a first-aid course (preferable) or buy one of the excellent first-aid books available and make yourself familiar with the contents. Keep a list of emergency numbers both in the first-aid box and next to the telephone.

Provide the house and the car with a first-aid box—the contents of these boxes should be checked at regular intervals and topped up when necessary.

I carry a mixed first-aid box as I find that it covers most eventualities. The contents of the boxes that follow are in addition to the usual dressings, tweezers, scissors, etc. There are now very good non-stick dressings and tape available which take the 'ouch' out of changing dressings. Many of the dressings 'breathe' which gives the wound a better chance to heal.

MIXED FIRST-AID BOX

ALOE VERA GEL: *for burns (minor), scalds, sunburn, insect bites, minor cuts and scratches, skin irritations.*

ARNICA CREAM: *homeopathic cream for bruises (not to be used if skin is broken).*

CHAMOMILE TEA-BAGS: *to calm tension, depression and anxiety, insomnia, internal inflammation such as gastritis, diarrhoea, cystitis, menstrual pain, PMS.*

GARLIC OIL CAPSULES: *to ease earache (see Earaches).*

GINGER CAPSULES: *to ease nausea, particularly travel nausea and sickness.*

INFUSED OILS: *(see Aromatherapy & Essential oils, Extraction of essential oils), choose from calendula, chamomile, golden seal, meadowsweet.*

IPECAC: *emetic for use when non-corrosive poisons have been swallowed. Follow instructions on label and get medical help as soon as possible.*

LAVENDER OIL: *treats minor burns, sunburn, scalds, insect bites, insect repellent, cuts, sores, tension headaches, stress. May be used undiluted.*

OINTMENTS: *for suggestions see Ointments.*

POWDERED HERBS: *see Herbs, Powdered herbs. Use for weeping open wounds and sores.*

RESCUE REMEDY: *see Bach Flower Remedies. Use to treat shock, pain and trauma.*

SLIPPERY ELM: *soothes sore stomach linings, eases diarrhoea, use for poultices.*

TEA-TREE OIL: *first aid in a bottle; powerfully antibacterial and anti-septic; may be used undiluted.*

TINCTURES: *choose from suggestions in Tinctures.*

WITCH-HAZEL, DISTILLED: *controls external bleeding; eases pain and inflammation from cuts, bruises, haemorrhoids, insect bites and stings.*

ESSENTIAL OIL FIRST-AID BOX

If you are a frequent traveller (particularly an overseas one) you may find it easier to carry this first-aid kit instead of the conventional one.

2 empty dropper bottles (for mixing)

2 eye droppers

15 ml bottle vegetable oil

15 ml bottle brandy

CHAMOMILE OIL: *use to treat the above problems externally and also to ease dull pain.*

GERANIUM OIL: *use with lemon oil to stop bleeding. Use as a nerve tonic when stressed. Use with lemon and lavender to repel insects.*

GINGER OIL: *for muscular pain and fatigue.*

GRAPEFRUIT OIL: *use to combat fatigue, depression and nervous exhaustion. Blend with geranium to counteract muscle stiffness.*

LAVENDER OIL: *may be used undiluted; is antibacterial, antiviral, antidepressant. Use for insect bites; as an insect repellent; and to treat bruises, minor burns and sunburn, headaches, and depression.*

LEMON OIL: *use with geranium oil to stop bleeding and prevent bacterial infection of wounds. A drop of oil in 1 cup (250 ml) of water is reputed to make the water safe to drink but I would hesitate to recommend this in countries such as India.*

PEPPERMINT *&/OR* GINGER OILS: *eases stomach cramps, travel sickness and nausea (see Travel).*

ROSEMARY OIL: *stimulates the central nervous system (and therefore the brain); gives clarity to the brain; eases the pain of muscles that are tired and stiff from sitting for long periods; inhalations ease the symptoms of colds, coughs, catarrh.* **Caution:** not to be used by epileptics or during pregnancy.

TEA-TREE OIL: *antibacterial, antiviral, antiseptic, antifungal. May be used undiluted. Use to treat abscesses, athlete's foot, cold sores, cuts, grazes, bites, ringworm, sunburn.*

TO USE THE OILS: *The essential oils may be used for compresses (see Compresses), fomentations (see Fomentations), massage (see Massage) or inhalations (see Inhalations).*

It's not recommended to take the oils internally but if you choose to, no more than 1 drop in 1 cup (250 ml) of water should be used.

Caution: Use 0.5–1 per cent only (see Aromatherapy & Essential oils, Blending chart) of ginger and peppermint oils.

HOMEOPATHIC FIRST-AID BOX

The asterisked remedies are those with the widest applications and are probably the most important to buy first (6^c–30^c potencies are appropriate for all first-aid situations).

*ARNICA: *use after any injury; for bruises, sprains, physical exhaustion and aching muscles.*

*HYPERICUM: *for painful cuts and wounds, falls on the spine, headache after a fall, banged fingers and toes, horsefly bites.*

*ARSENICUM: *for intense chilliness; restlessness and fear; weakness and exhaustion; burning pains, especially the eyes, throat and stomach.*

*FERRUM PHOS.: *for fear, nosebleeds, dizziness.*

•CANTHARIS: *for burns and scalds before blisters form, sunburn, hoarseness, loss of voice.*

•LEDUM: *for reducing pain and swelling from bites and stings, black eyes, severe bruising, puncture wounds especially where there is redness, swelling and throbbing.*

•NAT. MUR.: *for sneezy colds, runny nose, sinusitis, eczema, thrush, vertigo, exhaustion.*

•KALI SULPH.: *to ward off colds and boost the immune system; helps to clear the sinuses and yellow-green mucus conditions.*

ECHINACEA (6^x only): *for boils, septic conditions, and as an immune system booster.*

MAG. PHOS.: *for menstrual pain, abdominal pain.*

APIS MEL.: *for insect stings, stinging, burning pains, cystitis, arthritis.*

KALI. PHOS.: *for mental/nervous exhaustion, nervous indigestion, headache with humming in the ears after mental effort, giddiness.*

GELSEMIUM: *for influenza, sneezing, sore throat, shivering, difficulty in swallowing, running nose, vertigo.*

NUX VOMICA: *for nerves, nervous indigestion, ill-effects of over-eating/drinking, travel sickness, indigestion, itching piles, stuffy colds, raw throat, PMS.*

RHUS TOX: *for bruises, cold sores, eczema, sprains and strains, and tickling coughs.*

POWDERED HERBS

Some wounds such as weeping grazes, open sores and ulcers heal more quickly with the use of dry treatments. The following powder keeps the wound dry, prevents sepsis and accelerates healing.

Choose as many herbs as possible from the vulnerary list (see Vulneraries).

TO MAKE: *Dry the herbs, grind very finely and pass through a fine sieve. Store in an airtight jar in a dark cupboard.*

TO USE: *Sprinkle on wounds and cover with a dry dressing. Add to boiling water in the same way as a tea. Strain, use as a wound wash.*

Foot care

Most foot problems are a result of wearing ill-fitting shoes. There should always be a small gap between the end of the big toe and the end of the shoe to allow for movement when walking. Nylon stockings also cause problems as they don't allow the feet to breathe.

Special care needs to be taken when buying shoes for children as they are often unsure what a well-fitting shoe should feel like. Children can also grow out of shoes within 2 weeks or less of buying them as their bodies grow in unpredictable 'spurts'.

Modern 'joggers' are pretty deplorable as, unless they are fearfully expensive they are constructed entirely of synthetic materials and completely enclose the foot. Encourage the wearing of cotton socks and the use of a deodorant foot powder (below). The powder can be also sprinkled in the shoes overnight to sweeten them and help to kill bacteria.

ATHLETE'S FOOT (TINEA)

Wear cotton socks. Wash socks and foot towels separately using a few drops of tea-tree oil in the rinsing water. Dry the feet very thoroughly after washing.

ESSENTIAL OIL TREATMENT

Have you heard that athlete's foot is a fungal problem which is encouraged by wearing synthetic socks and enclosed shoes? Go barefoot as much as possible, particularly in the sunshine.

FOOT BATH BLEND

4 drops tea-tree oil

2 drops lavender oil

1 drop thyme or myrrh oil or 1 teaspoon (5 ml)
of either tincture.

TO MAKE & USE: *Sprinkle the oils on a bowl of water big enough for the feet. Stir well to disperse oils, soak the feet for 5–10 minutes. Dry well. Dust with foot powder.*

DEODORANT FOOT POWDER

6 drops tea-tree oil

6 drops lavender oil

3 drops myrrh oil (optional)

1 cup unperfumed talcum powder or cornflour

TO MAKE: *Drip the oils into the powder stirring constantly to prevent lumping and ensure even distribution. Store in an airtight container.*

TO USE: *Dust the feet liberally particularly between the toes.*

HERBAL TREATMENT

HERBAL FOOT RINSE

2 tablespoons (40 ml) cider vinegar

6 tablespoons (120 ml) warm water

TO MAKE: *Mix together.*

TO USE: *Wash feet in soap and water. Use cotton wool dipped in the foot rinse to thoroughly wet every part of the foot, particularly between the toes. Dry thoroughly. Dust with foot powder (herbal or essential oil).*

HERBAL FOOT POWDER

1/2 teacup calendula petals, dried and ground to a fine powder

1/4 teacup unperfumed talcum powder or cornflour

TO MAKE: *Mix together well, sift and store in a container with a well-fitting lid.*

TO USE: *After washing and drying, dust the feet thoroughly, particularly between the toes.*

FOOT BATHS

This is a treat for aching, swollen feet that have been walking or standing all day.

Use two bowls each big enough to immerse both feet. Fill one bowl with very cold water and the other with water as hot as can be borne. Add a handful of salt to each bowl, stir to dissolve. Alternate feet at 20 second intervals between the two bowls until the water is no longer hot.

Dry the feet and massage with 4 drops lavender oil and 4 drops rosemary oil in 1 tablespoon (20 ml) vegetable oil.

CORNS

It's possible to buy a hard black pumice-like treatment called a Chiropody sponge. If the corn is not too painful it may be removed by following the instructions in the packet. After treatment apply infused calendula oil (see Aromatherapy & Essential oils, Extraction of essential oils) to the area and either bandage or apply a non-stick dressing.

If the corn is too painful for the abrasive treatment the calendula oil may be massaged in morning and night, covered with a dressing. Lift the core out when soft enough. Poorly fitting shoes are almost invariably the cause of corns, so find the culprits and throw them out.

Fixed oils

Not to be confused with essential oils. These are natural, usually non-volatile oils occurring in the seeds, kernels, beans etc. of plants and extracted by presses, heat or chemicals. They are the oils that we use for cooking, making massage oils and other preparations. Cold-pressed oils are often perceived as being superior as the heat generated by the presses in this process is far less than that in the refining process, and more of the nutrients are preserved.

Fixed oils are classified as:

- **Non-drying:** These oils remain liquid at normal temperatures and don't form a film when exposed to oxygen. These are the most suitable oils to use for dry and normal skins and the main ones to use in massage oils. Some of these oils are almond (sweet), apricot, canola, castor, olive, palm, peach kernel, peanut, wheatgerm (non and semi-drying).
- **Semi-drying:** These oils dry to a soft film when exposed to oxygen. They are suitable for dry, combination and normal skins and should only be used in small quantities in massage oils. They include apricot (non and semi-drying), avocado, grape-seed, hazelnut, peach kernel (non and semi-drying), safflower, sesame, sunflower, wheatgerm.
- **Drying:** These oils dry quite quickly to a tough and elastic skin when exposed to oxygen. For this reason they are often included

in paints to shorten the drying time. Not suitable for inclusion in massage oils but may be added in small quantities to emulsified creams and lotions, as the process of emulsification alters the character of the oils. These oils include soya and linseed.

Fluid retention

Sudden or prolonged fluid retention in the legs can indicate a kidney or heart problem and to attempt self-help could be dangerous. A health professional should be consulted without delay. Fluid retention caused by cellulite, heat or plane flights may be dealt with using the following remedies.

INTERNAL TREATMENT

* Reduce salt intake.
* Dandelion leaf is a diuretic and contains potassium, which makes it far superior to most other diuretics.
* Drink 3 cups of dandelion leaf tea daily for 1 week (see Teas). Drink one cup daily for two weeks, discontinue for 1 week. This regime may be followed for as long as needed.

DAILY SUPPLEMENTS

* 1000 mg garlic oil capsules twice daily or 2 teaspoons 'Long-life juice' 2–3 times daily.
* 25 mg vitamin B6.
* 1 vitamin B complex tablet.
* 1000 mg vitamin C with bioflavonoids.

ESSENTIAL OIL TREATMENT

BATH & MASSAGE OIL
90 ml vegetable oil
20 drops juniper oil
20 drops geranium oil
20 drops grapefruit oil
TO MAKE: *Mix together in a 100 ml bottle. Leave for a few days to blend. Store in a cool, dark place.*

TO USE: *Add 2 teaspoons (10 ml) to a warm bath, stir well to distribute. Soak for at least 10 minutes, massaging the legs and hips while in the water.*

Use the blend also as a daily massage oil.

HERBAL TREATMENT

Celery seed extract as directed.

HOMEOPATHIC TREATMENT

All 6–30^c, take 4 times daily:
❧ Nat. mur., Apis mel.

Fomentations

Fomentations are a way of applying moist heat to areas of the body. They are used to draw pus or foreign bodies from the flesh or for relieving congestion. They can ease pain and relax spasms.

Be very careful not to burn the patient when applying a fomentation. Remember that a sore, bruised or abraded area will be very sensitive, test the heat on the inside of your wrist before applying the fomentation to the patient.

HERBS

Make a triple-strength tea of the chosen herb and follow the last three stages of Essential oils.

ESSENTIAL OILS

TO MAKE: *Add 5–10 drops (depending on the age of the patient) of the chosen essential oils to a small bowl of very hot, boiled water, agitate to spread the oils.*

Fold a piece of clean soft cloth in four and place on the surface of the water. Squeeze out until still wet but not dripping.

Apply as hot as can be borne, cover with plastic wrap. Fasten in place with a piece of towelling or strip of cloth.

Leave for 20 minutes, repeat frequently for the first 3–4 hours.

Frankincense (*Boswellia carteri*)

ESSENTIAL OIL ACTION

Anti-inflammatory, antiseptic, astringent, expectorant.

USE TO TREAT

Respiratory disorders, asthma, coughs, chronic bronchitis, bronchial catarrh. Calms anxiety, depression, nervous tension, stress, PMS. Use in skin-care preparations to tighten and tone older skin and retard the formation of wrinkles.

Galactagogues

Induce milk secretion.

HERBS

Basil, fennel, nettle.

Gallstones

The presence of gallstones may not be suspected unless the gall-bladder becomes inflamed. If there are bouts of colic, an increase in bloating and flatulence or nausea and discomfort after eating fatty foods then there is reason to suspect gallstones. An ultra-sound will detect them.

INTERNAL TREATMENT

- Eat a vegetarian diet that includes increased amounts of fibre, fruit and vegetables.
- 1 dessertspoon ground linseed daily, sprinkled on cereal or stirred into a glass of water. *Follow with another glass of water.*
- Avoid animal fats and sugar.
- Avoid all fried foods.
- Drink 6–8 glasses of lemon water daily (fill a jug with filtered or bottled water and float a chopped lemon in the water, leave for 2–3 hours before drinking).

DAILY SUPPLEMENTS

- ❧ 1000 mg vitamin C with bioflavonoids.
- ❧ 500 iu vitamin E (d-alpha tocopherol).
- ❧ Milk thistle as directed.

ESSENTIAL OIL TREATMENT

Treatment by essential oils is not indicated.

HERBAL TREATMENT

Drink dandelion coffee 3 times a day in place of ordinary tea or coffee.

HOMEOPATHIC TREATMENT

Consult a homeopathic practitioner.

Gardening

The use of herbs and essential oils will help to enrich and protect your garden without the hazards caused by chemical pesticides.

It's not always necessary to go to a lot of trouble making special mixtures unless there is a specific problem that needs particular herbs or oils. I used to enrich and protect the soil by stripping the leaves from herbs that I was pruning and sprinkling them around the garden as I worked. I would often end up with some prunings for re-planting, some for indoors to dry and store, some to enrich the compost heap, and the remainder for the garden.

If herbs are grown among vegetables and flowers they enhance the appearance of the bed and help the plants by acting as insect repellents.

ANTI-FUNGAL SPRAY

10 drops chamomile oil

6 drops tea-tree oil

¼ cup (60 ml) paraffin oil

2 cups (500 ml) water

TO MAKE: *Mix the essential oils with the paraffin oil. Leave for 2–3 days. Add the water while stirring constantly. Shake well before use.*

TO USE: *Add 2 tablespoons (40 ml) to 8 cups (2 litres) water, mix well and use to spray seedlings and plants.*

GENERAL ANTI-BUG & PEST SPRAY
5 drops peppermint oil
2 garlic oil capsules squeezed into mixture
5 drops citronella oil
½ cup (125 ml) paraffin oil
2 cups (500 ml) water
TO MAKE & USE: *As for Anti-fungal spray.*

COMFREY FERTILISER
Comfrey makes one of the best fertilisers for potatoes and tomatoes due to its high potash content. Put the leaves in a container and cover with water. Leave for 4–6 weeks until the leaves are completely rotted and use the diluted liquid on the soil around the plants and use the rotted leaves as mulch. Alternatively the leaves may be chopped and sprinkled around the plant as mulch where they will slowly rot into the ground.

CHAMOMILE SPRAY—TO PREVENT 'DAMPING OFF'
Chamomile is known as the 'Plant Doctor' as it seems to benefit weak or ailing plants growing near it.
TO MAKE: *Make a very strong tea of chamomile using 3 teaspoons dried chamomile, 1 cup (250 ml) boiling water. Leave for 24 hours. Strain and add 5 cups (1.25 litres) of cold water.*
TO USE: *Water onto weak plants to boost them or onto young seedlings to prevent 'damping off' (a fungal problem that rots seedlings at soil level).*

ELDERFLOWER SPRAY
TO MAKE: *See Chamomile spray.*
TO USE: *Spray on and around young plants to protect them against insects and caterpillars.*

GARLIC SPRAY

100 g garlic cloves

6 onions

6 very hot chillies

paraffin oil to cover

4 cups (1 litre) water

1 cup skim milk powder

TO MAKE: *Mince or blend garlic, onions and chillies well. Put in a non-plastic container and cover with paraffin oil, stand for 2–3 days. Add water, stir and strain through fine cloth. Mix the dried milk in thoroughly until there are no lumps. Store in a non-plastic container.*

TO USE: *Add 1–2 parts spray to 50 parts water (stronger if liked) spray on soil and plants to protect against aphids, ants, spiders and caterpillars.*

HERBAL FERTILISER & INSECT REPELLENT

Herbs: southernwood, wormwood, mint, tansy, feverfew, chamomile, nettle, elder, parsley, sage, dandelion

TO MAKE: *Use as many as possible of the listed herbs. Chop very finely, cover with boiling water, cover and leave for 2 weeks. Strain through fine cloth.*

TO USE: *Sprinkle the rotted herbs in the compost heap or around the vegetable garden. Spray the liquid wherever nutrients and insect repellents are needed.*

Gargles

Gargles are preparations for healing and soothing infected sore throats and laryngitis. They can be made from 1 teaspoon (5 ml) tincture of myrrh or ¼ teaspoon cooking salt added to 1 cup (250 ml) warm water; from a strong tea or decoction of herb; or from adding 1–2 drops of tea-tree oil to 1 cup (250 ml) of warm water. Stir well, gargle and spit gargle out. Don't swallow. See also Throat, sore.

Garlic (*Allium sativum*)

HERB PART USED

Bulb.

HERB ACTIONS

Anthelmintic, antiseptic, antispasmodic, antiviral, carminative, cholagogue, digestive, diuretic, expectorant, febrifuge, and hypotensive. Garlic loses much of its antibiotic property when dried or cooked and is best either eaten raw or in 'Long-life juice' (see 'Long-life juice').

USE TO TREAT

Discourages the growth of many bacteria and viruses. Has been used successfully to treat amoebic dysentery; mouth, ear and fungal infections; to normalise blood pressure; and for lung conditions. It is said to lower serum cholesterol levels. Widely used in cooking. Garlic is also very useful in the garden where the spray (see Gardening) can be used to control many pests.

ESSENTIAL OIL ACTION

As above.

Gelsemium (*Gelsemium sempervirens*) ❀ Homeopathic

Suited to people who suffer from 'nerves', and who worry about the most trivial tasks.

USE TO TREAT

Anxiety, colds, influenza, neuralgia, vertigo and writer's cramp.

Gentian root (*Gentiana lutea*)

HERB PART USED

Root.

HERB ACTIONS

Gentian is one of the best bitters to stimulate and tone the digestive system, the digestive juices and accelerate the emptying of the stomach.

USE TO TREAT

Flatulence, heartburn, indigestion. Stimulates the flow of gastric juices improving digestion and absorption of nutrients.[1] Has a reputation for raising the white blood-cell count. Gentian root is the main ingredient in the cocktail additive Angostura Bitters.

ESSENTIAL OIL

None.

Geranium (*Pelargonium graveolens*)

HERB PART USED

Leaves and flowers.

HERB ACTIONS

There are more than 230 varieties of pelargoniums but the most popular and widely used is *P. graveolens* known as rose geranium. The leaves and flowers are used mainly in cooking and rarely medicinally but the essential oil is used extensively.

ESSENTIAL OIL ACTION

Antiseptic, antidepressant, hormone-regulating properties, astringent and haemostatic. The essential oil is called either geranium or rose geranium.

USE TO TREAT

PMS and menopausal problems, cuts, abrasions and wounds. Balances sebum in the skin making it useful in skin care for all skin types. Problems of the urinary system such as kidney stones and urinary tract infections.

Ginger (*Zingiber officinalis*)

HERB PART USED

Rhizome.

HERB ACTIONS

Anti-inflammatory, appetiser, carminative, diaphoretic, stimulant.

USE TO TREAT

Poor circulation (tones the circulatory system), cramps and chilblains, travel and morning sickness. Promotes perspiration (use for colds, flu); stimulates digestion and eases indigestion, flatulence and colic. Tonic. Relieves aches and pains. Reduces inflammation and pain in arthritis, bursitis and similar conditions. Tones the cardiovascular system and reduces blood clotting

ESSENTIAL OIL ACTION

A powerful oil that shouldn't be used at dilutions more than 1 per cent (see the Blending chart in Aromatherapy & Essential oils). The rubefacient properties bring blood to the surface of the skin. Use 0.5 per cent in blends or compresses/fomentations.

USE TO TREAT

Arthritis, fibrositis, muscle pain, rheumatism.

Gingivitis

Inflammation and bleeding of the gums, caused largely by bacterial plaque. If allowed to continue it can lead to periodontitis (loose teeth and sometimes jaw bone damage). Other causes may include poor brushing and flossing that leaves impacted food in crevices, faulty fillings that have rough edges which allow food to collect. Hard-bristled toothbrushes can cause damage to the gums, allowing the entry of bacteria. Medium and soft bristles are preferable.

If the problem is long-lasting treat it in conjunction with treatment and advice from a periodontist or dentist.

INTERNAL TREATMENT

❧ Eat plenty of fruit, vegetables, wholegrain bread and cereals.

❧ Cut down (or cut out) the amount of sugar and refined carbohydrates.

❧ Drink lemonade using the *whole* ground-up lemon (for the bioflavonoids in the skin).

DAILY SUPPLEMENTS

❧ 5000–10 000 iu beta-carotene.

❧ 1000 mg vitamin C with bioflavonoids twice daily.

❧ 500 iu vitamin E (d-alpha tocopherol).

❧ 15 mg zinc.

❧ 1000 mg garlic oil capsules 3 times daily or 2–3 teaspoons 'Long-life juice' 3 times daily.

ESSENTIAL OIL TREATMENT

MOUTHWASH

¼ cup (60 ml) sherry

2 tablespoons (40 ml) brandy

8 drops peppermint oil

6 drops thyme oil

4 drops oil of myrrh or ½ teaspoon (2.5 ml) tincture of myrrh

1 teaspoon (5 ml) glycerine

TO MAKE: *Mix together in a jar. Leave for 5–6 days to blend. Strain through coffee-filter paper. Store in a dark bottle.*

TO USE: *Add 2 teaspoons (10 ml) mouthwash to ½ glass (125 ml) warm water, rinse mouth several times with the mixture; spit out. Repeat 3 times daily.*

HERBAL TREATMENT

Mix 1 teaspoon (5 ml) tincture of myrrh with ½ glass warm water, 'swoosh' the mixture around the mouth for 10–15 seconds before spitting out. Repeat 3 times daily.

HERBAL MOUTHWASH

1 cup (250 ml) brandy, sherry or cider vinegar

1 tablespoon crushed thyme leaves

1 tablespoon finely chopped peppermint leaves

4 cloves, bruised

½ teaspoon (2.5 ml) tincture of myrrh

TO MAKE: *Mix together in a jar with a well fitting lid. Leave for 1 week, shaking daily.*

   Strain through a sieve and then through coffee-filter paper.

TO USE: *Add 2 teaspoons (10 ml) to 2 tablespoons (40 ml) warm water, rinse mouth, spit out. Repeat 3 times daily.*

HOMEOPATHIC TREATMENT

Take 4 times daily:

- 𝕏 Gums, swollen—Apis mel. 30^c.
- 𝕏 Gums, inflamed—Calc. phos. 12^c.
- 𝕏 Mouth ulcers—Merc. sol. 12^c.

Ginkgo biloba (*Ginkgo biloba*)

HERB PART USED

Leaves.

HERB ACTIONS

Improves the blood supply and so oxygenation to the brain, improves mental performance and alertness, enhances memory, may be useful for senility and Altzheimer's disease. Relieves some types of hearing loss and 'ringing in the ears'. May improve problems such as haemorrhoids, varicose veins and restless legs caused by poor circulation. Increases energy, improves blood supply to the heart, helps to reduce high blood pressure.

ESSENTIAL OIL ACTION

None.

Ginseng (*Panax schinseng & P. quinquefolius*)

HERB PART USED

Root.

HERB ACTIONS

Adaptogen, antidepressive, tonic, increases physical and mental performance.

USE TO TREAT

Considered by some to be a panacea for all ailments but in fact ginseng isn't recommended for *acute* inflammatory diseases and if taken in large doses or for prolonged periods can cause depression and nervousness. Improves physical endurance and mental concentration, normalises menstruation. Raises low blood pressure to a normal level. Eases digestive disturbances. Helpful for chest complaints such as coughs and colds. Enjoys a reputation as an aphrodisiac and is a sexual restorative and tonic for men who are lacking in sexual energy.

ESSENTIAL OIL ACTION

None.

Ginseng, Siberian (*Eleutherococcus senticocus*)

HERB PART USED

Root.

HERB ACTIONS

Adaptogen, circulatory stimulant, tonic, vasodilator.

USE TO TREAT

Physical and mental stress to improve stamina and resistance to stress. Acts as a tonic for people who are run down or feeling weak and lacking in energy.

ESSENTIAL OIL ACTION

None.

Glandular fever (Infectious mononucleosis)

The Epstein-Barr virus (one of the herpes viruses) causes glandular fever. It is usually seen in young adults and has earned the nicknames 'kissing disease' or 'student flu'. Glandular fever begins as a flu-like condition that doesn't clear up—sometimes for months. During the acute stage the lymph glands (particularly in the neck) are usually swollen; there is also fever, muscular pain and weakness, sore throat and extreme fatigue. Apart from the swollen glands, there is a great deal of similarity between glandular fever and Chronic Fatigue Syndrome. See Chronic Fatigue Syndrome for treatment suggestions.

After the acute stage has passed, the symptoms are typified by extreme lethargy that can last for months. Patients may look perfectly well but this may not be the case—they must ensure they have adequate rest and good nutrition to help the body recover.

Glycerine

A natural substance found in animal and vegetable fats, usually obtained as a by-product of soap-making. Vegetable glycerine is available from specialist sources. It is syrupy in consistency, colourless, odourless, sticky and sweet. If used in small proportions in lotions, creams and toners it acts as an antibacterial, softener, lubricant and humectant (holding moisture to the skin). If more than 20 per cent is used in any recipe it will have the opposite effect and draw water *out* of the skin.

Golden seal (*Hydrastis canadensis*)

HERB PART USED

Rhizome.

HERB ACTIONS

Antiseptic, antibiotic, antifungal, antibacterial and antiviral, astringent, diuretic, immune-system enhancer, laxative, tonic. Stimulates the immune system.

USE TO TREAT

Infections and inflammations of all types. Congestion and catarrh of the mucous membranes, colitis, gastritis, loss of appetite. Stimulates bile production. Supports the lymphatic system during detoxification. The ointment will help to heal haemorrhoids, herpes, impetigo, scabies and ringworm. Sprinkle the powdered root directly onto open wounds to disinfect and promote scab formation. Use the tea as an eyewash for eye infections and irritations. A gargle will help to heal sore mouths and throats.

A tincture (see Tinctures) of golden seal is a very useful addition to the family medicine chest.

Caution: *Avoid during pregnancy.*

Gotu kola (*Centella asiatica*)

HERB PART USED

Leaves.

HERB ACTIONS

Tonic and blood purifier.

USE TO TREAT

Varicose veins and circulation problems in the legs. Has had considerable success in the treatment of arthritis. Tranquillising, sedative and anti-spasmodic.

Gout

An excessive build-up of uric acid in the body causes gout, the excess turning into crystals around joints. The joint most often affected is at the base of the big toe but gout can affect other toes, the knuckles of fingers and earlobes. Attacks of gout can cause excruciatingly painful inflammation and swelling and may be accompanied by high fever.

Gout is mainly an affliction of middle-aged men and is associated with living of the 'good life', namely consuming too much rich food (particularly red meat) and alcohol.

INTERNAL TREATMENT

- Eliminate alcohol, tea and coffee. Avoid red meat and cheese and increase consumption of fresh fruits, vegetables, wholegrain breads and cereals.
- Avoid shellfish, sardines, beans and kidneys.
- Drink 6–8 glasses of filtered or bottled water daily.
- Eat 225 g black cherries (fresh or canned) daily to lower uric acid levels.

DAILY SUPPLEMENTS

- 500 iu vitamin E (d-alpha tocopherol).
- 1000 mg vitamin C with bioflavonoids.
- Devil's claw as directed.

ESSENTIAL OIL TREATMENT

MASSAGE OIL

2 tablespoons (40 ml) vegetable oil

15 drops chamomile oil

10 drops geranium oil

5 drops peppermint oil

TO MAKE: *Mix well together in a small bottle.*

TO USE: *Massage the affected parts very gently with the slightly warmed oil.*

Cool footbaths (see Foot care) containing 2 drops each fennel, juniper and cypress oils

HERBAL TREATMENT

- 1 cup (250 ml) burdock and nettle tea 3 times daily.
- Devil's claw as directed.

✣ Celery seed extract as directed.

✣ Poultice (see Poultices) of mashed comfrey root.

HOMEOPATHIC TREATMENT

All 6–30ᶜ, take 4 times daily:

✻ Afraid of being touched—Arnica.

✻ Enlargement of finger joints—Calc. fluor.

✻ Suffering much pain—Lycopodium.

Grapefruit (Citrus paradisi)

ESSENTIAL OIL ACTION

Antibacterial, antidepressant, antiseptic, astringent, diuretic, detoxifier, stimulant, tonic.

USE TO TREAT

Acne and oily skin. Anxiety, depression, jet-lag, mental exhaustion, tension and stress-related problems, fluid retention, cellulitis, elimination of toxins, lymphatic-system stimulation.

Caution: *Mildly phototoxic.*

Graphites (Graphites) ✻ Homeopathic

Suited to people who are cautious and find decision making difficult.

USE TO TREAT

Constipation, dandruff, earache, eczema, hot flushes, PMS, psoriasis, sinus problems, styes, tinnitus.

Grief ❦ See Emotional & nervous problems, Grief

Gums ❦ See Gingivitis

Haemorrhoids (Piles)

These are varicose veins in the rectum just above the anus. The veins sometimes protrude from the anus and can bleed and be very uncomfortable. They are caused by restriction of the blood vessels in the area. This can occur in pregnancy, when constipated or adopting a squatting position for long periods. Genetic pre-disposition is also a factor. Avoid constipation and 'straining'. Don't sit on the toilet for long periods reading books! Do Kegel exercise to strengthen the pelvic-floor muscles (see Prostate).

INTERNAL TREATMENT

If constipation is a problem, a dessertspoonful of ground linseed or psyllium seed daily may cure it. Increase or decrease the amount when you have determined what is necessary for you. Eat a diet rich in fibre. Eat buckwheat porridge for the rutin content every morning.

DAILY SUPPLEMENTS

- 1 vitamin B complex tablet.
- 1000 mg vitamin C with bioflavonoids.
- 500 iu vitamin E.
- 15–30 mg zinc.
- Horse chestnut as directed.
- Gotu kola as directed.
- 500–750 mg bromelain 3 times daily between meals.

ESSENTIAL OIL TREATMENT

MASSAGE OIL

40 drops cypress oil

30 drops juniper oil

20 drops geranium oil

10 drops peppermint oil

TO MAKE: *Mix together in a small bottle.*

TO USE: *Add 4 drops to 1 tablespoon (20 ml) vegetable oil. Use to massage the anal area at least 3 times a day.*

Use 4 drops in a bowl of warm water large enough to sit in or 10 drops in a warm bath, agitate the water to disperse the oil. Soak for 10–15 minutes. Pat the anal area dry and dab with cold distilled witch-hazel.

HERBAL TREATMENT

꙾ Calendula and/or golden seal ointment with the above oils (see Ointments) massaged on to the affected area 3 times a day.

꙾ Apply cold compresses of distilled witch-hazel particularly after a bowel movement if there is discomfort and bleeding.

HOMEOPATHIC TREATMENT

Take 4 times daily:

꙾ Bleeding, itching, protruding—Calc. fluor. 12^c.

꙾ Burning soreness, some bleeding—Hamamelis 12^c.

꙾ Protruding with sharp, shooting pains—Ignatia 30^c twice daily.

꙾ If there is flatulence and bloating—Lycopodium 30^c twice daily.

Haemostatics

Help to stop bleeding.

HERBS

Calendula, plantain, sage, shepherd's purse, distilled witch-hazel, yarrow.

ESSENTIAL OILS

Chamomile, cypress, eucalyptus, geranium, lemon, rose.

Hair care ❧ See also Head lice

Commercial shampoos and conditioners are one way for multi-national companies to part us from our money. Many of these shampoos are so harsh that a conditioner is needed to give some semblance of gloss and manageability to abused hair. Look at old paintings and photographs of men and women in the past—their hair wasn't terrible and yet if we are to believe the commercials the only way to have reasonable hair is to use their products. In fact these products steadily weaken the hair by putting layer after layer of waxes and other chemicals on the hair shaft.

It takes about three weeks for natural shampoos to get rid of the chemical junk but after that you will have the hair that nature intended—sweet smelling, soft and shiny.

HEALTHY HAIR

❧ Avoid commercial shampoos or at least buy the most natural one you can find in a health-food shop. Even these shampoos can be improved and made to last longer by the addition of essential oils or concentrated herbal teas.

❧ Brace yourself! One of the best ways to ensure thick, healthy hair is to use only lukewarm water for shampooing and to use cold water (or herbal vinegar in cold water) for the final rinse. Rosemary vinegar is good for dark hair, chamomile for fair hair and lavender is lovely for all hair types.

❧ Buy the best hairbrush that you can afford. Pure bristle brushes are best but even these need checking by tapping the bristles on the palm of your hand to make sure that the ends of the bristles are rounded and not sharp. Gentle washing once a week will extend the life of your brush. Thirty to forty strokes are enough when brushing the hair. Bend over and brush from the scalp to the ends of the hair to distribute the oil evenly. Bending over also increases the blood supply to the scalp, which is beneficial to the hair follicle.

- Use a wide-toothed comb. Teeth that are too close together can pull out a lot of hair.
- If you pull your hair back in a style that causes tension for long periods of time you could develop a condition called traction alopecia. This means that you are losing your hair because you are pulling it out!
- Overuse of chemicals to colour the hair and using heat to dry your hair could result in brittle hair. If you don't do either of these and your hair is still brittle, look to your diet.
- Rinse the hair immediately after swimming, and shampoo it as soon as possible using a conditioning treatment before and after shampooing. Chlorinated water and seawater are both very damaging to hair.
- Don't do anything rough to your hair while it's wet. After shampooing, towel lightly and run your fingers through to arrange it. Wet hair is very elastic and can be badly damaged by rough handling, for example, by brushing and combing.
- Regular scalp massage can increase the flow of blood to the hair follicle and greatly improve the condition of your hair. Place all your fingers and both thumbs firmly on the scalp and move the skin on the scalp. Don't rub or you will merely pull hairs out which is rather counter-productive!

The following shampoos are soap based and because of this need an acid rinse to restore the acid balance of the hair and to get rid of the last traces of soap.

SHAMPOO BASE **1**

1/3 cup (packed) Lux soap flakes

4 cups (1 litre) very hot water (rainwater is best)

2 teaspoons borax

TO MAKE: *Mix all ingredients in a large jar and stir until dissolved. When mixed and slightly cooled add 40 drops lavender, 40 drops rosemary and 20 drops basil (optional) essential oils. Stir again really well to distribute.*

TO USE: *The mixture may go lumpy on standing so stir well before using.*

The shampoo can be decanted into a squeeze bottle or can just be scooped out of the jar as you need it. The squeeze-bottle method is best as this slippery mixture has a habit of sliding off your hands. Follow with a vinegar rinse.

SHAMPOO BASE 2

Use either fresh herbs or essential oils but remember that fresh herb teas 'go off' and the shampoo won't last as long as when using essential oils. Follow the shampoo with a vinegar rinse.

CASTILE SHAMPOO

3 tablespoons finely chopped fresh rosemary and lavender
1 cup (250 ml) water (rainwater is the best)
3/4 cup (185 ml) liquid castile soap (from health-food stores)
TO MAKE: *Simmer the herbs and water in a covered pan for 30 minutes. Stand overnight if possible. Strain.*

Simmer, covered, until reduced to 1/4 cup. Add to the castile soap, mix and bottle.

If using essential oils add 20 drops lavender, 10 drops rosemary and 10 drops basil (optional) essential oils to castile soap. Mix well.

ESSENTIAL OIL VINEGAR RINSE

2 tablespoons (40 ml) vinegar
20 drops lavender oil
20 drops rosemary oil
10 drops geranium oil (or lemon oil if hair is oily)
rainwater
TO MAKE: *Mix essential oils and vinegar together in a 300 ml spray bottle. Fill with purified or rainwater. Shake well before use.*
TO USE: *Rinse the hair after shampooing then spray it thoroughly with the vinegar rinse. Don't rinse out.*

HERBAL VINEGAR RINSE

TO MAKE: *Substitute the essential oils in the Essential Oil Vinegar Rinse with the same herbs. Fill a jar with the mixed herbs, cover with warm vinegar then with a vinegar-proof lid.*

Stand in hot sun or other warm place for 24 hours.

Strain the vinegar, add more fresh herbs and repeat the above process. Repeat once more if a very strong vinegar is desired.

TO USE: *Add 1–2 tablespoons (20–40 ml) vinegar to a 300 ml spray bottle.*

Rinse the hair with water after shampooing then spray thoroughly with the vinegar rinse. Don't rinse out.

MILK & HONEY TREATMENT

If your hair has become very dry through the use of harsh shampoos, bleaching, colouring, too much sun or through illness the following treatment will do much to restore it.

1 egg yolk, beaten
1 teaspoon (5 ml) jojoba oil
1 teaspoon (5 ml) runny honey
4 drops rosemary oil
dried milk powder to mix

TO MAKE: *Mix the first four ingredients. Add enough milk powder to make a soft paste.*

TO USE: *Massage into the hair and scalp. Cover the hair with a plastic shower cap and then with a hot towel. Leave for 20 minutes. Shampoo with a mild herbal shampoo.*

DAILY HAIR TREATMENT

This treatment is for everyday use on all hair types. The non-greasy oils will be absorbed into the hair shaft and will keep the hair smooth, glossy and healthy.

3 teaspoons (15 ml) lavender oil
2 teaspoons (10 ml) rosemary oil
1/2 teaspoon (2.5 ml) jojoba oil

TO MAKE: *Mix together in a small bottle. Shake to blend.*
TO USE: *Put a few drops on the palm of your hand. Rub your hands together and then rub through your hair.*

DANDRUFF

Dandruff is a common problem in which the skin of the scalp flakes causing white flecks to fall on clothes. It is usually caused by an excess of sebum that blocks the pore to the hair follicle and dries out to form little white flakes. There is also some evidence to suggest that dandruff may be a fungal infection. I don't recommend the use of commercial dandruff shampoos—they are very harsh and if they worked then you wouldn't need to keep using them year after year.

Before shampooing sprinkle salt through the hair and massage the scalp well. Follow with one of the above shampoos and finish with a vinegar rinse/spray. Shampoo every three days.

INTERNAL TREATMENT

- Eat lots of fresh fruit and vegetables and avoid refined carbohydrates and junk food.
- Cut down on animal fats and margarine.
- Eat lean red meat, shellfish and pumpkin seeds for their zinc content.

DAILY SUPPLEMENTS

- 1 vitamin B complex tablet.
- 50 mg vitamin B6.
- 10 000 iu beta-carotene.
- Selenium as directed.
- 2000 mg vitamin C with bioflavonoids.

ESSENTIAL OIL TREATMENT

ANTI-DANDRUFF SHAMPOO
Use one of the shampoo bases above.
1 cup (250 ml) shampoo base
20 drops rosemary oil

20 drops eucalyptus oil

20 drops lemon oil

TO MAKE: *Mix all ingredients together really well and mix again before use. Store in a squeeze bottle.*

TO USE: *Invert the bottle a few times to mix the oils with the shampoo. Shampoo the hair thoroughly paying special attention to the scalp, massaging with the pads of the fingers, not the nails. Rinse well and follow with the Essential Oil Vinegar rinse above.*

ANTI-DANDRUFF TONIC

1 cup (250 ml) water (rainwater if possible)

1 teaspoon borax

1 tablespoon (20 ml) distilled witch-hazel

2 teaspoons (10 ml) cider vinegar

20 drops lavender oil

20 drops rosemary oil

10 drops tea-tree oil

TO MAKE: *Mix the water and borax, stir until dissolved. Add remaining ingredients, bottle and shake well.*

TO USE: *Shake well before use. Part the hair and rub a little of the tonic onto the scalp using a cotton-wool ball. Repeat all over the scalp. Use the tonic every night.*

HOMEOPATHIC TREATMENT

30^c take once daily:

* ❀ Dry scales on scalp—Graphites.
* ❀ Moist dandruff—Sepia.

Hamamelis (*Hamamelis virginiana*) ❀ Homeopathic

USE TO TREAT

Chilblains, haemorrhoids, nosebleeds, piles, varicose veins.

Hand care

The skin on the hands contains very little oil and what little there is, is constantly being stripped away by detergents, soil from gardening, dust from housework and other jobs that stress the skin. It really pays to try to remember to use suitable gloves for work and to use a rich handcream whenever possible.

The following recipes are simple and inexpensive to make and will improve the condition of your hands.

LEMON, OIL & SUGAR SCRUB

TO MAKE: *Mix 2 teaspoons lemon juice and 2 teaspoons vegetable oil to a paste with 1–2 tablespoons sugar.*

TO USE: *Massage well into the hands and around the nails. Rinse off, pat dry and apply handcream.*

AVOCADO LAVENDER HAND CREAM

1 level tablespoon finely grated, firmly packed beeswax

2 tablespoons (40 ml) almond oil

2 tablespoons (40 ml) avocado oil

1 teaspoon (5 ml) glycerine

1½ tablespoons (30 ml) lavender tea or water

½ teaspoon (2.5 ml) borax

10 drops lavender oil

5 drops lemon oil

TO MAKE: *Melt the beeswax in a small bowl or jar over a pan of simmering water. When melted slowly add the almond and avocado oils taking care not to re-harden the wax. Take off the heat.*

Warm the glycerine and lavender tea or water to the same temperature as the oils and wax (feel the outside of the containers to compare) and add slowly to the waxes and oils, beating steadily the whole time. As soon as the two mixtures are incorporated stop beating or the mixture will separate.

Stir in the essential oils and pot the cream. Store in the refrigerator.

HAND & NAIL OIL

This oil will nourish the skin and nails. Use at least once a week, more if possible.

1½ tablespoons (30 ml) vegetable oil

½ tablespoon (10 ml) jojoba oil

60 drops borage (starflower) oil or evening primrose oil

20 drops palmarosa oil

5 drops geranium oil

2 × 500 iu vitamin E oil capsules

TO MAKE: *Prick the vitamin E capsules and squeeze into a dark coloured bottle. Add all the other ingredients and shake well.*

TO USE: *Shake well before use. Sprinkle a few drops onto the hands and massage in well, particularly around the nails, repeat as desired.*

Hangover

If you are going out for a 'night on the town' take the following supplements with a glass of milk before leaving home and again when you return. In addition drink *lots* of water as alcohol causes dehydration.

* 1000 mg vitamin C with bioflavonoids.
* 1 vitamin B complex tablet.
* 1000 mg borage (starflower) oil or evening primrose oil.
* Dry bread.
* 2 tablets milk thistle.
* Homeopathic Nux Vomica 30ᶜ as needed.

Hawthorn (*Crataegus monogyna*)

HERB PART USED

Berries, flowers, young stems and leaves.

HERB ACTIONS

Normalises the heart and blood pressure.

USE TO TREAT

Angina (dilates coronary blood vessels and increases coronary flow),[1] irregular heart beat, hardening of the arteries and other heart problems; lowering serum cholesterol levels and high blood pressure. This is the most widely used herb for cardiovascular problems.

ESSENTIAL OIL ACTION

None.

Hayfever

The many sufferers of hayfever spend months of every year (usually during spring) in misery with sneezing, streaming nose, sore throat and itchy eyes. Most of these people are reacting to grass, flower and tree pollens but many are allergic to dust, animal fur, mould spores and chemicals. Desensitisation therapy should be considered if the problem is severe.

INTERNAL TREATMENT

- Cut out all dairy products to reduce mucus.
- Drink 8 glasses of filtered or bottled water a day. Rinse eyes and nasal mucous membranes with sterile saline solution to remove pollen granules.
- Eat garlic and onions daily.

DAILY SUPPLEMENTS

- 25 mg vitamin B6.
- 1 vitamin B complex tablet.
- 500 mg vitamin C with bioflavonoids every 2 hours during an attack.
- 300 iu vitamin E (d-alpha tocopherol).
- 5000–10 000 iu beta-carotene.
- 1000 mg calcium/magnesium citrate.
- 15 mg zinc.
- Dong quai as directed.

✣ 1000 mg garlic oil capsules 3 times daily or 2 teaspoons 'Long-life juice' 3 times daily.

ESSENTIAL OIL TREATMENT

Sprinkle the following oil blends onto sea salt crystals in a little jar or cut small sheets of cloth (environmentally sound) or kitchen paper towels to fit a small tin and sprinkle with the blend. Re-sprinkle as often as necessary to keep the oils fresh. Make two sets of the 'sniffs' and alternate for maximum effect.

SALT SNIFFS

A

20 drops chamomile oil

20 drops eucalyptus oil

20 drops lemon oil

B

20 drops lavender oil

10 drops geranium oil

20 drops tea-tree oil

10 drops lemon oil

HERBAL TREATMENT

⁓ Make chamomile tea using chamomile tea-bags, save used bags and pop in the fridge to get really cold.

⁓ Drink 3 cups of the tea daily and place the cold tea-bags over the eyes to soothe itching and inflammation.

⁓ Add ¼ teaspoon salt to 1 brimming glass lukewarm water and use to douche the nostrils (see Douches, saline nasal).

HOMEOPATHIC TREATMENT

All 30ᶜ, take as often as needed until symptoms abate, then 4 times a day:

✸ Burning, watery eyes, runny nose—Euphrasia.

✸ Symptoms eased in the open air—Pulsatilla.

✸ Worse on waking—Silica.

Headaches

There are many reasons headaches develop, including indigestion, stress, muscle tension in the neck and back, eyestrain, tiredness, or nasal congestion. See also Migraine.

If a headache persists and a cause isn't obvious it would be advisable to seek professional help (an optician if you suspect eyestrain or a chiropractor if you feel that a spinal adjustment may be needed).

INTERNAL TREATMENT

❦ Foods that contain tyramine are often implicated in throbbing headaches or migraine and should be avoided. These foods include most alcoholic drinks, preserved meats (salamis, sausages, smoked meats, bacon and ham), all cheeses except cottage cheese, chocolate, soya sauce, sour cream and yeast concentrates. Other foods that may cause headaches are those containing monosodium glutamate (found in Asian food and many very salty foods), pickles and preservatives.

❦ Drink 8 glasses of filtered or bottled water daily.

DAILY SUPPLEMENTS

❧ 1000 mg garlic oil capsules 3 times daily or 2–3 teaspoons 'Long-life juice' 3 times daily.

❧ 400 iu vitamin E (d-alpha tocopherol).

❧ 500 mg magnesium.

❧ 1000 mg vitamin C with bioflavonoids.

Have you heard that sniffing the steam from heated vinegar can often bring relief from a headache?

ESSENTIAL OIL TREATMENT

MASSAGE & BATH BLEND

1 tablespoon (20 ml) vegetable oil

4 drops lavender oil

3 drops rosemary oil

1 drop peppermint oil

TO MAKE: *Mix the oils together in a little bottle.*

TO USE: *Massage a few drops on the temples and the nape of the neck. Add 2 teaspoons (10 ml) to a warm bath just before you get in, agitate the water to disperse the oil.*

HERBAL TREATMENT

- ❧ Drink 2 cups of dandelion coffee daily.
- ❧ 1000 mg milk thistle.
- ❧ 1000 mg white willow bark, for pain. These three herbs may be found as a combination in health-food shops.
- ❧ Chamomile or peppermint tea for headaches caused by digestive disorders.
- ❧ Rosemary tea for headaches caused by mental or physical exhaustion.
- ❧ Make a very cold compress using a strong lavender and rosemary tea or vinegar. Lie down and place the compress over the forehead. Replace it as it gets warm.
- ❧ Alternate hot and cold footbaths (see Baths) can also ease an aching head. Add 2 drops each lavender, basil and marjoram oil to the cold water, agitating well to disperse. Soak the feet for 5 minutes in each bath and repeat 2–3 times.
- ❧ A simple but often effective treatment is a vinegar inhalation. Heat a tablespoon or so of vinegar and inhale the steam.

HOMEOPATHIC TREATMENT

All 6–30ᶜ, take as often as liked during acute stage:

- ✷ Unable to tolerate light. Watery eyes—Euphrasia.
- ✷ Pain eased by bending head backwards—Hypericum.
- ✷ Headache with humming in the ears—Kali. phos.
- ✷ Misty vision or jagged lights before thudding headache—Nat. mur.
- ✷ Sudden, violent band of pain—Aconite.
- ✷ Throbbing headache—Belladonna.

Head lice

The same precautions need to be taken as those for fleas (see Pets, Dogs). If the nits (eggs) aren't destroyed then the problem will re-occur.

Wash all bedding and personal clothes in very hot water. Add 2 teaspoons (10 ml) eucalyptus oil to the rinsing water. Hang the bedding and clothes in the sun for a whole day turning them inside out at intervals so that every part of the material receives air and sun. Nits hatch out at 48-hour intervals so the treatment of clothes and bedding will need to be carried out every two days until the problem no longer exists.

Essential oil is the best way of dealing with head lice, and the percentage of oils is higher than that normally used. If there is any burning or discomfort to the skin, the amount of vegetable oil in the following blend should be increased by 1 tablespoon (20 ml).

ESSENTIAL OIL TREATMENT

SCALP & HAIR BLEND

40 drops eucalyptus oil

40 drops geranium oil

40 drops lavender oil

5 tablespoons (100 ml) vegetable oil

TO MAKE: *Mix together in a bottle, shake well and leave overnight.*

TO USE: *Massage thoroughly into the hair and scalp, cover with a shower cap and leave either all day or all night. Shampoo the hair and comb through with a fine-tooth comb (available from pharmacies) paying particular attention to the area behind the ears and at the back of the neck — this will help to get rid of nits.*

Repeat every 2 days for a week.

To prevent re-infestation use one of the shampoos in the Hair care section.

Heartburn

Indigestion, heartburn and acidity are all terms used to describe the minor gastrointestinal symptoms of nausea, discomfort, pain, bloating, heartburn and gas. Indigestion can be caused by some of the following: over-eating; eating too quickly; eating over-rich and/or spicy foods or eating while angry, stressed or overtired. If the abdominal pain is very severe it would be wise to seek professional help particularly as some of the symptoms are the same as for appendicitis.

INTERNAL TREATMENT

Avoid eating rich, spicy food and drinking tea and coffee. Don't eat at all if you are upset or angry. Don't over-eat or eat too quickly.

HERBAL TREATMENT

- 2–4 slippery elm tablets ½ hour before a meal.
- Bromelain and/or papain as directed.
- A cup of peppermint or meadowsweet tea after a meal.
- Gentian tablets or herbal bitters (from health-food store) 30 minutes before a meal.

HOMEOPATHIC TREATMENT

All 6–30^c unless indicated, take 3 times daily after meals:
- Burning sensation and acid reflux—Carbo. veg.
- Nerves about forthcoming events—Argent. nit.
- After food with wind; worse from late afternoon to early evening—Lycopodium.
- Burning pain relieved by warm drinks—Arsen. alb.
- Griping pain and sickness—Ipecac.
- Wants to vomit but unable to—Nux vomica.
- Nat. phos. and Nat. sulph. 12^c, 4 times daily.

Heart care ✿ See also Cholesterol

The following are suggestions to ensure that your cardio-vascular system stays in optimum health. If you already have a problem, the treatments should be discussed with your health-care professional and can be carried out as an adjunct to prescribed treatment.

Caution: *Don't stop taking medication or attempt to 'self-treat' if you have a heart condition requiring professional help.*

Until a woman reaches menopause she is less at risk of having a heart attack than a man (unless she is on the contraceptive pill and is also a smoker). There is an even greater risk for men if they have male blood relatives who have suffered from heart attacks before the age of sixty. After menopause the risk for women increases greatly. If you fit the above profiles there are lots of ways you can improve and/or maintain the health of your heart. The main factors to consider are:

- ❦ **Serum cholesterol levels:** Those people with high serum cholesterol levels are at much greater risk. See Internal treatment.
- ❦ **Smoking:** *Stop smoking.* Smoking has been shown to be a potent risk factor. Nicotine constricts the arteries, reduces the blood's oxygen-carrying capacity, stimulates the sympathetic nervous system and the heart, causing them to work harder than necessary. Women who take the contraceptive pill and smoke are specially at risk.
- ❦ **Stress levels:** Stress can be controlled by learning stress management techniques such as meditation and visualisation (see Relaxation) exercise (walking, swimming, cycling, etc for ½ to 1 hour 3–5 times a week). A strenuous game of squash or other similar activity taken once a week, however, can precipitate a heart attack rather than prevent one. Anger, feelings of rage and frustration, feelings of isolation and loneliness can potentially be very damaging to the heart. Relaxation and visualisation are excellent techniques for learning to cope with these feelings.
- ❦ **Drinking alcohol and coffee:** Alcohol and coffee add to the workload of the heart and adrenal glands, they also create higher stress levels.
- ❦ **High blood pressure:** See High Blood Pressure.

Did you know that sucking a teaspoon or two of sugar onto which a few drops of vinegar have been dripped can usually stop hiccoughs?

❧ **Thinning the blood to reduce the blood clotting and coating the artery walls:** See Daily supplements and Herbal treatment following.

INTERNAL TREATMENT

❧ Adopting a diet that is low in animal fats and saturated and polyunsaturated oils can reduce serum cholesterol levels. Use only olive or canola oil for cooking, don't fry anything, and if you crave something on your toast use avocado.

❧ Eat sardines, mackerel and salmon several times a week, and reduce your intake of red meat.

❧ Increase your consumption of fruit, vegetables and grains.

❧ Eat garlic and onions every day.

❧ Avoid all fried foods.

❧ Avoid all refined sugars such as those found in cakes, biscuits and sweets.

DAILY SUPPLEMENTS

❧ 1000 mg vitamin C with bio-flavonoids 3 times daily.

❧ 400 iu vitamin E (d-alpha tocopherol).

❧ 1 tablespoon (20 ml) linseed oil (flax oil).

❧ 1000 mg garlic oil capsules twice daily or 2–3 teaspoons 'Long-life juice' 3 times daily.

Did you know that more essential oil penetrates the skin if the skin is covered immediately after application?

ESSENTIAL OIL TREATMENT

Use the following blend to reduce stress and lower blood pressure.

'HAVE A HEART'

1 tablespoon (20 ml) vegetable oil

4 drops rosemary oil

4 drops bergamot oil

4 drops marjoram oil

2 drops lavender oil

TO MAKE: *Mix together.*

TO USE: *Either use the blend for massage or add 2 teaspoons (10 ml)*
of the blend to a warm bath, agitate the water to disperse the oils and
enjoy a soak for 15–30 minutes.

'HEART CARE'

This blend will help to create and maintain healthy circulation.

1 tablespoon (20 ml) vegetable oil

4 drops geranium oil

4 drops lavender oil

4 drops ginger oil

2 drops black pepper oil

TO MAKE: *Mix together.*

TO USE: *Either use the blend for massage or add 2 teaspoons*
(10 ml) of the blend to a warm bath, agitate the water to disperse the
oils and enjoy a soak for 15–30 minutes.

HERBAL TREATMENT

- ✻ Drink ginger decoction (see Decoctions) once or twice a day and
  use ginger in cooking.
- ✻ 1 tablespoon ground linseed sprinkled on cereal or yoghurt or
  stirred into a glass of water and drunk, *followed by a further*
  glass of water.
- ✻ Hawthorn (see Hawthorn) is a heart tonic and has also been
  shown to reduce serum cholesterol. It is available in health-food
  shops. Take as directed.

HOMEOPATHIC TREATMENT

Consult a homeopathic practitioner.

Hepar sulph. (*Hepar sulphuris*) ✻ Homeopathic

Suited to those who are physically hypersensitive and mentally irritable. Also those who are overly sensitive to pain in general, irritable,
discontented and easily angered.

USE TO TREAT

Abscess, acne, athlete's foot, croup, earache, eczema, sinusitis, tonsillitis.

Hepatics

Stimulate and strengthen the liver.

HERBS

Burdock, dandelion, garlic, milk thistle, peppermint, rosemary, sage, thyme.

ESSENTIAL OILS

Chamomile, cypress, lemon, peppermint, rosemary, thyme.

Hepatitis

Hepatitis means inflammation of the liver. *All types of hepatitis need to be treated seriously and with the help of a physician.* There are several types of hepatitis caused by related viruses. The most common are A, B and C. All types of hepatitis are contagious and great care needs to be exercised with regard to hygiene and close physical contact with others. The symptoms can include fatigue, flu-like symptoms, fever, jaundice, loss of appetite and/or nausea, enlarged liver and dark urine.

Hepatitis A is usually found in children and young adults who acquire it from faecal matter and food contaminated by flies. The incubation time is 2–6 weeks. This type of hepatitis can vary in severity, causing very mild illness in young children but more serious illness in adults. It is usually non-fatal.

The first symptoms are similar to flu or other viral infection, pain may develop in the liver area and jaundice may follow (the whites of eyes turn yellow and urine becomes dark orange or brown).

Careful washing of hands with soap and water after going to the toilet, before preparing food or eating, and avoiding contaminated water supplies can prevent hepatitis.

Hepatitis B is transmitted through blood, saliva and sexual secretions and infected needles, like those used for tattoos, acupuncture and injecting drugs. Personal items such as toothbrushes and razors shouldn't be shared. Hepatitis B can also be passed from infected mothers to their babies at birth.

Hepatitis B infection is usually more severe than hepatitis A and can cause severe, permanent damage to the liver or even death. There are few symptoms from this type of hepatitis and 75 per cent of carriers will never feel ill.

Hepatitis C is transmitted in the same way as hepatitis B. Most infected people do not develop any significant symptoms or illness at the time of infection. Some may have flu-like illness about 6–8 weeks after exposure and many will develop long-term chronic inflammation or cirrhosis of the liver.

The signs during the acute phase may include jaundice, abdominal pain, fever, diarrhoea, nausea and feeling unwell. During the chronic phase the symptoms may include intolerance to fatty food, weight loss, extreme fatigue, pain in the liver area.

Bed rest is essential during the acute stage of all types of hepatitis. Activity should be resumed slowly and carefully. Avoid over-exertion.

Body brushing twice daily will improve circulation and excretion through the skin. This in turn relieves the liver of some of its work.

Learn how to manage stress. Read the Relaxation section but if possible, attend a meditation group before attempting to meditate alone. Rest as soon as you feel tired. Find an understanding person to talk to about your feelings.

INTERNAL TREATMENT

A good diet is essential for hepatitis sufferers to give your liver the best possible chance to heal. Cell regeneration is enhanced by an alkaline diet (most fruits and vegetables become alkaline during the digestive process).

Try to reduce or avoid the following:

🦎 alcohol, tobacco, chocolate, tea and coffee.

✖ all red meat and dairy foods (cow's milk, cheese, butter, yoghurt (however, soya or goat's milk yoghurt is good for the liver), cream and ice cream) — use soya milk as a cow's milk substitute.

✖ foods with high levels of sugars, preservatives and artificial colourings.

Ensure that you consume or use as much of these as possible:

✖ olive and canola oils are the only fats to be eaten.

✖ mainly fruits (not citrus), nuts, vegetables, wholemeal bread and cereals.

✖ very small amounts of free-range chicken and free-range eggs, and fish.

✖ eat vegetable proteins such as tofu, tempeh, chickpeas, beans and soya beans.

✖ 3 cups of dandelion coffee daily (from health-food stores).

✖ 6–8 glasses bottled or filtered water daily.

✖ fruit and vegetable juices may be tolerated better than solid food when the liver is inflamed. Avoid carrot and spinach juice as they may irritate the liver. The best juices are lemon, apple, pineapple, pear, celery and beetroot.

DAILY SUPPLEMENTS

✖ Drink 3 cups daily of dandelion coffee in place of regular tea and coffee (see Dandelion).

✖ Milk thistle as directed is the most effective liver herb for protection and helping with regeneration of liver cells.

✖ 1000 mg vitamin C with bioflavonoids twice daily.

✖ Take a course of astragalus as directed. When the course is finished, follow with ½ teaspoon (2.5 ml) fluid extract of echinacea 3 times daily.

✖ 1000 mg garlic oil capsules 3 times daily or 2–3 teaspoons (10–15 ml) 'Long-life juice' 3 times daily.

ESSENTIAL OIL TREATMENT

'ANTIVIRAL' MASSAGE OIL

½ cup (125 ml) olive and almond oil mixed

40 drops chamomile oil

15 drops tea-tree oil

15 drops eucalyptus oil

10 drops cypress oil

TO MAKE: *Mix together in a bottle, shake well. Leave for a few days to blend.*

TO USE: *Massage over the whole body (except the tender bits) once daily after bathing or showering. A professional lymphatic massage using the oil blend is very helpful.*

HERBAL TREATMENT

As well as the herbs recommended above, chamomile (*Matricaria recutita*) and golden seal (*Hydrastis canadensis*) are both anti-inflammatory in their action.

HOMEOPATHIC TREATMENT

All 6–30^c unless indicated, take 3 times daily:

- With pain and swelling—Bryonia.
- If tight waistbands are unbearable—Mercurius cor. 12^c, Lycopodium, Lachesis 12^c or Nat. sulph.

Herbal housekeeping

Essential oils and herbs have many roles in keeping a home sweet smelling and germ free. They act as antibacterial and antiviral agents and sweeten clothing, air and surfaces.

BLOCK PERFUME FOR DRAWERS & CUPBOARDS

1 tablespoon (20 ml) lemon or lemongrass oil

1 teaspoon (5 ml) clove or eucalyptus oil

1 teaspoon (5 ml) lavender oil

1 kg beeswax

TO MAKE: *Break or cut the beeswax into pieces as small as possible. Melt over a very low heat, taking care not overheat and burn. Allow*

to cool but not to set. Stir in the mixed essential oils. Pour the wax
into empty milk cartons or other containers. When the wax is cold
and firm but still soft enough to cut, tear the carton away and cut the
wax into blocks.

Wrap in tissue and place in drawers and cupboards.

If the perfume starts to fade, the block may be scratched to release
more of the oils.

LEMON ALL-PURPOSE CLEANER

1$^{1}/_{2}$ cups biodegradable phosphate-free washing powder
4 cups (1 litre) hot water
1 teaspoon (5 ml) lemon oil
1 teaspoon (5 ml) eucalyptus oil
20 drops thyme oil

TO MAKE: Mix the laundry powder with the hot water. Stir gently
until dissolved. Allow to cool. Add the essential oils to the soap
mixture, stirring slowly but well to incorporate. Bottle and label.
Invert the bottle once or twice before use to mix oils and liquids.

TO USE: Add 1 teaspoon (5 ml) to 4 cups (1 litre) warm water to
clean rubbish bins, cupboards, floors, toilet seats and toilet bowls,
baths and washbasins, and bathroom vanity surfaces.

GREEN MUSCLE

This mixture cleans grease and stains, and disinfects and deodorises.

$^{1}/_{4}$ cup bicarbonate of soda
8 cups (2 litres) hot water
2 tablespoons (40 ml) vinegar
1 teaspoon (5 ml) lemon oil
1 teaspoon (5 ml) eucalyptus oil
1 tablespoon (20 ml) cloudy ammonia

TO MAKE: Mix the bicarbonate of soda and hot water. Cool. Combine
the vinegar and essential oils. Add the ammonia. Mix well, bottle and
label.

TO USE: Spray or sprinkle on a cloth to clean working surfaces, sinks,
greasy floors, shower recesses, baths, floor and wall tiles.

VACUUM CLEANER & CARPET FRESHENER

This powder will keep carpets looking and
smelling fresh. For those with dogs and cats,
it has the bonus of absorbing pet smells and,
if used regularly, will help to repel fleas.

3 cups bicarbonate of soda
4 tablespoons (80 ml) borax
30 drops lavender oil
20 drops eucalyptus oil
20 drops lemon oil
20 drops pine oil

TO MAKE: *Mix the powder thoroughly and then drip the oils in
slowly while stirring to prevent lumps forming. Store in a jar or
container with a sprinkler lid.*

TO USE: *Sprinkle the powder lightly onto the carpet. Leave overnight
or for as long as possible before vacuuming. Sprinkle a little into the
vacuum bag to absorb musty, stale odours.*

Did you know that if you
sprinkle a little of the
carpet freshener powder
into smelly shoes, leave
overnight and shake out in
the morning it will
deodorise them?

HERBAL AIR FRESHENER 🌿 See also Air fresheners

*Something as simple as a huge bowl or vase full of mixed herbs looks
lovely and gives a fresh, inviting fragrance to the living room. Most of
the herbs last for a long time after cutting. Mix as many as possible
of the heavily scented herbs — geranium, lavender, rosemary, lemon
verbena (the scent lasts for years) and, for colour contrast, add some
scented grey herbs such as wormwood and southernwood.*

Herbal ice cubes

These cubes are particularly useful if you have young people or
sportspeople in your household. The ice cubes provide an instant
method of easing the pain of cuts, abrasions, minor burns, sprains
and reduce inflammation. They also contain antibacterial and antiviral herbs to prevent infection.

TO MAKE: *Fill a jug with a mixture of as many as possible of the
following freshly chopped fresh herbs or half-fill with dried,
crumbled herbs. If you don't have all the herbs it doesn't matter:*

calendula, chamomile, comfrey leaf, lavender, mallow, plantain, rosemary, sage, thyme and yarrow.

Fill the jug with boiling water, cover and leave to go cold.

Strain the herbs through a sieve, squeezing to extract as much liquid as possible.

Strain once more through coffee-filter paper.

Freeze in ice-cube trays and when frozen put cubes into a freezer bag labelled with the name of the herb and date.

TO USE: **As Compresses:** *drop 3–4 cubes in enough water to melt them.*

As Fomentations: *drop 3–4 cubes in enough boiling water to melt them. For treating cuts, abrasions, minor burns and inflammations, wrap as many cubes as needed in a handkerchief or piece of clean cloth and apply to the wound.*

Herbalism & Herbs

Herbs have been used as medicine and food since prehistoric days when humans and animals were entirely dependent on the land for their survival and health.

The main aim of herbal medicine is the prevention of illness and the treatment of the underlying cause of illness rather than merely curing the symptom. For instance, a headache may be caused by a digestive problem; if an aspirin or other painkiller is taken the headache may disperse but will return again. Herbal treatments will treat the whole digestive system and the headaches won't recur.

During the nineteenth century, chemists began isolating the active principles from plants. Allopathic medicine uses these isolates, arguing that the active principle will work faster and more efficiently than the whole herb. The resulting drug is also more 'predictable' than the whole herb. In some ways this may be true but by isolating the active principle a powerful and usually toxic product is obtained. As these resultant drugs are usually in pill or capsule form they are easy to take and very easy to overdose on.

The whole plant, on the other hand, has its own built-in 'safety barrier' and, as far more of the whole plant has to be used, the amount of active principle being released into the bloodstream is much smaller, is taken over a longer period of time and, hence, is much safer.

Wherever possible it's preferable to use herbs and their oils for both prevention and long-term cure and to save the allopathic drugs such as antibiotics for life-threatening or emergency situations.

There is something wonderful about making your own remedies. I have far more faith in the tinctures, creams, ointments and lotions that I have made myself than the ones that I have to buy. I know that on a very deep level that the healing process begins when I first start to prepare the ingredients, visualise the problem and how the herbs and oils will slowly and gently make the changes in my body. You will find that the making of the tinctures, teas, etc. is no more diffi-cult than making a casserole and, in some instances, far easier.

If you can't grow and use your own fresh herbs, buy only from the most reputable and reliable sources. Many purchased dried herbs are worthless, particularly the soft-leafed varieties which, unless they are less than twelve months old and have been carefully dried and stored, will have lost some or all of their therapeutic value. Look for bright, strong colours in the dried plant—if the herbs are a uniform greyish green and very crumbly don't buy them. Roots, bark and seeds are a much safer buy as they stay in good condition for much longer. Avoid buying imported herbs as they may have reduced potency. I would make an exception for good quality, well known and reputable brands of herbal teas. I have used these to make preparations on rare occasions when I haven't been able to use fresh herbs.

Methods for making herbal preparations will be found under sep-arate headings throughout the book. If you find a remedy that you would like to make yourself in preference to buying, please take time to familiarise yourself with the properties of each herb and ingredient (see under their own alphabetical headings). You will then begin to establish a connection with the remedy before you even make it.

Always remember to keep a record of the recipe and to label the preparation carefully with the name, date and whether the remedy is for internal or external use.

Herbs—drying & storing

If herbs aren't correctly dried and stored they lose both their therapeutic value and their flavour. The quicker the herbs dry the better their colour and flavour will be. However, herbs mustn't be subjected to direct sunlight (with the exception of roots) or high temperatures as the aromatic properties will be lost.

Pick the herbs on a dry, sunny morning when the dew has dried off the plant. Pick only enough herbs to deal with immediately. Most herbs are at their best flavour-wise and therapeutically just before they bloom—marjoram and oregano are among the few exceptions as the flowers and leaves are both useful.

Choose a drying area that is airy and dust free—a screened verandah is usually perfect. Failing this you can dry the herbs on the floor of the oven with the temperature set as low as possible and the door slightly ajar. An electric dehydrator is a perfect way to dry herbs provided that it is thermostatically controlled and can be set to about 35°C.

Microwave drying is not suitable, as the highly volatile oils are driven off and you end up with tasteless herbs and a nice smelling house. The only time to use the microwave for drying is when you want to preserve colour and form and not aroma.

LEAVES & FLOWERS

Don't wash the herbs unless they are very dirty. Tie them in small bunches and hang in a suitable area. If dust or flies are a problem the bunches may be enclosed in bags made from muslin, old lace curtains or something similar. If you have space, the herbs will dry very well spread out on insect screens or in the oven as described above.

To save space the leaves may be stripped from the stems (dry the straight stems to use as kebab sticks or as kindling for the fire).

The material is dry when leathery crisp but not so crisp that it crumbles to dust.

ROOTS, BARK & STEMS

Wash, dry and chop the roots into quite small pieces to speed up the drying process. The oven or dehydrator is perfect for these parts of the plant but, unlike the leaves, roots, bark and stems may be dried in the sun. Be aware though that if the sun is very hot, the outside may dry to form a skin and the inside will stay moist so start them off in the cooler part of the day.

SEEDS

Cut the whole seed head off, put it head-down in a brown paper bag or fine muslin bag. Fasten the bag at the top and hang in a warm, airy room. The seeds may take up to two months to become totally dry and should be checked from time to time for insects.

LARGE LEAVES & PODS

The easiest way to dry large leaves such as mullein, comfrey and borage and pods such as chillies, is to thread a large needle with strong thread or dental floss and push the needle through the end of the stem of the leaf or pod. Hang the thread in the same way as a washing line and arrange the leaves so that they don't touch.

STORAGE

Glass jars are the safest way to store dried herbs. The jars give protection from damp, dust and insects and allow you to see that the contents are in good condition. If the herbs were under-dried a mist may form on the glass. Label the jars with the name of the herb and the date that they were dried, store the jars in a dark cupboard and check them regularly. Only keep very small jars of herbs out for cooking as light quickly destroys the flavour and properties. Dried herbs stay potent for about 12 months. After this time empty the contents of the jars onto the garden or compost heap and you will be ready to refill the jars with this year's crop.

TO DRY FLOWERS IN THE MICROWAVE

2 pieces of thin board or thick cardboard to fit your microwave tray

2 pieces of blotting paper the same size as the board

4 or 5 strong elastic bands

herbs or flowers

TO MAKE: Place a sheet of blotting paper on one sheet of board.

Arrange the material for pressing without having pieces touching.

Place the other sheet of blotting paper over this and then place the remaining board on top.

Fasten together with the elastic bands using two or three each way.

Heat on defrost setting for 5 minutes, allow to cool before looking at the herbs.

If they are not sufficiently dry, repeat the process.

Herb oil base

Herb oils are among the most useful, easy and pleasant preparations that you can make. They can be used in massage oils, baths, skin-care products, insect repellents, ointments or used alone.

Another name for this type of oil is *infused* herbal oil and shouldn't be confused with essential oil (see Aromatherapy & Essential oils, Extraction of essential oils). The oils made using the following methods are safe, inexpensive and therapeutic.

If you want your finished oils to have a stronger aroma and action you can add a few drops of essential oil. Store the oils (carefully labelled) in a cool, dark place. Refrigeration of the oils will retard oxidisation and rancidity and will ensure a much longer life.

METHOD 1

TO MAKE: Chop herbs finely (see following lists for suitable herbs), place in a non-aluminium double-boiler pan or a heatproof bowl over a pan of simmering water and cover with a mixture of olive, grape-seed and/or canola oil until the herbs are submerged.

Add 1 tablespoon (20 ml) vinegar to every 4 cups (1 litre) oil. Stir well, cover with a lid and leave for 1–2 hours.

Heat the oil to no more than 45°C, if hotter some of the properties will be lost. Turn off the heat.

Repeat the heating several times over a period of 24 hours.

Carefully strain the oil, first through a sieve and then through muslin. If you want a very strong oil, the process may be repeated once or twice more using the same oil but adding fresh herbs each time. Don't add vinegar though.

Store the finished oil in a dark bottle if possible. Keep refrigerated.

METHOD 2

A crockpot is useful for making a large amount of oil and has the added advantage that (if used on its lowest setting) it never overheats the oil.

TO MAKE: *Place the herbs in the crockpot, cover with oil as described above, put the lid on and leave for 24 hours on the lowest setting.*

Strain the oil squeezing the herbs to extract as much oil as possible and pour back into the crockpot with fresh herbs. Repeat the first stage, then strain the oil, squeezing to extract as much oil as possible. Pour back into pot with fresh herbs and repeat.

Follow the last 2 steps in Method 1.

METHOD 3

The following is a method that has been employed by herbalists for centuries, it feels very magical and earthy but works best if you live in a country where there are long, hot sunny days.

TO MAKE: *Put the herbs in a glass jar, cover with warm oil until the herbs are completely submerged, cover with a tight lid and leave in a sheltered and sunny place in the garden, window box or on the veranda for 2 weeks. Shake the jar at least twice daily. Have as little air space as possible in the jar or mould may be encouraged to grow in the condensation that will form on the glass and the inside of the lid. Bring the jar in at night (if you remember). Strain the herbs from the oil through a sieve and then through muslin, and bottle.*

If you want a super strong oil you can repeat the process and leave for another 2 weeks.

TO USE: *Incorporate into massage oils, ointments, bath oils, skin care preparations, insect repellents or use alone.*

SUGGESTED HERBS

- **Skin oil:** chamomile, calendula, elderflower, lavender, rosemary, rose, jasmine.
- **Massage oil:** chamomile, geranium, jasmine, lavender, marjoram, rosemary, rose.
- **Healing ointments:** calendula, comfrey, lavender, mallow, plantain, rosemary, sage, thyme, violet, yarrow.

Herpes

The herpes virus is present in 30–100 per cent of all adults and there are over 70 viruses in the herpes family. The main ones are Herpes zoster that causes chickenpox and shingles; Epstein-Barr which is a variety of herpes zoster and causes mononucleosis (glandular fever) and Herpes simplex which causes painful blisters on the lips (cold sores), vulva, anus or buttocks (these blisters turn into sores that take up to two weeks to heal). The virus is recurrent and the frequency is largely dependent on the health of the immune system. It can be triggered from the dormant state by stress, trauma, minor infections and over-exposure to sun.

The sores are highly infectious during the weeping stage.

INTERNAL TREATMENT

- Eat foods containing lysine (an amino acid that helps reduce the incidence of and/or prevent herpes infection).[1] Foods such as chicken, potatoes, free-range eggs, sea food, low-fat milk and cheese, and brewer's yeast contain lysine.
- Eat lots of fresh fruit and vegetables and fibre-rich foods.
- Avoid foods containing a lot of arginine (an amino acid needed by the virus) such as chocolate and nuts.

DAILY SUPPLEMENTS

* 1 vitamin B complex tablet.
* 1000 mg vitamin C with bioflavonoids twice daily at the first signs of and during an attack.
* 500 iu vitamin E (d-alpha tocopherol).
* 25 mg zinc.
* 500 mg lysine.

ESSENTIAL OIL TREATMENT

Dab blisters and sores with 1 drop of neat tea-tree, manuka or lavender oil.

HERBAL TREATMENT

* If the skin or infected area is very sensitive use aloe vera gel or hypericum ointment. Repeat three times daily.
* Dab tincture of myrrh frequently onto lip lesions.
* A recent report states that lemon balm (melissa) is useful in helping to heal the blisters and sores of genital herpes. Use it as an ointment (see Ointments) or an infused oil (see Aromatherapy & Essential oils, Extraction of essential oils).

HOMEOPATHIC TREATMENT

All 6–30ᶜ, take 4 times daily:
* Blisters containing clear liquid—Nat. mur.
* Red, itchy and inflamed—Rhus. tox.

Hives (Urticaria)

Hives are angry, red, raised welts that usually itch intensely. They are triggered by allergic reactions that release histamine into the system. It is sometimes quite difficult to know what has caused the problem but insect venom, food allergies, chemical allergies and stress factors need to be examined. If the problem persists it may be necessary to find a professional who specialises in this complaint.

DAILY SUPPLEMENTS

- ❧ 1000 mg vitamin C with bioflavonoids 3 times a day.
- ❧ 1000 mg garlic oil capsules 3 times daily or 2–3 teaspoons 'Long-life juice' 3 times daily.

ESSENTIAL OIL TREATMENT

Apply a compress (see Compresses) using chamomile oil. Repeat every few hours. If the rash covers a large area it may be more appropriate to soak in a lukewarm bath to which you have added ½ cup of bicarbonate of soda and 8 drops of chamomile oil.

HERBAL TREATMENT

Make a tea of chamomile, cool to lukewarm and use as a compress on the affected area. If the rash covers a large area, soak in a lukewarm bath to which you have added 1 litre very strong chamomile tea mixed with ½ cup bicarbonate of soda.

HOMEOPATHIC TREATMENT

Take often until welts begin to subside, then take 4 times daily till clear:

- ❀ Made worse by warmth or exercise—Urtica urens 12^c.
- ❀ Intensely itchy, worse at night—Apis 30^c.

Homeopathy

Homeopathy is a system of medicine developed by Samuel Hahnemann in the first half of the nineteenth century. It uses the principle of treating a disease with minuscule amounts of a substance (vegetable, mineral or animal and sometimes bacteria and viruses) that produces the same symptoms as the disease. The remedies are prepared by progressively diluting the material. Each dilution is shaken (succussed) vigorously before being further diluted, this is called potentisation. The more dilute the remedy with each potentisation, the more powerful it becomes.

Some homeopaths and aromatherapists are of the opinion that homeopathic remedies and essential oil remedies shouldn't be used at the same time. Others, including me, would say that the two kinds of therapy may be used to treat a problem but avoid using eucalyptus, camphor, tea-tree, peppermint, rosemary and thyme oils while taking homeopathic remedies.

The homeopathic remedies in this book apply mainly to acute conditions. For complex or long-standing problems you would be advised to consult a homeopathic practitioner. See also Introductory notes at the front of this book.

Hormone imbalance 🌿 See Menopause and Menstruation

Hypericum (Hypericum perforatum) 🌸 Homeopathic

USE TO TREAT

Abscesses, acne, bruises, crushed fingers, horsefly bites, spinal injuries, sunburn.

Hypertensives

Raise blood pressure.

HERBS

Broom, hawthorn berries (normalises), gentian, garlic (normalises).

ESSENTIAL OILS

Clary sage, hyssop, rosemary.

Hypotensives

Lower blood pressure.

HERBS

Hawthorn berries (normalises), lime blossom, garlic (normalises).

ESSENTIAL OILS

Lavender, marjoram, melissa, ylang-ylang.

Ignatia (*Ignatia amara*) ✿ Homeopathic

Suited to sensitive and emotional people who try to avoid crying in front of others; to those who hate being reprimanded but are very self-critical; and who sigh frequently.

Use to treat

Acute emotional stress; grief, anger, fear, croup, depression, fainting, fright, sharp headache, sciatica.

Immune system (Depressed)

The immune system defends our body from invasion by harmful organisms that reproduce to the point where they become a threat. It is an immensely complex system that is still not fully understood.

If you suffer from Chronic Fatigue Syndrome, cancer, candidiasis or recurring colds and flu you are possibly suffering from a depressed immune system. To enhance this system we need to stay positive, laugh and hug a lot, have plenty of good nutritious food, recreation and enough restful sleep. The following suggestions will also be useful in the strengthening process.

Did you know that having a bath in a darkened bathroom by candlelight or with even no light at all is very energy raising and stress reducing?

INTERNAL TREATMENT

- ❧ Eat a low protein, high carbohydrate diet with lots of fresh fruit and vegetables.
- ❧ Use only canola or olive oil for cooking and dressings.
- ❧ Drink 6–8 glasses bottled or filtered water daily.
- ❧ Eliminate milk and milk products from your diet.
- ❧ Avoid all junk and processed food; cut down on tea, coffee and red meat.
- ❧ Cut down or give up smoking and alcohol.

DAILY SUPPLEMENTS

- ❧ 1 teaspoon astragalus fluid extract 3 times daily for 6 weeks then change to echinacea.
- ❧ ½ teaspoon (2.5 ml) echinacea fluid extract 3 times daily.
- ❧ 1000 mg vitamin C with bioflavonoids 3 times daily.
- ❧ 5000–10 000 iu beta-carotene.
- ❧ 2 vitamin B complex tablets.
- ❧ zinc lozenges as directed.

ESSENTIAL OIL TREATMENT

IMMUNE BOOSTER BLEND
1 teaspoon (5 ml) lavender oil
60 drops rosewood oil
20 drops black pepper oil
20 drops tea-tree oil
TO MAKE: *Mix together in a small bottle.*
Label and store in a cool dark place.
TO USE: *Add 10 drops to a warm bath, agitate water to disperse oil.*
Relax in the bath for 20 minutes.
or
Add 14 drops to 1 tablespoon (20 ml) vegetable oil. Use for massage.
or
Add 20 drops to 2 tablespoons (40 ml) vodka in a 100 ml spray
bottle, mix and add 100 ml water. Shake well before spraying room.

or

Use a few drops on water in an essential oil burner.

HERBAL TREATMENT

Marshmallow root decoction.

HOMEOPATHIC TREATMENT

Consult a homeopathic practitioner who will tailor a specific course of remedies.

Immuno-stimulants

Strengthen the body's defences to infection.

HERBS

Calendula, echinacea, eucalyptus, astragalus, garlic, golden seal.

ESSENTIAL OILS

Garlic, lavender, manuka, ravensara, rosewood, tea-tree.

Impetigo

Impetigo is a highly contagious skin infection, which is produced by the streptococcus bacterium. It usually affects children but it sometimes affects adults. It causes weeping blisters, which crust over and can appear on the face, hands and legs.

Because impetigo is so contagious it's important to obtain treatment from a health practitioner. Staphylococcal bacteria may infect the blisters and the patient may need antibiotic treatment. Golden seal, echinacea and myrrh ointment (see Ointments) is effective used as an adjunct to orthodox treatment.

DAILY SUPPLEMENTS

- 1000 mg vitamin C with bioflavonoids (6 times a day for adults, twice a day for children over 5 years of age).
- 1000 mg garlic oil capsules 3 times daily for adults, once daily

for children over 5 years of age (or 2 teaspoons 'Long-life juice'
3 times daily, once daily for children over 5 years).
❧ ½ teaspoon liquid extract of echinacea 3 times daily for adults,
half the dose for children, or as directed.

HOMEOPATHIC TREATMENT

All 6–12ᶜ, take 4 times daily:
❀ Oozing eruption with thick yellow crust—Antimonium crud.
❀ Scabby, oozy eruption—Graphites.
❀ Very itchy with small clustered blisters—Mercurius.

Impotence

Impotence sometimes results from physical causes that may respond
to surgery, but mainly has emotional or mental sources. Anxiety
about sexual 'performance' and other stresses, for example, those
related to work or money are important factors to consider.

There are clinics and/or sex counsellors which specialise in treating
impotence but the following suggestions may prove helpful.

Daily meditation and visualisation (see Relaxation) is useful as a
relaxation technique.

Remember that alcohol may increase desire but definitely *reduces*
performance.

DAILY SUPPLEMENTS

❧ 1000 mg vitamin C with bioflavonoids.
❧ 1 vitamin B complex tablet.
❧ 500 iu vitamin E (d-alpha tocopherol).
❧ 20 mg zinc.

ESSENTIAL OIL TREATMENT

'LOVING TOUCH'
4 tablespoons (80 ml) vegetable oil
20 drops sandalwood oil
10 drops neroli or orange oil
10 drops clary sage oil (not if you have been drinking)

TO MAKE: *Mix the oils together in a little bottle.*

TO USE: *An understanding needs to be reached that for as long as it takes (maybe a week, maybe much longer) you and your partner will give each other full body massages using this blend. There will be no expectation of intercourse taking place, just a sharing of a non-threatening, loving, sensual and sensuous experience. Allow time for anxiety and stress to lessen and enjoy the shared experience of closeness. When it's time it will happen!*

HERBAL TREATMENT

The following herbs are available from health-food shops, sometimes as a blend: damiana (valuable for strengthening the male reproductive system), Asiatic ginseng, saw palmetto.

HOMEOPATHIC TREATMENT

All 6–30^c, take 3 times daily unless otherwise indicated:
* Where there is stress, anxiety and fear of failure—Argent nit.
* Generally run down and anaemic—Cal. phos.
* Depressed—Kali phos.
* Loss of interest in sex—Sepia.

Indigestion 🌿 See also Heartburn

Persistent indigestion needs to be investigated by a health professional. Occasional indigestion may be the result of eating too quickly, eating fatty or over-rich food, or eating when emotionally upset.

INTERNAL TREATMENT

* Avoid drinking liquids with food as they dilute the digestive juices.
* Pay attention to noticing which foods cause indigestion and avoid them.

DAILY SUPPLEMENTS

Acidophillus capsules as directed.

Did you know that a teaspoon of the cocktail additive Angostura Bitters taken half an hour before a meal can help to prevent indigestion?

ESSENTIAL OIL TREATMENT

1 drop only peppermint oil mixed with ½ teaspoon sugar in 1 glass warm water sipped directly after a meal. *Never* exceed the 1 drop of essential oil.

HERBAL TREATMENT

✷ Take herbal bitters as directed 15–20 minutes before a meal (see Bitters).

✷ Drink a cup of strong peppermint tea after a meal.

HOMEOPATHIC TREATMENT

✷ Nervous excitement—Argent. nit. 30^c, twice daily.

✷ Flatulent, chilly people—Carbo veg. 12^c, three times daily.

✷ Heartburn with colic early evening—Lycopodium 30^c, twice daily.

Infants ❦ See Babies

Influenza ❦ See Colds & Influenza

Inhalations

A therapeutic steam treatment for ailments such as sinus problems, coughs, colds and excessive mucus relating to the respiratory tract. Herbs, essential oils or substances such as menthol crystals are added to hot water, and the steam inhaled. This steam is carried through the airways to the lungs, soothing, decongesting and exerting a healing effect.

Inhalations can be made with fresh or dried herbs or essential oils. Put a bowl on a folded towel on a table, half fill with boiling water. Sit close to the bowl. Cover it and your head with a big towel. Add a good handful of the chosen herbs or 3–6 drops essential oils to the bowl and breathe the steam for 5–10 minutes. Add 2–3 more drops of oil or more herbs if the mixture weakens.

As the process involves boiling water, take great care with the very young, the very old, sick or frail. A good system is to place the bowl of boiling water in the bathroom washbasin and to sit the patient very close to the basin with the towel covering both the basin and the patient's head. If the patient is a baby, sit with them on your lap very close to the steam.

Insect repellent 🦎 See Ross River Virus

Insomnia

True insomnia is the habitual loss of sleep on a regular basis; the occasional 'bad night' doesn't qualify. However, if you start to worry that you *might* not sleep then the chances are that you won't and this in turn may become insomnia. If you begin to toss and turn, get up and do something—staying in bed will only increase your anxiety levels.

Jumpy and edgy feelings that can create sleeplessness are often caused by positive ions which can be dispersed by taking a warm (not hot) shower or by walking barefoot on grass just before going to bed.

If you have been suffering from insomnia for some time, the following method may work for you. It needs to be done when you don't have any critical work to do and you shouldn't drive a car or other machinery. *For one night only*, instead of going to bed, find small, simple jobs to do around the house—just keep active enough to stay awake and continue this during the next day. By the time bedtime comes you should be able to fall into bed and *sleep*.

Using the essential oils and herbs recommended below will greatly increase your chances of having a sweet sleep.

DAILY SUPPLEMENTS

Try taking 1 skullcap or valerian capsule and 2 calcium citrate tablets with a milk drink 30 minutes before retiring for the night. Don't use valerian continuously for more than 3 weeks; have a 1-week break before recommencing.

🦎✹

Have you heard that pre-bedtime baths and showers should be taken warm, not hot, to ensure a good night's sleep?

Essential oil treatment

'SLEEP EASY'

1 tablespoon (20 ml) vegetable oil

3 drops lavender oil

3 drops clary sage oil

2 drops marjoram oil

TO MAKE: *Mix the oils together.*

TO USE: *Massage a few drops on the temples and the nape of the neck.*

Add 2 teaspoons (10 ml) to a warm bath just before getting in, agitate the water to disperse the oil.

Sprinkle 2–3 drops on a wet flannel, squeeze and then rub gently over your body.

Herbal treatment

- Make a small herb pillow containing crushed hops and lavender and slip it into your pillowcase with your pillow.
- Fill a small muslin bag with fresh or dried, chopped lavender and marjoram, hang it under the tap as the bath is running and then use it as a wash cloth.

Homeopathic treatment

All 6–30^{c}, take 3 times daily or 1 hour before bed:

- Very restless in bed—Aconite.
- Overtired, bed feels hard and uncomfortable—Arnica.
- Overtired from mental exhaustion—Kali phos.
- Overexcited—Coffea.

Intertrigo

A rather unpleasant smelling bacterial infection that develops in dark, warm, sweaty areas such as the groin where skin is in contact with skin. It can affect anyone; but babies, the overweight and the elderly are particularly prone to it especially if hygiene is neglected.

Wash the area 2 or even 3 times a day using cottonwool dipped in a small bowl of lukewarm water to which 4 drops of tea-tree oil have been added. Dry the skin carefully and gently with a soft towel as the affected skin is often fragile and will have been weakened further by the infection.

INTERTRIGO POWDER

¹/₂ cup BP (British Pharmaceutical) grade unscented talcum powder (available from pharmacies)

¹/₂ cup cornflour

20 drops tea-tree oil

20 drops lavender oil

20 drops rosemary oil

TO MAKE: *Add the oils, a few drops at a time, stirring constantly to prevent lumping. Store in an airtight container.*

TO USE: *Use cotton wool dipped into the powder to dust the area, discard and use fresh cotton wool each time.*

Ipecac. (*Ipecacuanha*) ✿ Homeopathic

USE TO TREAT

Asthma, bronchitis, morning sickness, nausea and vomiting, travel sickness.

Irritable Bowel Syndrome

The symptoms of irritable bowel syndrome (also known as spastic colon or nervous bowel) are characterised by colicky pain in the lower abdomen, abdominal bloating and cramping, constipation/ diarrhoea, flatulence and sometimes heartburn.

It seems to be a result of physical and/or mental stress and, perhaps, lack of fibre. This would indicate that an assessment of diet and stress levels needs to be made. Seek professional diagnosis before home treatment is commenced.

INTERNAL TREATMENT

✿ Avoid *all* wheat and dairy products for 6–8 weeks to see if you have an intolerance to these foods. If there is a marked improvement, introduce either wheat or dairy products once

more. If the symptoms return you will know which is the culprit
and be able to avoid these foods.

❧ Eat muesli or other wholegrain cereal for breakfast with ¼–½
cup 'live' yoghurt and 1 dessertspoonful of either ground
psyllium seed or linseed sprinkled over it. These seeds draw
moisture from the wall of the bowel and swell to form a
mucilage that creates a firm, but not dry stool.

❧ Eat fresh, unprocessed foods including lots of fruit and
vegetables (it may be better to cook fruit and vegetables while
symptoms persist). Cut down on red meat. Eat free-range chicken
or fish and a couple of free-range eggs a week.

❧ Avoid fried and fast foods, sugary food, alcohol and spicy foods.

DAILY SUPPLEMENTS

❧ 1–2 capsules (0.2 ml) enteric-coated peppermint oil (available
from pharmacies) taken between meals.

❧ 10 000 iu beta-carotene.

❧ 400 iu vitamin E (d-alpha tocopherol).

❧ 10 mg zinc.

❧ 1000 mg garlic oil capsules 3 times daily or 2–3 teaspoons
'Long-life juice' 3 times daily.

ESSENTIAL OIL TREATMENT

MASSAGE BLEND
1 tablespoon (20 ml) vegetable oil
4 drops chamomile oil
4 drops marjoram oil
4 drops peppermint oil
TO MAKE: *Mix the oils together.*
TO USE: *Massage the abdomen daily in an anti-clockwise movement.*

HERBAL TREATMENT

❧ 1000 mg milk thistle.

❧ 1 cup (250 ml) ginger decoction (see Decoctions) 2–3 times a
day.

☞ 1 valerian or skullcap tablet or 15 drops of tincture 2–3 times a day if you feel that the problem is stress related. Continue for 1 month only, discontinue for 1 week before resuming.

HOMEOPATHIC TREATMENT

All 30^c unless indicated otherwise, take 4 times daily:
- With diarrhoea brought on by worry—Argent. nit.
- Flatulence and colic after drinking alcohol—Nux vomica.
- Nat. phos. 12^c and Nat. sulph. 12^c.

Itching (Pruritis)

Pruritis is a general term for itching. The most awkward itch is that of the anus or of the vulva as you can't complain of it and you can't scratch it in public. Wear underclothes made from natural fibres and don't wear very tight trousers or jeans. Wash the area thoroughly after going to the toilet.

ESSENTIAL OIL TREATMENT

ANTI-ITCH BLEND
1 tablespoon (20 ml) vegetable oil
2 drops lavender oil
2 drops chamomile oil
TO MAKE: *Mix the oils together.*
TO USE: *Massage the itching area after bathing, showering or washing.*

HERBAL TREATMENT

Fill a bath or very large basin with enough warm water to cover the lower hips. Add 1 cup bicarbonate of soda and, if possible, a litre of very strong chamomile tea. Sit in the bath for up to 10 minutes. Dry gently and apply the essential oil treatment recommended above.

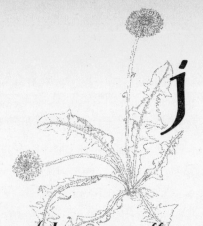

Jasmine (*Jasminium officinale & J. grandiflorum*)

HERB PART USED

Flowers.

HERB ACTIONS

In pot-pourris or as fresh flowers in the house. A lovely infused oil can be made from the flowers using the method in Aromatherapy & Essential oils, Extraction of essential oils.

ESSENTIAL OIL ACTION

Antidepressant, anti-inflammatory, antiseptic, aphrodisiac, expectorant. Jasmine oil is often called the 'King of Oils'. It is very expensive but an infused oil is an acceptable substitute. If you have time and lots of fresh plant you may like to try your hand at enfleurage (see Aromatherapy & Essential oils) to extract the pure essential oil. The flowers should be collected at night when the perfume is strongest.

USE TO TREAT

Anger, anxiety, depression, frigidity, impotence, stress-related problems. The oil is used in childbirth to massage the lower abdomen and lower back in the first stage of labour and then after the birth to help to expel the afterbirth. Jasmine is known as an aphrodisiac and the alluring perfume certainly helps to allay the anxiety and fear that often accompanies unsure lovers.

Jasmine is one of the best anti-depressant oils and even one drop in 100 ml of massage oil can have a profound 'spirit-lifting' effect.

Caution: *Use only after the fifth month of pregnancy. Not suitable for children.*

Jojoba oil (*Simmondsia chinensis*)

A yellow waxy oil pressed from the bean of the desert plant. The oil contains a waxy substance, similar to collagen, which penetrates deeply into the skin, giving it a silky, smooth feel. Use 10 per cent concentration in blends for all skin preparations and for treating acne, eczema, inflamed skin and psoriasis.

Juniper (*Juniperus communis*)

HERB PART USED

Berries.

HERB ACTIONS

Antiseptic, carminative, diuretic, rubefacient, stomachic, tonic.

USE TO TREAT

Digestive problems due to insufficient hydrochloric acid, gastro-enteritis, stomach cramps, rheumatism and gout.
Caution: *Not to be used during pregnancy or by those with kidney problems.*

ESSENTIAL OIL ACTION

Antibacterial, anti-infective, antirheumatic, antiseptic, astringent, detoxifying, disinfectant, tonic.

USE TO TREAT

Acne, boils, eczema. Arthritis, gout, rheumatism, poor muscle tone. Cellulite, fluid retention, obesity, poor circulation. Bronchitis, coughs, colds, flu, sinusitis. Diarrhoea, flatulence, haemorrhoids, varicose veins. PMS, urinary tract infections.
Caution: *Not to be used during pregnancy or by those with kidney problems.*

Kali. bich. (*Kalium bichromicum*) ❦ Homeopathic

USE TO TREAT

Catarrh, ear infections, lung infections, migraine, nausea, sinus problems, sore throat.

Kali. phos. (*Kalium phosphoricum*) ❦ Homeopathic

Suited to those who tend to be irritable, low spirited and indifferent to people and occasions. They are often unmotivated and disinclined to do mental or physical work.

USE TO TREAT

Depression, exhaustion after intensive study, emotional and physical exhaustion, headaches with humming in the ears, impotence, nervous indigestion.

Kaolin

Kaolin, a very fine clay powder with great absorption properties, is used cosmetically and therapeutically as a base for poultices, packs and masks. It is particularly good for oily skins as it will absorb oil from the skin. Kaolin is used commercially for making porcelain, soap, paint and paper.

Kidney care

The kidney tissue is responsible for taking excess water, unwanted bodily chemicals, toxins and toxic chemicals from the blood. This, however, is only a very small part of the vast number of functions performed by the kidneys. If any kidney function is compromised a whole range of serious problems can arise, so take good care of your kidneys.

One of the helpful things that we can do to ease the load on the kidneys is to dry-brush massage our skin daily (see Skin, Dry-brush massage).

The emphasis in treatments outlined below is placed on keeping the kidneys in optimum condition. If there is an existing condition or if a problem is suspected (pain in the kidneys or blood in the urine) a health professional must be consulted.

INTERNAL TREATMENT

❧ If you are a smoker you need to stop smoking as nicotine reduces the blood supply to the kidneys.

❧ Eat a low protein diet. Cut down on meat (red meat in particular) and cheese.

❧ Drink at least 6 glasses of filtered or bottled water every day. Never allow your system to become dehydrated as this places a huge load on the kidneys.

❧ Cut out or down on coffee drinking.

ESSENTIAL OIL TREATMENT

DIURETIC OIL BLEND

1 tablespoon (20 ml) vegetable oil

4 drops geranium oil

4 drops rosemary oil

4 drops cedarwood oil

2 drops fennel oil

TO MAKE: *Mix together.*

TO USE: *Either use the blend for massage or add 2 teaspoons (10 ml)*

*of the blend to a warm bath, agitate the water to disperse the oils and
enjoy a soak for 15–30 minutes.*

HERBAL TREATMENT

- Dandelion leaf is an excellent and safe diuretic. Unlike most other diuretics dandelion contains lots of potassium to safeguard the heart. Drink the leaves as a tea or eat the young leaves in soups, salads and sandwiches.
- Parsley is also a diuretic and may be used in the same way as dandelion.

HOMEOPATHIC TREATMENT

Apis 30^c and Cantharis 30^c can be used to tone the kidneys. If there is an ongoing problem it's wise to consult a homeopathic practitioner.

Labour 🌿 See Pregnancy

Lanolin, anhydrous

Also known as 'wool fat'. This is a sticky, yellow grease obtained by boiling the shorn wool of sheep. This fat is very close in composition to the sebum in human skin and because of this compatibility is a valuable lubricant and moisturiser.

There is a possibility of the fat containing traces of organophosphates as a result of sheep grazing on pasture that has been sprayed with these chemicals. The acceptable level of pesticides in lanolin as set by the US Food and Drug Authority should be no more than five parts per million. I don't recommend the use of lanolin in nipple creams as the baby might receive an unacceptable level (for its bodyweight) of pesticide when feeding from the breast. For other preparations this level appears to pose less of a problem than, say, petroleum jelly, which would be the obvious substitute.

Lanolin is often sold as 'hydrous lanolin' which means that water has been beaten into it to make it less glutinous and easier to use. All the recipes in this book use 'anhydrous' (no water added) lanolin.

Some people are allergic to lanolin.

Laryngitis & Hoarseness

Laryngitis is inflammation of the voice box or the vocal chords. This can lead to hoarseness or temporary loss of voice. Try to rest the voice completely as long as the condition persists (see also Throat, sore).

DAILY SUPPLEMENTS

- ✇ 4000 mg vitamin C with bioflavonoids taken in 2 doses at onset of problem, then 2000 mg daily for as long as needed.
- ✇ ½ teaspoon (2.5 ml) fluid extract of echinacea in 2 tablespoons (40 ml) water 3 times a day.
- ✇ 1000 mg garlic oil capsules three times daily or 2–3 teaspoons 'Long-life juice' 3 times daily.
- ✇ Suck zinc lozenges as directed.

ESSENTIAL OIL TREATMENT

1

2 drops benzoin oil

3 drops lavender oil

1 drop thyme oil

TO USE: *Use as an inhalation (see Inhalations).*

2

3 drops chamomile oil

3 drops sandalwood oil

2 drops lemon oil

1 tablespoon (20 ml) vegetable oil

TO USE: *Massage over throat. Cover entire area with a scarf or warm cloth.*

HERBAL TREATMENT

TO MAKE: *Make a strong tea (see Teas) of sage, add 1 tablespoon (20 ml) cider vinegar and 1 teaspoon honey. Alternate with ¼ teaspoon salt in 1 glass of lukewarm water.*

TO USE: *Gargle 6 times daily.*

HOMEOPATHIC TREATMENT

Take 3 times daily:

* Following cold, damp weather—Carbo veg. 12^c.
* Hoarseness with laryngitis—Phosphorus 30^c.
* Hard, dry cough, voice loss—Phosphorus 30^c.
* Tickling throat, barking cough—Drosera 30^c.

Lavender (*Lavandula officinalis*)

HERB PART USED

Flowers, leaves.

HERB ACTIONS

Antibacterial, antidepressant, antifungal, anti-inflammatory, antiseptic, antiviral, deodorant, insect repellent. The flowers are one of the most used ingredients in pot-pourris, sachets and sleep-pillows and are used for their calming and welcoming perfume. Lavender water is used for easing headaches and stress. A tea is effective as a douche to treat thrush and other vaginal infections.

ESSENTIAL OIL ACTION

Antibacterial, antidepressant, antifungal, anti-inflammatory, antiseptic, antiviral, deodorant, insect repellent.

Lavender oil is probably the most important and versatile essential oil having such a wide variety of uses and being very safe to use.

USE TO TREAT

All emergency situations such as bites, stings, wounds, minor burns, sprains, sunburn, bruises, headaches and stress. Helps to relieve pain, stimulates new cell growth. Strengthens the nervous system. Use to treat acne, athlete's foot and ringworm, psoriasis, sores and spots. Asthma, bronchitis, coughs, colds, croup, flu, laryngitis, sinusitis, sore throats, whooping cough. Aching muscles, arthritis, gout, sciatica. Helps to boost the immune system. Headache, migraine.

Labour pain, period pain, PMS. Lavender is used also in perfumery, soap making and cosmetics.

Lavender spike (*Lavandula spica*)

The perfume of this lavender is similar to *L. officinalis* but sharper and more like rosemary. Has similar properties to its gentler cousin, but it is suggested that as it is more aggressive it may therefore be more valuable therapeutically. It's higher in thujone (a toxic ketone) than *L. officinalis* and so a smaller proportion should be used. I prefer *L. officinalis* as the perfume and action is softer and gentler.

Legs ✤ See Restless legs

Lemon (*Citrus limonum*)

HERB PART USED

All.

HERB ACTIONS

Astringent, detoxifying, refrigerant. A drink made from the *whole* pulped lemon—peel, pith and juice—is rich in vitamins A, B, C and bioflavonoids; the oil in the skin also stimulates the production of white blood corpuscles that protect us from infection. Drop a chopped lemon, with honey to taste and water, into a blender and blend until fine. Drink the pulp as well as the liquid particularly if you have a cold threatening or have a fever. The drink needs to be made fresh as it becomes bitter on standing.

The peel may be candied for use as a confection or in fruit cakes. The juice is used to treat rheumatism and to reduce the size of kidney and gallstones. The raw juice held in the mouth will stop the bleeding from gums and tooth sockets.

Cosmetically the juice is used diluted as an astringent for oily skin, a bleach for discoloured skin, and a rinse for oily and/or fair hair.

ESSENTIAL OIL ACTION

Antibacterial, antifungal, antiseptic, astringent, detoxifying, insect repellent.

USE TO TREAT

Fever, to lower blood pressure, to boost the immune system. Acne, chilblains, cuts. Asthma, catarrh, colds, coughs, flu, sinusitis, sore throats. Depression, 'nerves', lethargy. Add to wound washes and to distilled witch-hazel to stop bleeding and prevent sepsis. Use in air sprays to prevent the spread of infection.
Caution: *Not suitable for children. Phototoxic. Skin irritant—use 0.5–1 per cent only.*

Lemon balm (*Melissa officinalis*)

HERB PART USED

Leaves.

HERB ACTIONS

Antispasmodic, antidepressive, calmative, carminative, diaphoretic, emmenagogue, hypotensive, stomachic. Lemon balm has been used to flavour many well known alcoholic drinks such as Chartreuse and Benedictine. It lends itself well to cooking when a subtle lemon flavour is wanted. The leaves don't dry well so it's better to either use the fresh or frozen leaves. Lemon balm is a tranquillising herb.

USE TO TREAT

Anxiety, depression. Colic, heart flutters, stomach nerves and high blood pressure. The ointment may be useful to treat genital herpes. Nausea and flatulence. Give hot teas to ease flu, colds, fevers, mumps and headaches. This is an excellent herb for calming young children as the action is effective but gentle.

ESSENTIAL OIL ACTION

Antiallergenic, antidepressant, antispasmodic, carminative, digestive, febrifuge, hypotensive, nervine, sedative, stomachic, sudorific, tonic, uterine. The oil of lemon balm is usually sold as melissa. It is a very expensive oil as the plant contains lots of water and little oil—huge quantities of plant are needed to obtain a small amount of oil.

USE TO TREAT

High blood pressure, and for slowing rapid heartbeat, and reducing depression, nervousness and insomnia and easing shock. Use to regulate menstrual cycles. Given the cost of the pure essential oil, melissa would be useful when made as an infused oil (see Aromatherapy & Essential oils, Extraction of essential oils).

Caution: *The oil needs to be treated with more respect than the herb as some of the constituents can cause skin irritation—use at ¹/₂–1 per cent only.*

Leukorrhoea

A thick white or colourless vaginal discharge which is non-infectious and may merely be a slight increase of the normal vaginal secretions. If there is irritation or infection, thrush should be suspected.

ESSENTIAL OIL TREATMENT

Not recommended.

HERBAL TREATMENT

Douche (see Douches) with 1 teaspoon (5 ml) tincture of myrrh in 1 cup (250 ml) warm water or 1 teaspoon (5 ml) cider vinegar in 1 cup (250 ml) water.

HOMEOPATHIC TREATMENT

All 30ᶜ, take 3–4 times daily:
* With irritation, rawness and burning—Cantharis and/or Kreosotum.

🌿 With symptoms of thrush—Nat. mur.

🌿 With the consistency of cream—Pulsatilla.

Lice 🌿 See Head lice

Linseed (Flaxseed) (*Linum usitatissimum*)

HERB PART USED

Seed.

USED TO TREAT

Constipation—linseed absorbs liquid and creates a soft, bulky stool that is easy to expel. Linseed oil is also the richest food source of alpha linolenic acid (see Omega-3 fatty acids). Linseed oil needs to be bought in a small light-proof bottle and kept refrigerated as it becomes rancid very quickly.

Lips

The skin on the lips is very thin and lacking in oil glands, in consequence they can dry out in sun and wind and develop cracks and lines. The following lip salve is for use all the year round to protect against dryness.

'LEMON LIPS'

3 1/2 tablespoons firmly packed tablespoons finely ground beeswax

2 tablespoons (40 ml) light sesame or almond oil

1 tablespoon (20 ml) wheatgerm oil

1 teaspoon (5 ml) castor or jojoba oil

10 drops lemon oil

1/2 teaspoon (2.5 ml) glycerine

TO MAKE: *Melt the beeswax in a very small pan taking care not to overheat and/or burn. Add the sesame, wheatgerm and castor or jojoba oils slowly—don't overheat. Take off the heat and allow to cool a little but not begin to set. Add the remaining ingredients and mix until no drops of glycerine are visible. Pot quickly before the mixture sets.*

Liquorice (Glycyrrhiza glabra)

HERB PART USED

Root.

HERB ACTIONS

Antibiotic, antiviral, demulcent, diuretic, expectorant, laxative.

USE TO TREAT

Respiratory tract infections, coughs, mucous congestion, lung congestion, viral infections. Supports the immune system, appears to be particularly useful in the treatment of viral hepatitis, adrenal insufficiency, inflammation and allergies. Liquorice is often added to medicines to make them more palatable.

Caution: *Long-term use of liquorice isn't recommended as it can lead to sodium retention, potassium deficiency and high blood pressure. An increased amount of potassium rich foods (such as bananas and potatoes) should be eaten while using liquorice.*

ESSENTIAL OIL ACTION

None.

Liver health

The liver is the main organ of metabolism and as such is largely responsible for our health and energy. It is the largest internal organ and the most complex, as it is the organ that filters our blood (more than a litre a minute) of toxins and breaks them down into substances that can be excreted via urine or faeces. It manufactures heparin which helps the blood to clot, bile (which helps with the absorption and digestion of fats and excretion of toxic substances) and creates chemical changes in proteins, fats and carbohydrates that enables them to be used by the body. These are a *very* small number of the functions that this remarkable organ performs.

Because of high-fat/low-fibre diets, exposure to toxic chemicals, overindulgence in alcohol and tobacco and other factors, the incidence of 'sluggish liver' and gall-bladder problems is very high in the more affluent nations of the world. Some symptoms of a sluggish or otherwise malfunctioning liver include fatigue, allergic reactions, digestive problems, a feeling of 'being under the weather' and PMS.

If you feel that your liver is compromised, the following suggestions should help it to recover. If, however, the problem is cirrhosis or hepatitis a health practitioner should be consulted before embarking on a course of self-help.

❧ Dry-brush massage daily before bathing or showering (see Skin care, Dry-brush massage).

❧ Milk thistle (*Silybum marianum*) is one of the most potent treatments for the liver. It is used to supply important nutrients and to treat cirrhosis, chronic hepatitis (see Hepatitis), gallbladder inflammation and other problems of the liver. It has the ability to block the effect and reduce the damage caused by liver toxins including alcohol and drugs.[1] (see Herbal treatment below).

INTERNAL TREATMENT

❧ Eat lots of fresh, steamed or raw vegetables; grains; pulses; nuts; fresh fruit (particularly pineapple).

❧ Drink fresh juices such as beetroot, carrot or lemon juice, all of which increase the flow of bile (which helps with the excretion of waste products).

❧ Cut down on red meat (avoid fatty meat). Eat fish and free-range chicken.

❧ Avoid all fried foods, fast foods and foods containing refined sugars.

❧ Restrict fat consumption to 1 teaspoon butter and 1 tablespoon (20 ml) monounsaturated olive or canola oil a day (this includes what is used in cooking, dressings, sauces and the 'hidden' fats in biscuits, cakes and sweets).

❧ Use low-fat dairy foods (skim milk and low-fat cheese).

❧ Drink 8–10 glasses of filtered or bottled water daily, cut down on tea, avoid coffee and alcohol.

DAILY SUPPLEMENTS

- ❧ 1000 mg vitamin C with bioflavonoids twice daily.
- ❧ 1 vitamin B complex tablet.
- ❧ 1000 mg choline.

ESSENTIAL OIL TREATMENT

MASSAGE OIL

½ cup (125 ml) vegetable oil

40 drops rosemary oil

20 drops chamomile oil

15 drops peppermint oil

5 drops cypress oil

TO MAKE: *Mix together in a bottle, shake well. Leave for a few days to blend.*

TO USE: *Massage over the whole body (except the tender bits) once daily after bathing or showering. A professional lymphatic massage using the oil blend is very helpful.*

HERBAL TREATMENT

- ❧ Dandelion coffee 3 times daily.
- ❧ Milk thistle as directed.

HOMEOPATHIC TREATMENT

Consult a homeopathic practitioner.

'Long-life juice'

This juice is delicious. It will counteract excessive blood clotting, help control diabetes, lower cholesterol and blood pressure and keep flu and cold bugs at bay. In addition, it can help to reduce inflammation. It can be used as a substitute in any of the complaints that recommend garlic oil capsules.

Make a fresh batch every 3–4 days. Don't refrigerate it unless the weather is really warm.

Take 2–3 teaspoons (10–15 ml) 3 times daily. I enjoy eating the chopped mixture but if this doesn't appeal, just drink the juice.

1 very finely chopped onion

4 very finely crushed garlic cloves

juice of 1 lemon

2–3 teaspoons finely grated ginger

runny honey to cover

TO MAKE: *Put the onion, garlic and ginger in a jar, pour the lemon juice over. Mix well.*

Pour honey into the jar until the contents are well covered, stir and add more honey if needed. Put a lid on the jar. Leave for 2–3 hours before use.

Lycopodium (*Lycopodium clavatum*) ✾ Homeopathic

Suited to people who are cowardly and insecure even though they are intense, hard working and have a sharp intellect; and who are nervous in social situations, fear rejection and being alone.

USE TO TREAT

Acidity and heartburn, cystitis, gout, hiccoughs with heartburn, indigestion, period pain, PMS.

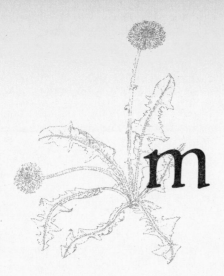

Mandarin (*Citrus nobilis*)

ESSENTIAL OIL ACTION

Antiseptic, antidepressant, antispasmodic, detoxifying, stimulant, tonic; can be used throughout pregnancy.

USE TO TREAT

To prevent or treat stretch marks. Eases anxiety, depression, fear, insomnia. Eases stomach cramps, digestive problems and PMS. A useful oil for children of all ages, can be used as a tummy massage oil to ease colic, produce 'burps' and ease hiccoughs.

Manuka (*Leptospermum scoparium*)

ESSENTIAL OIL ACTION

Antiviral, antifungal, antibacterial, antiseptic, disinfectant, immuno-stimulant. This oil is distilled from the wood of a New Zealand native tree. It is as gentle and versatile as lavender and tea-tree with (to my nose) a slightly more pleasant aroma than tea-tree.

USE TO TREAT

Urinary tract infections, trichomonas, candida, thrush; may help to heal genital herpes. Abscesses, ringworm, athlete's foot, corns, warts.

Coughs, bronchitis, colds. Cold sores, mouth ulcers, gingivitis, bad breath, tonsillitis. Acne, boils, burns, sunburn. ME and other auto-immune problems. In general, manuka oil is non-irritant and may be used undiluted over small areas of the body.

Marjoram (*Origanum majorana*)

HERB PART USED

Leaves and flowers.

HERB ACTIONS

Antispasmodic, calmative, carminative, diaphoretic, expectorant, stomachic, tonic.

USE TO TREAT

Sinus problems, laryngitis and respiratory problems as an inhalation although the essential oil probably works more efficiently than the whole herb. Used in cooking marjoram acts as a digestive, reducing abdominal and intestinal cramps. It has a reputation for being anti-aphrodisiac. A well known culinary herb, with a similar but less pungent flavour to oregano, it is mostly used in bean, cheese and tomato dishes.

ESSENTIAL OIL ACTION

Anaphrodisiac, antibacterial, antifungal, antiseptic, antispasmodic, antiviral, digestive, expectorant, sedative.

USE TO TREAT

Respiratory and sinus problems. Sedative, use for insomnia. Lowers high blood pressure, eases pain and stiffness in over-used muscles, menstrual cramps, rheumatism, arthritis and stiff joints generally. Use in baths to treat the early symptoms of colds and flu. The oil is con-sidered one of the best for dulling the pain of grief.

Marshmallow (*Althea officinalis*)

HERB PART USED

Root and leaf.

HERB ACTIONS

Astringent, demulcent, emollient, expectorant. The root is soothing and healing.

USE TO TREAT

Ulcers (internal and external), digestive problems, bronchitis, laryngitis, coughs, emphysema, catarrh. A powerful remedy for infections of the urinary system. Stimulates white blood cell production.

ESSENTIAL OIL ACTION

None.

Massage

Massage is beneficial to the body and to the emotions. It stimulates and improves the functions of the circulatory and lymphatic systems increasing the elimination of toxins and improving muscle and skin tone. It soothes and stimulates the nervous system resulting in a feeling of well being and relaxation.

The molecules of essential oils used in massage are small enough to pass through the skin. From there they are absorbed into body fat, then into the blood stream and carried to all the systems of the body.

The aromas of the oils when breathed in are carried to the limbic portion of the brain and also partially absorbed into the body through the lungs. The oils seem to work more beneficially when applied externally rather than when taken internally as the stomach is bypassed and the oils aren't affected or diluted by gastric juices.

Essential oils are used in therapeutic massage by professional aromatherapists but home massages can be very satisfactory.

Massage doesn't always mean the massaging of the entire body — foot massage (reflexology) is a powerful therapy because all the body systems have nerve endings in the feet. These systems are stimulated through foot massage. A similar effect can be experienced from a reflexology massage of the hands and ears.

Individual areas such as shoulders, abdomen, legs and other areas suffering from localised problems can benefit greatly from massage.

The essential oils (with the exception of lavender and tea-tree) must never be used undiluted (see dilution chart in Aromatherapy & Essential oils). Instructions for making a herbal massage oil will be found under Herb Oil Base.

MASSAGE OIL BASE

½ cup (125 ml) Herb Oil Base or

4 tablespoons (80 ml) grapeseed oil

2 tablespoons (40 ml) almond oil

1 tablespoon (20 ml) avocado oil

1 teaspoon (5 ml) wheatgerm oil

TO MAKE: *Mix together and add to one of the essential oil blends that follow.*

TO USE: *Massage oils are nicest to use if slightly warm. A small bowl can be heated first before adding the massage oil.*

GENERAL ACHES & PAINS

15 drops juniper oil

15 drops rosemary oil

10 drops lavender oil

5 drops black pepper oil

5 drops ginger oil

TO MAKE: *Mix together and add to the Massage oil base. Shake well.*

ANTI-CELLULITE

20 drops fennel oil

15 drops juniper oil

10 drops grapefruit oil

5 drops geranium oil

TO MAKE: *Mix together and add to the Massage oil base. Shake well.*

ARTHRITIS *&* RHEUMATISM ❦ See Arthritis

BACK PAIN

20 drops juniper oil

10 drops rosemary oil

10 drops cypress oil

10 drops black pepper oil

TO MAKE: *Mix together and add to the Massage oil base. Shake well.*

CALMING

20 drops bergamot oil

15 drops lavender oil

5 drops cedarwood oil

5 drops sandalwood oil

5 drops ylang-ylang oil

TO MAKE: *Mix together and add to the Massage oil base. Shake well.*

FATIGUE

20 drops basil oil

15 drops marjoram

15 drops rosemary

TO MAKE: *Mix together and add to the Massage oil base. Shake well.*

MUSCLE SORENESS

20 drops marjoram oil

10 drops lavender oil

10 drops chamomile oil

10 drops rosemary oil

TO MAKE: *Mix together and add to the Massage oil base. Shake well.*

MUSCLE TONER

15 drops rosemary oil

15 drops juniper oil

10 drops cypress oil

10 drops black pepper oil
TO MAKE: *Mix together and add to the Massage oil base. Shake well.*

POOR CIRCULATION

25 drops rosemary oil
10 drops black pepper oil
10 drops eucalyptus oil
5 drops ginger oil
TO MAKE: *Mix together and add to the Massage oil base. Shake well.*

REFRESHING

20 drops bergamot oil
10 drops lavender oil
10 drops geranium oil
10 drops grapefruit oil
TO MAKE: *Mix together and add to the Massage oil base. Shake well.*

ROMANTIC

15 drops ylang-ylang oil
15 drops bergamot oil
12 drops geranium oil
5 drops petitgrain oil
3 drops black pepper oil
TO MAKE: *Mix together and add to the Massage oil base. Shake well.*

SWEET SLEEP

20 drops chamomile oil
15 drops lavender oil
10 drops marjoram oil
5 drops sandalwood oil
TO MAKE: *Mix together and add to the Massage oil base. Shake well.*

Meadowsweet (*Filipendula ulmaria*)

HERB PART USED

Flowers.

HERB ACTIONS

Antirheumatic, anti-inflammatory, antacid, astringent, diaphoretic, diuretic. Contains salicylates that act to ease pain in a similar way to aspirin without having the undesirable side effects of that drug.

USE TO TREAT

Rheumatism, fevers and pain in muscles and joints. An excellent remedy for easing heartburn, acidity and disturbed digestion. Protects and soothes the mucous membranes of the digestive tract. Is said to help in the treatment of urinary tract infections.

ESSENTIAL OIL ACTION

Make an analgesic and anti-inflammatory infused oil to treat joint pain, rheumatism, arthritis and all similar conditions.

Measles

This is a serious childhood viral disease as it can lead to secondary infections of the eyes, ears and chest. Professional advice must always be sought but there are also measures that can be taken at home to reduce the discomfort of the symptoms.

Early symptoms can be mistaken for a cold with an accompanying cough. After 3–4 days white spots appear on the insides of the cheeks followed by a rash that spreads and often joins together. The child can feel very unwell and has a cough and fever. Keep the room at a steady temperature and the lighting fairly dim.

Follow the treatment suggested for chickenpox (see Chickenpox). See also Rubella.

Meditation ❦ See Relaxation

Melanoma

I include melanoma in this book in order to stress that there is no known and proved alternative treatment for this condition. There is anecdotal evidence of various herbal 'cures' but you put your life at risk if you use these remedies alone and refuse orthodox treatment.

Melanoma is a type of cancer that usually starts in the pigment cells found in the outer layers of the skin. It tends to spread in the outer layer of skin before moving to deeper layers where, if not treated, the cancer cells may break away and be carried to other parts of the body. It looks like a freckle with a wavy or irregular edge. It may have a variety of colours including brown, black, blue, red or occasionally light grey. At first a melanoma is usually flat but may become raised as it grows. If you are at all concerned about changes in a mole or freckle you should consult a doctor immediately. The sooner that treatment begins, the more successful it is likely to be.

Exposure of the skin to the sun's harmful ultraviolet rays is the most significant factor in the development of melanoma and Australians have the highest rate of melanoma in the world. Exposure during childhood is the greatest risk with as few as five or six incidents of sunburn in childhood, increasing the risk of developing melanoma as an adult.

Treatment involves removal of the melanoma and a thorough examination to see whether the cancer has spread elsewhere (see also Cancer and Skin care).

While undergoing orthodox treatment it is also appropriate to boost your immune system using the recommendations listed under Immune system.

Protecting your skin from ultraviolet rays can reduce the risk of developing melanoma or other forms of skin cancer. To be SunSmart (a registered campaign name started in Victoria, but now adopted as an 'umbrella' logo in most states) the Australian Cancer Society recommends the following:

* Avoid being in the sun between 10 a.m. and 3 p.m.
* Use shade whenever possible.
* Wear a broad-brimmed hat or a legionnaire-style cap.
* Wear protective clothing.
* Use maximum-protection sunscreen (SPF30 broad spectrum) on skin not covered by clothing.
* Wear sunglasses that conform to the Australian Standard AS 1067 (1990).
* Check your skin regularly.
* See your doctor if you notice any unusual skin changes.
* Encourage work places, schools and sports organisations to promote a SunSmart policy.

Menopause

Menopause is the time when periods and ovulation cease. It is one of the biggest changes that occur in a woman's life. If periods stop abruptly it can be a profound shock and makes the adjustment more difficult even though the hormonal changes will have been happening for several years before.

When physical symptoms are coupled with other major changes such as re-entering the workforce; children leaving/having left home (or being at a stage in their lives when they may be difficult); or parents ageing (and maybe becoming sick or helpless); it can be a stressful and emotional time.

Western cultures don't afford respect to the 'getting of wisdom', the emphasis instead being on the importance of youth, sex and beauty. The rounded gentle beauty of the older woman is largely ignored or derided. By contrast, traditional cultures treat their older women with respect and reverence, valuing them for their wisdom.

Making a psychological shift at this stage of the life cycle is crucial to achieve grace, productivity, peace and self-worth. Having passed through the phases of daughter and mother, you now reach the precious time when you find your own realm and pass on the wisdom that you have learned over the years. Believe me, the 'grandmother years' are to be cherished. This is the precious time to enjoy the 'Change of Life'!

Many authorities assure us that there is no reason why women should suffer from unpleasant menopausal symptoms but the depressing fact is that many women have a really unhappy and uncomfortable time. If your life is being ruined or dominated by mood swings; depression; hot flushes; sweating; dryness of the skin, mucous membranes and vagina; anxiety; insomnia; loss of libido or any of the other symptoms accompanying menopause the use of some or all of the following suggestions may bring relief.

INTERNAL TREATMENT

❧ Walk daily to help to increase bone density and to prevent osteoporosis.

❧ Avoid coffee, alcohol, salt and salty foods, full-cream dairy products and meat fat, fried and junk foods, and chocolate.

❧ Eat a healthy diet with lots of fresh fruit and vegetables, wholegrain bread and cereals. Many plants contain oestrogenic/progesterone-like properties that can reduce the symptoms of oestrogen and progesterone deficiencies. A few of these foods are tofu, tempeh, soya beans and soya milk and (to a lesser extent), pumpkin, corn, carrots, garlic, olive oil, chickpeas, beetroot, alfalfa, potatoes, sesame seeds, sunflower seeds and sweet potato.

❧ Eat foods containing the anti-ageing essential fatty acids to promote hormonal balance. These are found in olive and canola oils, avocados, sunflower and sesame seeds, wheatgerm (must be fresh and stored in the freezer), mackerel, herrings, sardines, salmon and tuna.

DAILY SUPPLEMENTS

❧ 500–1000 mg vitamin C with bioflavonoids.

❧ 200–400 iu vitamin E (d-alpha tocopherol).

❧ 10 000 iu beta-carotene.

❀ 500–1000 mg calcium/magnesium citrate.

❀ high-potency vitamin B complex tablet.

❀ 1000–2000 mg borage (starflower) oil or evening primrose oil.

❀ 15 mg zinc.

ESSENTIAL OIL TREATMENT FOR HORMONAL BALANCE

'CHANGE' MASSAGE & BATH OIL

15 drops clary sage oil

15 drops geranium oil

10 drops bergamot oil

95 ml vegetable oil

TO MAKE: *Mix together in a 100 ml bottle.*

TO USE: *Massage a little into the body after a bath or shower and before bed.*

Add 1 tablespoon (20 ml) to a warm bath, agitate to disperse the oils. Soak in the bath for as long as you wish.

HERBAL TREATMENT

❧ Drink a cup (250 ml) of sage tea twice daily.

❧ 2 capsules passionflower or 1 dropper tincture up to 4 times a day to help calm nerves.

❧ There are excellent herbal combinations available in health-food shops. Look for one that contains some or all of the following herbs: false unicorn root, chaste tree, dong quai, fennel, black cohosh.

❧ There are creams available that contain wild yam, flaxseed oil, essential oils, vitamin E oil and a homeopathic wild yam remedy. The cream is massaged onto areas such as the abdomen and inner thighs and from there is absorbed into the system.

HOMEOPATHIC TREATMENT

All 6–30ᶜ, take once daily:

❦ Fair-haired women—Pulsatilla.

❦ Dark-haired women—Sepia.

✻ Hot flushes, mostly of the face—Graphites.
✻ With sweating—Sepia.

Menstruation

While menstruation isn't an illness, many women suffer from menstrual problems such as bloating, uterine cramps, pelvic pain, constipation, backache, headaches, fatigue and other unpleasant and incapacitating symptoms.

The use of relaxation, meditation, visualisation, herbal and homeopathic remedies, essential oils and supplements have proved a blessing to many women, changing both their attitude and the physical symptoms associated with menstruation. These suggestions may be helpful.

ABSENCE OF, OR SCANTY PERIODS (AMENORRHOEA)

Lack of periods or scanty periods can be caused by the onset of menopause, weight loss and/or anorexia, over-exercising, stress, illness and pregnancy. The first and most important thing to ascertain is that you aren't pregnant. If menstruation stops suddenly consult a gynaecologist. If stress is the problem, the sections on Stress and Relaxation may be helpful.

DAILY SUPPLEMENTS

§ 400 iu vitamin E (d-alpha tocopherol).
§ 1000 mg borage (starflower) oil or evening primrose oil.
§ 1000 mg vitamin C with bioflavonoids.

ESSENTIAL OIL TREATMENT

MASSAGE OIL BLEND
1 tablespoon (20 ml) vegetable oil
6 drops lavender oil
4 drops clary sage
4 drops chamomile oil
2 drops rosemary oil

TO MAKE: *Mix together.*

TO USE: *Massage the abdomen and lower back once or twice daily.*

HERBAL TREATMENT

The following herbs taken singly or in combination are helpful for this problem, blue cohosh, false unicorn root (a paramount toner and stimulator of the reproductive system, which will balance and tone the system and is particularly useful for ovarian pain and delayed menstruation), squaw vine, dong quai.

Caution: *The above treatments are not to be used during pregnancy.*

PAINFUL PERIODS (DYSMENORRHOEA) & HORMONAL IMBALANCE

Painful periods can sometimes indicate pelvic disease but are often caused by hormonal imbalances. It is thought that the uterus producing an excessive amount of prostaglandins causes the severe backache and cramping. It's important to avoid constipation.

DAILY SUPPLEMENTS

- ✻ 1000 mg vitamin C with bioflavonoids.
- ✻ 500 mg calcium/magnesium citrate.
- ✻ 400 iu vitamin E (d-alpha tocopherol).
- ✻ 2000–4000 mg borage (starflower) oil or evening primrose oil.

ESSENTIAL OIL TREATMENT

MASSAGE OIL BLEND

6 drops chamomile oil

6 drops cypress oil

4 drops clary sage oil

1 tablespoon (20 ml) vegetable oil

TO MAKE: *Mix together.*

TO USE: *Massage once or twice daily over the abdomen and lower back.*

* Add 5 drops of geranium oil and 5 drops of clary sage oil to a bath. Agitate the water well and soak for 10 minutes.

HERBAL TREATMENT

❧ Black cohosh, cramp bark, chaste tree, wild yam and dong quai. They may be found singly or as a combination in tablet form in health-food stores.
❧ Willow bark as needed to control pain.

Caution: *The above essential oil and herbal treatments are not to be used during pregnancy.*

HOMEOPATHIC TREATMENT

All remedies are 6–30^c, take as required before and during periods:
* Tearful and tense with sore breasts—Pulsatilla.
* Painful menstruation—Mag. phos. and/or Chamomilla.
* Acute and sudden painful cramps—Belladonna.

HEAVY BLEEDING

If the problem persists, professional help must be sought as there may be a more serious reason for it. Heavy bleeding can be caused by a pelvic infection, endometrial polyps, endometriosis, uterine fibroids, thyroid abnormalities or can happen for no apparent reason. It can lead to anaemia.

Bleeding between periods must always be treated with suspicion and professional help sought.

DAILY SUPPLEMENTS

* 1000 mg vitamin C with bioflavonoids.
* 5000–10 000 iu beta-carotene.
* 200–400 iu vitamin E (d-alpha tocopherol).
* Iron-rich foods.

ESSENTIAL OIL TREATMENT

Avoid antispasmodic oils (see Antispasmodics).

MASSAGE OIL BLEND

1 tablespoon (20 ml) vegetable oil

6 drops cypress oil

6 drops geranium oil

6 drops lemon oil

TO MAKE: *Mix together.*

TO USE: *Once or twice daily, massage the abdomen and lower back. Add 5 drops cypress and 5 drops lemon oil to a warm bath, agitate to disperse the oils, soak for 10 minutes.*

HERBAL TREATMENT

- ½–1 teaspoon (2.5–5 ml) fluid extract of shepherd's purse (a first-rate remedy for easing internal bleeding).
- Dong quai as directed.

HOMEOPATHIC TREATMENT

All 30ᶜ, take 3–4 times daily:

- Try Phosphorus and/or Ferr. phos. or Sabina.

Merc. sol. (*Mercurius solubilis*) ❋ Homeopathic

USE TO TREAT

Abscesses, athlete's foot, earache, itching skin, mouth ulcers, sore throat, thrush, toothache.

Migraine

Migraine is *not*, as so many people imagine, merely a bad headache. In 50 per cent of cases you get forewarning of the severe, often incapacitating pain by signs such as flashing lights or blurring of the vision, numbness or tingling on one side of the body or sudden fatigue or anxiety.

Most migraines seem to be caused by a sudden constriction of the blood vessels surrounding the brain, followed by dilation as the blood forces its way through. This contraction and dilation causes inflammation and intense pain.

Migraine is often accompanied by any or all the following: nausea and/or vomiting, sensitivity to light, tunnel vision, severe pain around one eye or one or both sides of the head. The headaches can often last for 3 days.

There seems to be a very diverse range of causes of migraine which need to be examined in an attempt to find and hopefully correct the condition.

Food allergy seems to be the major cause with chocolate, cheese, alcohol (especially red wine) and dairy products being some of the main offenders. It's a simple matter to eradicate these items in turn to see if an improvement is effected. If these foods are not the culprits, the sufferer would be well advised to seek the help of a specialist in allergy testing as the potential list of food allergens is very long and a specific routine has to followed.

Relaxation training and bio-feedback have been shown to reduce the frequency and severity of attacks that are triggered by stress. See also Stress and Relaxation.

Migraine sufferers would be advised, after eliminating food allergies as a reason for their suffering, to try some or all of the following suggestions. (See also Headaches.)

INTERNAL TREATMENT

See above.

DAILY SUPPLEMENTS

- ✻ 1 vitamin B complex tablet.
- ✻ 50 mg niacin.
- ✻ 2000 mg borage (starflower) oil or evening primrose oil.

ESSENTIAL OIL TREATMENT

Essential oil treatments are best used as preventative measures as, by the time a migraine has begun, the sufferer can often not bear to be touched and can't tolerate smells.

If, however, the patient is open to the treatment, hot fomentations (see Fomentations) on the back of the neck using marjoram oil will help in the very early stages when the blood vessels are constricting. Cold compresses (see Compresses) of lavender on the forehead may help when the blood vessels are dilating.

HERBAL TREATMENT

ॐ Feverfew is now being used extensively in the treatment of migraine, see Feverfew for more information. Its effects may not be felt for a month or so, so it's important to persevere.

Caution: *The leaves of the fresh herb occasionally cause soreness of the mouth. Feverfew mustn't be used during pregnancy.*

ॐ Valerian is an antispasmodic and sedative herb that often reduces the severity of a migraine attack.

HOMEOPATHIC TREATMENT

All 6–30^c, take as often as required:

* Sudden and violent with throbbing, pounding pain—Belladonna.
* Beginning behind the neck, moving over the head to one eye—Silica.
* Blurred vision before headache—Kali. bich.

Milk thistle (*Silybum marianum*)

Also known as St Mary's Thistle.

HERB PART USED

Seeds.

HERB ACTIONS

Powerful antioxidant, anti-inflammatory, antiallergenic. A potent liver protectant. Helps to prevent liver destruction and enhance liver function.

USE TO TREAT

Cirrhosis, acute and chronic hepatitis, inflammation of the bile duct. May be useful to treat food intolerances and skin conditions due to poor liver function. Has been used to reduce the side-effects of chemotherapy.

ESSENTIAL OIL ACTION

None.

Minerals ✹ See also Vitamins

CALCIUM

What it can do: needed for strong bones and teeth. Needed, together with magnesium, for a healthy heart. Can help to alleviate insomnia and nervousness.
Main sources: milk, cheese, broccoli, legumes, green-leafed vegetables, nuts, seeds.
Herbal sources: alfalfa, anise, dandelion greens, nettle, watercress.

IODINE

What it can do: improve energy, mental function and weight control. Promote healthy nails, teeth, skin and hair.
Main sources: oily fish, beef liver, eggs, peanuts, wholewheat flour, lettuce, spinach, green pepper, milk products, poultry, grains and cereals.
Herbal sources: cayenne, peppermint.

IRON

What it can do: cure and prevent iron-deficiency anaemia, give added resistance to disease, help to prevent fatigue, improve skin tone.
Main sources: liver (calf's liver in particular but no more than 100 g daily because of the high vitamin A content), kidney, heart, egg yolk, legumes, dried apricots and other dried fruits, shellfish.
Herbal sources: dandelion greens, garlic, land and watercress, nettle, parsley.

MAGNESIUM

What it can do: act as an anti-depressant, support the cardiovascular system, and help prevent calcium deposits in kidneys and gallbladder. Relieve indigestion that is due to an excess of stomach acid.

Main sources: nuts, shrimps, soya beans and tofu, tempeh, soya sauce, wholegrains, green-leafed vegetables.

Herbal sources: cayenne, dandelion greens, parsley, red clover, watercress.

PHOSPHORUS

What it can do: help to give healthy bones, gums and teeth, assist the body in using some of the vitamin B complex vitamins. It is involved in the production of energy from food and can help to relieve arthritic pain.

Main sources: milk, cheese, butter, nuts, wholegrain cereals, poultry, eggs, meat, fish and legumes.

Herbal sources: alfalfa, cayenne, dandelion greens, garlic, sage, watercress.

POTASSIUM

What it can do: regulate the balance of water and acidity in the blood, send oxygen to the brain and improve clear thinking, balance the body's water and normalise heart rhythms.

Main sources: fresh fruit, wholegrains, and vegetables.

Herbal sources: dandelion greens, parsley, watercress.

ZINC

What it can do: improve wound healing, help to reverse taste loss, help prostate problems, may decrease cholesterol deposits, improve mental alertness and improve fertility.

Main sources: ginger root, lamb chops, steak, split peas, brazil nuts, non-fat dried milk, egg yolk, wheatgerm, peanuts, peas, turnips, parsley, potatoes, carrots, beans and corn.

Herbal sources: dandelion greens, garlic, nettle, rosemary.

Mint ❧ See Peppermint, Spearmint

Morning sickness ❧ See Pregnancy

Mosquito repellent ❧ See Ross River Virus

Mouth ulcers ❧ See Ulcers

Mouthwashes ❧ See Bad breath

Mullein (*Verbascum thapsus*)

HERB PART USED

Leaves, flowers.

HERB ACTIONS

Anodyne, antispasmodic, demulcent, diuretic, expectorant, vulnerary.

USE TO TREAT

Use a tea or tincture made from the leaves to treat asthma, colds, coughs, hoarseness, bronchitis, bronchial catarrh, whooping cough. Stomach cramps, urinary tract infections, diarrhoea, colitis.

The flowers are used to treat skin inflammations and wounds.

ESSENTIAL OIL ACTION

No essential oil but an infused oil (see Aromatherapy & Essential oils) of the flowers is a useful remedy to relieve pain and to treat ear infections, insect bites, bruises, sore joints and haemorrhoids.

Multiple sclerosis (MS)

The causes of multiple sclerosis are still a mystery after 120 years of research. There are theories suggesting viral, immune disturbances or autoimmunity causes. Some research suggests that nutrition plays a key role in the causes of MS as diets high in milk and gluten are common in areas where there is a high rate of MS.[1] Norwegian studies have found that there was a higher incidence of MS in inland farming communities where the diet was much higher in animal and dairy products than for coastal dwellers who consumed high levels of cold-water fish. Another interesting observation is that the highest incidence of MS occurs in the higher latitudes (of both northern and southern hemispheres).

It is a chronic disease affecting twice as many women as men and usually striking between the ages of 20 and 50 years. The sheaths that surround the nerves become inflamed and progressively degenerate. MS can affect muscles, eyesight, speech and bladder and bowels. It is an unpredictable disease—relapses and remissions are common. Only about one in five sufferers will experience severe disability.

MS is not contagious or infectious and not a fatal disease. It is not inherited (people may inherit a susceptibility to the disease, but not the disease itself) and is not a mental disease.

Exercise and physiotherapy can reduce the symptoms and maintain joint flexibility and balance, and stress can be managed by several methods (see Relaxation).

Chronic fatigue affects many MS sufferers. Work out if there is time of day when your energy levels are at their best and reserve vital jobs for this time. Pace yourself and get plenty of rest.

There is a lot of help available through many organisations. These can be found through your GP, the local hospital or the telephone directory under Multiple Sclerosis Society.

It is neither helpful nor health promoting to mix with people (some doctors included) who are pessimistic about MS as negativity can be destructive to health while positivity can be health enhancing.

A low-fat diet devised by Dr Roy Swank, professor of Neurology, University of Oregon Medical School seems to have had very convincing results. Dr Swank has been successfully treating patients since 1948. He claims that a diet containing less than 15 g a day of saturated fats and high in polyunsaturated fats produced less relapses, an increased life expectancy and higher energy levels. The recommendations for the diet are included below along with (in brackets) comments and/or suggestions from others.

INTERNAL TREATMENT

✳ A saturated fat intake of no more than 15 g a day (butter, hard cheeses, palm and coconut oil and fat on meat). This means careful reading of food labelling as processed meats, bread, biscuits and cakes, for example, often contain saturated fats.

✳ A daily intake of 40–50 g of polyunsaturated oils. *Not including margarine, shortening or hydrogenated oils.* (I would suggest using only monounsaturated virgin olive oil and cold-pressed canola oil.)

✳ At least 1 teaspoon cod liver oil daily. (Dr Andrew Weil, MD, [see bibliography] recommends blackcurrant oil, 500 mg twice a day as being preferable.)

✳ A normal amount of protein (Dr Weil recommends limited protein intake).

✳ The consumption of fish three times a week or more. (Sardines, salmon, mackerel, herring, tuna are best.)

✳ Eat a diet that is rich in fresh fruits and vegetables—with as wide a variety as possible.

✳ Eat 6 small, rather than 3 large, meals daily.

✳ Eat plenty of wholegrain cereals in breads, muesli and brown rice.

✳ Snack on fruit and nuts rather than biscuits and cakes.

✳ Use skimmed milk and yoghurt in preference to full cream milk. If intolerance to milk is a problem use goat's or soya milk instead.

✳ Eat only very lean meat with no skin and keep the consumption of meat to one or, at the most, two meals a week.

✳ Eat meals containing pulses (peas, beans and lentils) in preference to meat.

✳ Eat 1–2 dessertspoons daily of linseeds sprinkled on yoghurt or cereal.

✳ Avoid caffeine drinks, tobacco and alcohol, all of which have a bad effect on the nervous system.

DAILY SUPPLEMENTS

- Antioxidant formula as directed.
- 1 vitamin B complex tablet.
- 1 multivitamin tablet.
- 400 iu vitamin E (d-alpha-tocopherol).
- 30 mg Co-enzyme Q twice daily.

ESSENTIAL OIL TREATMENT

Use any of the massage oils recommended for sore muscles, stress, depression, etc. as needed.

HERBAL TREATMENT

Herbal remedies need to be tailored to suit the individual. Consult a herbalist or naturopath who will assess your needs and prescribe accordingly.

HOMEOPATHIC TREATMENT

Consult a homeopathic practitioner.

Mumps

A viral infection characterised by swollen glands on one or both sides of the jaw. Adult *males* should try to avoid contracting mumps as it can lead to swelling and inflammation of the testicles and possibly cause sterility.

The treatment suggested for chickenpox may be followed. The compresses may be laid on the swollen glands to offer relief.

Muscular aches & pains   ❦ See Massage

Myrrh (*Commiphora myrrha, C. molmol*)

HERB PART USED

Resin.

HERB ACTIONS

Anticatarrhal, antifungal, astringent, antiseptic, anti-inflammatory, expectorant. The resin is crushed and used as a fixative in mixtures for perfumes, incenses, pot-pourris, sachets, pillows and other scented products. The crushed resin is also used to make a tincture that is used in toothpaste, ointments, creams, lotions and mouth-washes to heal gingivitis, mouth ulcers and cold sores.

ESSENTIAL OIL ACTION

Anticatarrhal, antifungal, astringent, antiseptic, anti-inflammatory, expectorant. Myrrh oil is difficult to dissolve in anything other than a fixed oil.

USE TO TREAT

Slow-to-heal wounds, boils, athlete's foot, cuts, chapped skin, gin-givitis, mouth ulcers and cold sores, ringworm, sores and ulcers. Pulmonary antiseptic; use inhalations or massage to treat catarrh, coughs, bronchitis and sore throats.

Nat mur. (*Natrum muriaticum*)  Homeopathic

Suited to insecure, nervy, irritable people who worry about the future and who are emotionally sensitive but have difficulty expressing emotions. They are often sensitive to heat and the sun, but feel better in the open air.

USE TO TREAT

Colds, cold sores, eczema, grief and suppressed emotions, RSI, incontinence, irregular periods, migraine, PMS, sinusitis, thrush, urticaria, vertigo.

Nausea

Nausea is the feeling of wanting to vomit. There are many causes for nausea but the most likely ones are:

- If the vagus nerve in the stomach becomes irritated, a reflex action of the nerve makes one want to vomit.
- A severe shock, such as seeing an accident or smelling something putrid, can stimulate the nervous pathway from the brain.
- An overloaded liver due to eating over-rich food.

There are several remedies that will help to ease the discomfort of nausea (see also Pregnancy, Morning sickness).

INTERNAL REMEDIES

Ginger capsule or tea, chamomile or peppermint tea.

TRAVEL NAUSEA ❦ See Travel

INDIGESTION NAUSEA

Sip tea of any of the following herbs: aniseed, fennel, peppermint.

NAUSEA DUE TO SHOCK

- ❦ Sip lemon balm tea and use deep breathing to steady the nerves.
- ❦ Massage lavender oil on the pulse points and inhale the aroma deeply.
- ❦ Sniff marjoram oil direct from the bottle.

HOMEOPATHIC TREATMENT

Nausea and vomiting—Ipecac.

Neroli (*Citrus aurantium, var. amara*)

ESSENTIAL OIL ACTION

Antidepressant, antiseptic, antispasmodic, aphrodisiac, sedative.

USE TO TREAT

Shock, intestinal cramps, nervous tension, PMS, menopausal depression. Induces deep relaxation; calms palpitations and nerves, fear and shock; use to treat insomnia, acne, eczema, scars, stretch marks, sensitive skin, PMS, menopausal symptoms.

Nervines

Strengthen the nervous system.

HERBS

Chamomile, lavender, lemon balm, marjoram, rosemary, skullcap, valerian.

ESSENTIAL OILS

Chamomile, lavender, marjoram, melissa, rosemary, sandalwood, vetivert.

Nervous tension ❦ See Emotional & Nervous problems

Nettle (*Urtica dioica*)

HERB PART USED

Leaves.

HERB ACTIONS

Astringent, diuretic, galactagogue, haemostatic, tonic.

USE TO TREAT

Anaemia, poor circulation, poor appetite, poor milk flow in nursing mothers. Increases urine flow. Eases haemorrhoids and lessens excessive menstrual flow. Use in hair treatments and as a fertiliser in the garden.

ESSENTIAL OIL ACTION

None.

Nettle rash ❦ See Hives

Neuralgia

Neuralgia is a pain originating in a nerve that radiates from the central nervous system. The pain, especially when in the face, can sometimes be intense.

DAILY SUPPLEMENTS

1 vitamin B complex tablet.

ESSENTIAL OIL TREATMENT

MASSAGE OIL BLEND

1 tablespoon (20 ml) St John's Wort oil

3 drops lavender oil

3 drops chamomile oil

2 drops clove or marjoram oil

TO MAKE: *Mix the oils together.*

TO USE: *Massage a few drops along the affected nerve. Apply a cold compress (see Compresses) using 1 drop of each oil. Sometimes heat works better than cold—try and see which works best for you.*

HERBAL TREATMENT

❧ Zostrix is a cream available in pharmacies. It contains capsaicin, an extract from chillies, and is helpful in temporarily relieving the pain of neuralgia, arthritis and the after-pain associated with shingles.

❧ Take 2 willow bark capsules or 2 droppers of the tincture to ease pain and relax the nerves.

❧ Apply alternate hot and cold fomentations and compresses using teas of mixed lavender, vervain, and rosemary. Drink hot teas of mixed lavender, vervain and rosemary. If you don't have all the herbs just use what you have.

❧ Fill a hot water bottle with boiling water. Put enough frozen peas in a plastic bag until it's about the size of a tennis ball. Fasten with a rubber band. Hold the ball with a cloth or wear a glove and massage the painful nerve or joint with the icy-cold bag for a minute or two. Now hold the hot water bottle on the area for the same length of time. Keep alternating the two for 10–15 minutes. This treatment often brings dramatic relief.

❧ An alternative to the frozen peas method is to buy from the pharmacy 2 gel-filled plastic packs that can be either frozen or heated. Keep one in the freezer and heat the other as recommended. Use in the manner described above.

HOMEOPATHIC TREATMENT

All 6–30ᶜ, take 2–4 times daily:

🦋 Pain only during the day—Actaea rac.

🦋 Flushed, throbbing face—Belladonna.

🦋 Pain in jaw—Chamomilla.

Nose, blocked

If you don't have all these oils you can use what you have but keep the proportions the same.

> 2 teaspoons (10 ml) cajuput oil
>
> 2 teaspoons (10 ml) eucalyptus oil
>
> ½ teaspoon (2.5 ml) peppermint oil
>
> 20 drops clove oil
>
> 20 drops thyme oil
>
> TO MAKE: Mix all together in a small dropper bottle.
>
> TO USE: Sprinkle a few drops on a tissue and sniff or use as an inhalation (see Inhalations).

Nosebleeds

Sit the patient in an upright chair and ask them to pinch their nostrils firmly at the point before the bony part begins and to breathe through their mouth. Apply ice-cold packs (some frozen peas in a small bag are good) to the bridge of the nose and the back of the neck.

Try releasing the pressure and the cold packs after 5 minutes. If the bleeding continues, repeat the treatment.

If the bleeding doesn't stop after the above treatment medical help needs to be sought. If the bleeding happens frequently and for no apparent reason a doctor should be consulted.

HOMEOPATHIC TREATMENT

Take often during acute stage:

🦋 Particularly in children—Ferr. phos 12ᶜ.

🦋 Frequent—Hamamelis 12ᶜ.

🦋 Phosphorus 30ᶜ.

Nux vom. (*Nux vomica*) ❦ Homeopathic

Suited to thin, dark, nervy, irritable, quick tempered people who get sick from overindulgence in food or mental work.

USE TO TREAT

Acidity, colic, constipation, diarrhoea, fainting, flatulence, gall-bladder problems, influenza, insomnia, over indulgence, PMS, raw throat, travel sickness. Use after surgery (medical and dental) to clear anaesthetic from the system.

Oils ✿ See Aromatherapy & Essential oils

Ointments

Ointments are fun to make. A homemade ointment can, if carefully made, be superior to any commercial product. The herb oil can be made from either single or mixed herbs. Tinctures and essential oils may be added to strengthen the properties of the ointment.

Useful ointments include:

- ✿ **Comfrey:** for use on bruises, sprains, strains and to accelerate healing of fractures, cuts, ulcers and wounds.
- ✿ **Calendula:** a prime first-aid remedy for wounds, cuts, sores, abrasions, sore nipples, ulcers, sprains and to reduce inflammation and pain from measles and chickenpox spots.
- ✿ **Plantain:** for insect stings and bites of all kinds. (I don't use plantain alone but always put three times as much calendula and plantain as other herbs in a mixed healing cream.)

HERBAL HEALING OINTMENT

3 level tablespoons finely grated, firmly packed beeswax

80 g anhydrous lanolin (available from pharmacies)

4–5 tablespoons (80–100 ml) Herb oil base (see Herb oil base)

2 teaspoons (10 ml) tincture of myrrh (to make, see Tinctures)

2 teaspoons (10 ml) tincture of calendula (to make, see Tinctures)

20 drops mixed tea-tree or manuka and lavender oil

TO MAKE: *Melt the beeswax over a very low light, taking care not to overheat.*

Add the lanolin, stir until melted.

Slowly add the herb oil (see Herb oil base) made from herbs from the vulnerary list (see Vulneraries), don't re-harden the wax. Take off the heat, cool slightly.

Mix together the tinctures and essential oil and add slowly while stirring thoroughly to incorporate until the mixture is just beginning to thicken. Pour into jars.

ESSENTIAL OIL OINTMENT

3 level tablespoons finely grated, firmly packed beeswax

80 g anhydrous lanolin (available from pharmacies)

4–5 tablespoons (80–100 ml) Herb oil base

1 teaspoon (5 ml) tincture of myrrh

20 drops lavender oil

5 drops rosemary oil

5 drops thyme oil

TO MAKE: *Make as Herbal ointment above.*

Omega-3 essential fatty acids

These are found mainly in some fish oils and can be made by the body from alpha linolenic acid found principally in linseeds (flax) and linseed and canola oils.

They are a group of hormone-like unsaturated fatty acids that reduce inflammation, suppress blood clotting and thin the blood. Oily fish such as mackerel, sardines, salmon or tuna are good sources of omega-3 acids but if you don't like oily fish you can use ground linseed (flax) or linseed (flax) oil instead. As linseed oil (flax oil) becomes rancid very quickly it should be purchased in small quantities and stored out of the light and in the refrigerator. Use omega-3 oils regularly if you are in a 'heart attack risk' category, if you suffer from arthritis or an immune-system insufficiency complaint.

Orange (*Citrus aurantium*)

PART USED

Whole fruit.

HERB ACTIONS

Carminative, stimulant, stomachic, tonic.

USE TO TREAT

Used in drinks and the flesh is eaten for the vitamin C content and its delicious refreshing flavour. Oranges can be made into pomanders with cloves stuck into the flesh, the whole then rolled in spices. The pomander is hung in wardrobes and rooms to act as an air freshener and insect repellent.

ESSENTIAL OIL ACTION

Antibacterial, antidepressant, antiseptic, antispasmodic, detoxifying.

USE TO TREAT

Acne, cellulite, oily skin. Anxiety, stress, insomnia. Bronchitis, chills, colds, coughs, flu. Diarrhoea, constipation, flatulence, indigestion, nausea.

The oil has many of the properties of neroli oil but a different odour and may be used for several of the same purposes if neroli is too expensive. This is a 'happy' oil that brings sunshine into your day. As with most of the other citrus oils (bergamot excepted), orange oil keeps well for only about six months (buy little and often).

Caution: *Use only 1 per cent dilution. Do not use for extended periods. Phototoxic, avoid use on skin before exposure to sunlight.*

Oregano (*Origanum vulgare*)

HERB PART USED

Leaves and flowers.

HERB ACTIONS

See Marjoram.

USE TO TREAT

Poor digestion of food and to generally improve digestion. Eases headaches caused by digestive problems. Use to treat respiratory complaints, menstrual abdominal cramps, insomnia. A popular culinary herb. Oregano is pungent and a little goes a long way.

ESSENTIAL OIL ACTION

Oregano oil has too many potential hazards to recommend its use. It's a close relative of marjoram, which may be used as a substitute for oregano.

Osteoarthritis ✣ See Arthritis

Osteoporosis

Osteoporosis is a condition where the bones become porous and thin and are at risk of fracturing. Unfortunately, the first signs of osteoporosis are when a fracture occurs as until the condition is advanced there is no pain.

Women are five to six times more likely than men to develop osteoporosis. Until menopause they are continually renewing their skeletal structure. After menopause the oestrogen level and the amount of calcium retained by the bones drops. The condition appears to be hereditary with fine boned, small women being most at risk. Young women who are athletes or gymnasts, for example, can also risk developing osteoporosis if they have a low amount of body fat, as there is less stress on the bones and it is this stress that increases bone density.

There are many things that we can do to prevent getting osteoporosis. Recent studies show that if the problem has already occurred, there are ways to prevent it from worsening and may even help to reverse some of the damage.

Weight-bearing exercise such as walking, dancing and running is probably the most important factor in both prevention and retardation of osteoporosis as it provides changes in the metabolic processes implicated in calcium loss. If this exercise is done outdoors you will reap the additional benefit of increased vitamin D, which stimulates the absorption of calcium, from the action of the sun on your skin. The length of time that you exercise is more important than how strenuous it is—an hour of gentle walking is considered better than 15 minutes of very fast walking.

INTERNAL TREATMENT

There is one school of thought which states that eating calcium rich foods such as milk and cheese (particularly in childhood and adolescence) can prevent or minimise osteoporosis. Dr Andrew Weil in his book *Natural Health, Natural Medicine* takes an opposite view and states a high protein diet is contra-indicated and that consuming large quantities of milk and other dairy products can be counter-productive and result in a further loss of calcium through increased excretion of calcium in the urine. He strongly supports the weight-bearing exercise programme as being the best way to avoid and possibly regress osteoporosis. Encourage your family to exercise and to eat plenty of calcium and magnesium-rich foods such as broccoli, legumes, green-leafed vegetables, nuts and seeds to help to guard against osteoporosis (see Vitamins and Minerals).

- Cut down (or out) all refined sugars such as are found in biscuits, cakes, sweets and carbonated drinks.
- Limit the consumption of coffee, salt and alcohol as they can all cause calcium loss.
- Eat fresh fruit and vegetables every day to ensure an ample supply of vital trace elements.

DAILY SUPPLEMENTS FOR THOSE WHO ALREADY HAVE OSTEOPOROSIS

- 1000 mg calcium/magnesium citrate (citrate appears to inhibit the formation of kidney stones).

⚸ 1 mg folic acid.

ESSENTIAL OIL TREATMENT

Not appropriate.

HERBAL TREATMENT

If menopausal or if oestrogen deficiencies are apparent it will be appropriate to take herbal remedies for menopause (see Phyto-hormones and Menopause).

HOMEOPATHIC TREATMENT

Consult a homeopathic practitioner.

Oxymel

Oxymel is a honey mixture used as a base for herbal extracts. It acts as a soothing syrup and disguises the sometimes unpleasant taste of the herbs.

TO MAKE: *Boil 2 cups (500 ml) honey and ½ cup (125 ml) cider vinegar to a thick syrup taking care not to let it burn. Cool.*

TO USE: *To each 3 parts oxymel add 1 part tincture or triple-strength tea or decoction.*

DOSE: *½–1 teaspoon (2.5–5 ml) as needed, according to age.*

Pain

There is increasing attention being paid to the long-term management of chronic pain. The emphasis is on ways in which pain can be decreased or 'lived with' without resorting to addictive and/or damaging drugs. Pain, stress, fatigue and depression are closely connected and each has a profound effect on the others.

There is a theory that there is a 'gate' located in the spinal cord that can prevent pain signals from reaching the brain where they will be recognised as pain.[1] Stress and focusing on pain and fatigue seem to keep the gate open. It seems that various methods (see below) can close the gate. The body can also produce morphine-like substances known as endorphins that help to close the gate naturally. Endorphins appear to be released through massage, heat and cold, physical therapy, medications and exercise. Being positive also seems to play an important role in their production.

There is no single answer to the management of pain. The breaking of the pain/stress/depression cycle will vary with each individual and will also depend on the circumstances at the time. Some strategies will work well for a time and then lose their efficacy and a new method will need to be tried. With persistence, the cycle can almost always be broken. Help is now available to manage pain through the use of psychological strategies and/or pain clinics.

PSYCHOLOGICAL APPROACHES TO PAIN

Psychological studies have shown that although chronic pain has a physical component, it can be successfully controlled using mental strategies.[2]

In order to become proficient at pain management you need to become acutely aware of the mental processes associated with feeling pain. When you first begin driving a car, you need to observe every movement, this feels very clumsy. After a while the movements become automatic but the initial slow process was necessary in order for the skill to be mastered. In order to control pain, a similar process must happen. For example:

- Find an equivalent sensation similar to that being experienced, rating the pain level on a scale of 1–10 by comparing it with previously experienced pain. If you rate it against the worst pain you have ever experienced, you may find it quite bearable.

- Start writing down what your pain-related beliefs are, for example, 'what is the worst thing that can happen?', 'can I cope with the pain?', 'can I control the pain?'. In answering these questions, many people believe that they can neither cope with nor control the pain. However, research shows that one's beliefs about coping have a direct influence on pain intensity.[3] Therefore, efforts to change your beliefs about coping and controlling the pain will modify it. For more information contact your family GP or a psychologist who can refer you to a pain clinic. For those who would like to try some mental strategies on their own The following techniques are listed in order of effectiveness.[4] The comments on the strategies are my interpretations and I have often found cognitive activity to be the most effective for me.

MENTAL STRATEGIES

- **Pleasant imagery:** visualising a beautiful place and the things that are happening there, for example, a walk on a beach or through a forest, a river carrying the pain away.

* **Neutral imagery:** visualising a scene that isn't very stimulating or involving, for example, shopping or listening to a (boring) speech.
* **External focus of attention:** such as watching television or slides, reading, going to the movies, visiting with friends.
* **Rhythmic cognitive activity:** a mental exercise such as counting slowly backwards from 100 or 200 in threes, that occupies your mind to the exclusion of everything else.
* **Giving attention to the site of the pain:** Here are two examples but the most powerful are those that you devise for yourself.
  * imagining a shape and colour i.e. a red ball the size of a cricket ball; cooling the colour to pale green or blue and shrinking the size of the ball to a pea or smaller.
  * giving the pain a shape and form (a goblin) and imagining something that will incapacitate and drive the form from your body.

PHYSICAL APPROACHES TO PAIN

Acupuncture, yoga, TENS (Transcutaneous Electrical Nerve Stimulation), chiropractic and the Alexander technique are all disciplines that are useful for the relief of pain.

ESSENTIAL OIL TREATMENT

Essential oils used in baths and massage can be helpful to ease pain and the depression and stress that result from pain. Look under relevant headings i.e. Analgesics, Anti-inflammatories, Antispasmodics, Rubefacients, Calmatives, Sedatives or under complaints such as Arthritis, Burns.

HERBAL TREATMENT

Look under appropriate headings and complaints as for essential oils.

HOMEOPATHIC TREATMENT

Consult a homeopathic practitioner.

Palmarosa (Cymbopogon martini)

HERB PARTS USED

Grassy leaves.

HERBAL ACTIONS

Not known.

ESSENTIAL OIL ACTION

Antiseptic, antiviral, bactericidal, digestive stimulant, febrifuge, tonic.

USE TO TREAT

Intestinal infections, anorexia, anxiety, nervous exhaustion and stress-related conditions. In my opinion this is the most important skin oil for all types of skin. It moisturises, regulates production of sebum, regenerates skin cells, helps to heal acne, dermatitis, scars and sores. It is a useful oil to use in soap both for its effect on the skin and because the perfume is more persistent than that of most essential oils and is less likely to be destroyed by the caustic solution.

Pap smear

A procedure taken to determine whether abnormal cells are present in the cervix. Some women are resistant to having this test done as it involves a quite intimate procedure; if you are one such, then please, find a clinic with women doctors in attendance and surrender. The test should be done every two years and every year if you have a high risk factor until the age of 70. See also Cervical dysplasia.

Parsley (Petroselinum crispum)

HERB PART USED

Leaves for cooking. Seeds for essential oil. Seeds, root, leaves and stem are used medicinally.

HERB ACTIONS

Antispasmodic, carminative, diuretic, emmenagogue, expectorant, one of the best sources of vitamin C.

USE TO TREAT

Kidney stones and urinary tract infections. Its antispasmodic properties make it a valuable digestive aid—don't leave the decorative parsley on the side of the plate, eat it at the end of the meal! A tea from the leaves is used to treat late menstruation, jaundice, asthma, bronchitis, coughs, conjunctivitis and styes.
Caution: *Do not use if there is inflammation present in the kidneys.*

ESSENTIAL OIL ACTION

The oil may be used in massage, baths, compresses and fomentations to treat any of the above problems but as the oil is moderately toxic I prefer to use the fresh herb.
Caution: *Not to be used during pregnancy.*

Passionflower (*Passiflora incarnata*)

HERB PARTS USED

Whole plant.

HERBAL ACTION

Anodyne, antispasmodic, diaphoretic, sedative, hypnotic. A natural tranquilliser with none of the 'morning-after' effects of pharmaceutical tranquillisers.

USE TO TREAT

Colic, muscular spasm, pain, seizures and hysteria. Eases the pain of neuralgia and shingles. Helps to cure temporary insomnia.

ESSENTIAL OIL ACTION

None.

Patchouli (*Pogostemon patchouli*)

HERB PARTS USED
Leaves.

HERB ACTIONS
Dried leaves used in pot-pourris and sachets. In India the leaves are laid between clothes and bolts of cloth to act as an insect repellent.

ESSENTIAL OIL ACTION
Anti-inflammatory, antidepressant, antiseptic, deodorant, fungicidal, cell-regenerator, insect repellent.

USE TO TREAT
Acne, athlete's foot, chapped skin, eczema (weeping), mature skin. Depression, anger, insomnia, impotence, PMS. The heavy musky odour of this oil lingers for a long time making it a useful fixative. Use sparingly or it will overpower all other oils. If using in a blend for someone else, check first to see if they like the smell.

Pepper, Black ❦ See Black pepper

Peppermint (*Mentha piperita*)

HERB PART USED
Leaves.

HERB ACTIONS
Antibacterial, antiparasitic, anti-inflammatory, antispasmodic, antifungal.

USE TO TREAT
Headache, nerves, insomnia and migraine. When drunk as a tea with elderflower and yarrow it makes a first-rate treatment for influenza.

The clean, fresh taste of peppermint tea appeals to most people and is a good drink to enjoy after a meal as it cleanses the digestive tract of unwanted bacteria, relaxes the muscles of the digestive tract and eases indigestion.

Essential oil action

Analgesic, anti-inflammatory, antimicrobial, antiseptic, antispasmodic, antiviral, astringent, carminative, cholagogue, emmenagogue, expectorant, febrifuge, hepatic, nervine, stomachic, sudorific, vasoconstrictor.

Use to treat

Acne, dermatitis, ringworm, scabies. Neuralgia, muscular pain. Asthma, bronchitis, sinusitis. Catarrh, colds and influenza. Headaches and colds with lavender in inhalations (see Inhalations). Use enteric-coated peppermint oil (from pharmacies) for irritable bowel syndrome, colic, intestinal cramp.

This oil should never be used at more than 0.5–1 per cent. Not to be used in pregnancy or for the very young.

Perfumes

See Colognes and Aromatherapy & Essential oils, Enfleurage

Period pain

See Menstruation

Petitgrain (*Citrus aurantium bigardia* & other citrus varieties)

Herb parts used

Leaves and tips off the twigs from the bitter orange tree. The flowers of this tree are used to produce neroli oil.

Essential oil action

Antidepressant, antiseptic, antispasmodic, deodorant.

USE TO TREAT

Anxiety, depression, insomnia and lift the spirits. Acne, oily skin, oily dandruff, cellulite, fluid retention. Nausea, indigestion and flatulence. Unlike many of the citrus oils, petitgrain isn't phototoxic and so can be used on the skin even if it is to be exposed to sunlight. Petitgrain has many of the properties of neroli (being from the same tree) and, even though the perfume isn't quite the same (I prefer it to neroli), it is a perfectly acceptable and very much cheaper substitute. It can be used for long periods of time. As an ingredient in deodorants it is both a refreshing perfume and works quite well.

Pets

Pets can benefit greatly from herbs, oils and homeopathic remedies but remember that their sense of smell is very acute and the strong scent of essential oils, if not sufficiently diluted, may be quite distressing to them.

While I was writing this book, my daughter with whom we were staying was given a nice little dog called Casey. Neither we (nor the previous owner) had any idea that Casey was pregnant and we continued to be ignorant until the day that the pups were born! The fast building of a whelping box and the general trauma upset Casey so much that after the birth she became really savage—trying to bite anyone that went near the box. I sprinkled lavender oil in the vicinity of the bed and within 10 minutes she had completely calmed down. Another strong reminder of the power of essential oils.

Caution: *Some pets are highly sensitive to essential oils, in particular eucalyptus and tea-tree. If in doubt, use herbal treatments in preference to essential oils.*

ABSCESSES
ESSENTIAL OIL TREATMENT

Clean the area with a solution of 1 teaspoon salt in 1 cup (250 ml) boiled water. Apply a fomentation (see Fomentations) using 4 drops lavender or tea-tree oil every 3–4 hours until the abscess bursts. Keep the area clean using alternate lavender and tea-tree oil, using 1 drop every 3–4 hours.

Herbal treatment

Follow the suggestions for the above treatment using a strong tea of calendula, sage or oregano. When the abscess bursts, apply healing ointment (see Ointments) to the area.

Homeopathic treatment

All 30^c, give 3 times daily:
* Skin sensitive to touch—Hepar sulph.
* Tense and painful—Hypericum 30^c.

Arthritis

Mix finely chopped dandelion root and parsley and mix with the food.

ARTHRITIS MASSAGE OIL

½ *cup (125 ml) vegetable oil*
8 drops rosemary oil
8 drops eucalyptus oil
12 drops lavender oil
8 drops ginger oil

TO MAKE: *Mix together in a bottle. Shake well.*

TO USE: *Reach under the coat to the skin and massage the affected joints and the spine with long, firm but gentle movements.*

Bad breath

If there is a lot of tartar build-up on the teeth there is nothing that will get rid of the foul breath until the tartar has been removed by a veterinarian.

Once the teeth are clean, it's a fairly simple matter to keep them that way by using one or all of the following suggestions.
* Don't feed a diet of soft food. Dogs and cats need hard biscuits and bones to help to keep the teeth clean.

- Avoid milk and milk products—lactic acid has been implicated in tartar build-up.
- Feed raw (*never* cooked) bones two or three times a week. If the bone is meaty it will be the only meal required that day.
- *If* the animal will allow it, you can clean the teeth daily with the following tooth powder.

TOOTH POWDER FOR DOGS

¹/₄ cup bicarbonate of soda

2 tablespoons salt

1 drop myrrh oil

1 drop peppermint oil

TO MAKE: *Mix the bicarbonate of soda and the salt. Mix the oils into the powder stirring constantly. Sieve if necessary to avoid 'hot spots'.*

TO USE: *Dip either damp cotton wool or the softest toothbrush into the powder and gently clean the teeth and gums. Follow by offering the dog a drink of water.*

BRONCHITIS

Keep the animal in a warm, comfortable environment. Apply fomentations (see Fomentations), using 2 drops of eucalyptus oil. Rub the warm wet cloth over the chest and back. Repeat 4 hourly.

HOMEOPATHIC TREATMENT

All 30ᶜ, give 4 times daily:

- Hoarseness and cough—Phosphorus.
- Rattling mucous and sickness—Ipecac.
- Cough and wheezing on exposure to cold air—Hepar sulph.

BURNS & SCALDS

Immerse the burnt area in a bath of cold water. If the burn is on the head either use cold, very wet compresses or baste the head with cold water. Continue for 10 minutes. Sprinkle drops of lavender oil on the burn, give Rescue Remedy (see Bach Flower Remedies) for as long as the animal is in shock.

If the burn is severe seek the help of a veterinarian as soon as possible, in the meantime use lavender oil.

CUTS & BITES

Trim the hair or fur from around the wound if necessary. Bathe with a solution of 2 cups (500 ml) water, ½ teaspoon salt and 4 drops tea-tree oil.

Drip 1–2 drops of lavender oil, depending on size of the wound. Repeat every 4 hours.

HOMEOPATHIC TREATMENT

Give 4 hourly:
* Ferrum phos. 12^c.
* Rescue Remedy: use a few drops of Ledum 30^c and/or Hypericum 30^c to bathe the wound.

EAR PROBLEMS

Ear shaking or scratching can be a symptom of infection, a build-up of wax or a grass seed in the ear. The following oil will help to loosen the wax or grass seed and bring it to the outside of the ear where it can be removed. *Never* poke anything into the ear. If the problem persists consult a veterinarian.

EAR DROPS

1 tablespoon (20 ml) vegetable oil

2 garlic oil capsules squeezed into the vegetable oil

4 drops lavender oil

TO MAKE: *Mix together in a tiny bottle. Shake well.*

TO USE: *Using an eye-dropper, drip 5 drops of the formula into each ear every 4 hours. Massage around the base of the ear to help the oil to penetrate. Remove excess oil or wax that has come to the external ear with cotton wool dipped in a mixture of 1 part distilled witch-hazel in 3 parts water.*

FLEAS

It's useless to treat your pet for fleas unless you treat their surroundings at the same time. Fleas spend most of their life on carpets, in sand or animal bedding and only jump onto humans or animals to feed from the host's blood. The life-cycle of the flea is about 2 weeks so treatments need to be diligently carried out for this length of time.

Brisk brushing the coat of the dog or cat and combing with a flea comb *every day* will really upset the fleas as they don't like to be disturbed. Visiting dogs with fleas can undo all your good work and I caused a few raised eyebrows when, having declared my home a 'flea-free zone', I asked all visitors with dogs to leave them at home or in the car if there was a chance that they had fleas!

FLEA-BAN CARPET POWDER

3 cups bicarbonate of soda

4 tablespoons borax

40 drops lavender oil

20 drops citronella oil

20 drops cypress oil

TO MAKE: *Mix the powder thoroughly and then drip the oils in slowly while stirring to prevent lumps forming. Store in a jar or container with a sprinkler lid.*

TO USE: *Sprinkle the powder onto the carpets at night, vacuum the following day. Repeat every 2–3 days for 2 weeks, then once a week.*

ANTI-FLEA OIL BLEND FOR FLEA COLLARS

1 teaspoon (5 ml) eucalyptus oil

1 teaspoon (5 ml) cedarwood or pennyroyal oil

1 teaspoon (5 ml) citronella oil

4 garlic oil capsules, pierced and squeezed into the formula

1 teaspoon (5 ml) thyme oil

1½ tablespoons (30 ml) vodka

TO MAKE: *Mix together in a small bottle. Shake well to combine.*

TO USE: *Soak a cloth collar in 1–2 teaspoons (5–10 ml) of the formula, allow to dry before using on the animal. The flea collar will need to be re-treated every month in order to be effective.*

The collar won't work as well on large dogs as the fleas have a large area in which to get away from the smell of the oils

BEDDING: *Wash bedding in very hot water, rinse in cool water to which you have added 1–2 teaspoons (5–10 ml) eucalyptus oil. Hang in the sun to dry.*

BEDS: *Scrub baskets and wooden beds with hot water, rinse with cool water to which you have added 1 teaspoon (5 ml) of the flea-collar oil blend. Leave all day in the sun to dry.*

SHAMPOOING: *Add 2–4 drops of the oil blend to 1–2 tablespoons (20–40 ml) shampoo (depending on the animal's size). Add a further 2–4 drops to the final rinse.*

BETWEEN SHAMPOOS: *Add 4 drops of anti-flea oil blend to a small bowl of water. Soak a flannel, wring some of the water out. Rub through the animal's coat in the opposite direction to the hair growth paying particular attention to the areas behind the ears, above the tail and the back of the neck. If the hair is fairly short, a flea comb may be used.*

GARDEN: *Plant as many of the following herbs as possible around the areas where the dog spends much of its time. The herbs can also be dried and used to stuff a mattress cover to use as a dog or cat bed. Use fennel, pennyroyal, rosemary, rue, tansy and garlic.*

Spray sandy areas with 1 teaspoon (5 ml) eucalyptus oil in 4 litres of water every day for 2 weeks.

Phosphorus (*Phosphorus*) ❀ Homeopathic

Suited to tall, slender people with delicate, fair complexions. They are bright, cheerful and open with quick perceptions, over-imaginative and dramatic.

USE TO TREAT

Bronchitis, cough, heartburn, laryngitis, nosebleed, styes, vomiting.

Phytohormones

'Plant hormones': these are hormone-like substances that can be used in situations that are currently treated with pharmaceutical synthetic/natural pharmaceutical hormones such as oestrogen, progesterone and testosterone. The herbal treatments aren't as strong as prescribed hormones but neither do they appear to carry the risks or side effects. Phyto-oestrogens have a peculiar capacity to reduce an over-active level or increase an underactive level of oestrogen in the body making them suitable for both PMS (oestrogen excess) and menopausal symptoms (oestrogen deficiency).

Dr John Lee's recent research (see Bibliography) also demonstrates that natural progesterone such as found in wild yam (*Dioscorea villosa*) preparations is important for naturally balancing women's hormones.

Some of the most notable plants are:

- **Oestrogen-like activity:** soya beans (soya milk, tofu, tempeh as well as beans), dong quai, false unicorn root, fennel, hops, liquorice.
- **Progesterone-like activity:** chaste tree, ginseng, and wild yam.
- **Testosterone-like activity:** ginseng, damiana, saw palmetto.

Pimples

If you suffer from persistent outbreaks of pimples your diet may be inadequate or you may suffer from constipation resulting in a build up of toxins. *Never squeeze pimples* as the bacteria will spread and cause a further outbreak, squeezing can also cause scarring.

INTERNAL TREATMENT

- Drink 6–8 glasses of filtered or bottled water every day.
- Make sure that you eat several serves of fruit and vegetables daily.
- If you suffer from constipation, sprinkle 1–2 dessertspoons of linseeds or psyllium seed over breakfast cereal or over yoghurt.
- Eat 2–4 cups 'live' yoghurt daily.
- Avoid fatty and fried foods, and spices.

DAILY SUPPLEMENTS

- 1000 mg vitamin C with bioflavonoids.
- 10 000 iu beta-carotene.
- 1 vitamin B complex tablet.
- 1000 mg garlic oil capsules 3 times daily or 2–3 teaspoons 'Long-life juice' 3 times daily.

ESSENTIAL OIL TREATMENT

Apply 1 drop of tea-tree or garlic oil directly onto the pimple.

HERBAL TREATMENT

- Washing the area with a strong tea of calendula petals will prevent the spread of infection. Follow with a dab of calendula ointment.
- Dabbing the pimple with a cut clove of garlic is a proven way of getting rid of pimples but, because of the smell, you might like to reserve this treatment for a time when you are alone.

HOMEOPATHIC TREATMENT

- Pustules that have yellow tops—Kali. sulph and/or Hepar Sulph.
- Blistery pimples—Rhus. tox.
- To cleanse the blood—Echinacea.
- Caused by allergy, stress or emotions—Nat. mur.

Pine (*Pinus sylvestris, P. pinaster*)

HERB PART USED

Needles. The seeds found in pine cones are edible, nutritious and delicious.

ESSENTIAL OIL ACTION

Antibacterial, antirheumatic, antiseptic, antispasmodic, deodorant, disinfectant, stimulating.

USE TO TREAT

Pulmonary complaints such as colds, catarrh, coughs, bronchitis and sinusitis. In massage oils pine warms stiff, tired, overworked muscles. Most people have enjoyed a bath containing pine bath crystals, using the circulatory stimulating properties to refresh and invigorate, to clear mental exhaustion and dispel depression and anxiety.

Caution: *Pine oil can be a skin irritant. Use only 0.5–1 per cent in blends and 2–3 drops in a bath blended with 1 teaspoon (5 ml) vegetable oil or full cream milk.*

Planetary signs of herbs & oils

Many of the great herbalists (Culpeper being the main one) attributed planetary signs to the plants. There are differing opinions as to which herb goes with which planet. The lists below are for your pleasure and if you 'resonate' better with some herbs or oils not listed under your sun sign then maybe the ones that appeal to you are allied more with your moon or rising sign.

These plants and oils can be used in any of the preparations that you make for yourselves, family and friends, and make a more personal and unique statement.

Rosemary is considered esoterically to be one of the most powerful plants. If you can't obtain one of the suggestions below then you can replace it with rosemary.

SUN SIGN	ESSENTIAL OILS	HERBS
ARIES	frankincense, ginger, petitgrain, black pepper	*fennel, ginger, pine, juniper, frankincense*
TAURUS	cardamom, patchouli, rose, thyme, ylang-ylang	*oak moss, patchouli, rose petals, vanilla bean*
GEMINI	dill, lavender, lemongrass, mints	*clover, dill, lavender, lemongrass, peppermint*
CANCER	chamomile, lemon, palmarosa	*eucalyptus, jasmine, lemon balm, myrrh, sandalwood*

LEO	frankincense, lime, neroli, orange, petitgrain, rosemary	*cinnamon, frankincense, juniper, nutmeg*
VIRGO	clary sage, cypress, melissa, patchouli	*caraway, cypress, lavender, peppermint, patchouli*
LIBRA	cardamon, rose geranium, palmarosa, ylang-ylang	*catnep, chamomile, marjoram, mugwort, rose petals*
SCORPIO	black pepper, cardamon, pine	*basil, cumin, ginger, myrrh, pine*
SAGITTARIUS	clove, rosemary, sandalwood	*cedar, clove, frankincense, juniper, sassafras*
CAPRICORN	cypress, myrrh, patchouli, vetivert	*comfrey, cypress, oak moss, vervain, vetivert*
AQUARIUS	cypress, lavender, patchouli, benzoin	*benzoin, lavender, mints, nutmeg, patchouli*
PISCES	jasmine, sandalwood, ylang-ylang	*eucalyptus, jasmine, lemon, sage, sandalwood, ylang-ylang*

Plantain (*Plantago lanceolata, P. major*)

HERB PART USED

Leaves, seeds.

HERB ACTIONS

Astringent, demulcent, diuretic, expectorant, haemostatic.

USE TO TREAT

Bleeding, encourage healing and ease the pain of insect bites, cuts, scratches, haemorrhoids and sores. Use teas to treat bronchitis, catarrh, coughs, colds and all respiratory problems. The seeds of *Plantago psyllium* are used to treat constipation and are used in many proprietary brands sold for this purpose. Use double quantities of plantain leaf in infused oil for healing ointments.

ESSENTIAL OIL ACTION

None (see above for use of infused oil).

Post-natal depression ❧ See Pregnancy

PMS (Pre-menstrual syndrome/tension)

This troublesome problem affects one third of all women to a greater or lesser degree and occurs anything up to two weeks before bleeding begins. The symptoms can be mood swings, stress and tension; headaches and fatigue; depression, irritability and forgetfulness; weight gain, abdominal bloating and breast tenderness.

A wide variety of hormonal changes cause PMS but the most common cause seems to be excessive oestrogen and low progesterone production. This causes symptoms such as irritability, mood swings, nervous tension and anxiety.

Use a body brush to skin-brush before showering. Begin at the feet and using a circular motion work up the legs, body and arms. This stimulates the lymphatic system.

INTERNAL TREATMENT

- Eat lots of complex carbohydrates such as wholegrains, beans, fruit and vegetables as they help to excrete the excess oestrogen from the body.
- Cut out alcohol, tea and coffee during the time when the symptoms are most pronounced.
- Cut out refined carbohydrates and foods such as biscuits, cakes and sweets.
- Cut down on dairy foods.

DAILY SUPPLEMENTS

- 1 vitamin B complex tablet.

- ✿ 100 mg vitamin B6.
- ✿ 2000–3000 mg borage (starflower) oil or evening primrose oil.
- ✿ 500 mg vitamin C with bioflavonoids twice daily.
- ✿ 250 iu vitamin E (d-alpha tocopherol).
- ✿ 400–600 mg magnesium.
- ✿ 15 mg zinc.
- ✿ 2 capsules dong quai 3 times a day; discontinue a few days prior to menstruation and recommence when menstruation has finished.
- ✿ 1000 mg garlic oil capsules 3 times daily or 2–3 teaspoons 'Long-life juice' 3 times daily.

Essential oil treatment

DEPRESSION & IRRITABILITY
20 drops chamomile oil
10 drops bergamot oil
10 drops petitgrain oil
¼ cup (60 ml) vegetable oil
TO MAKE: *Mix together in a small bottle.*
TO USE: *Massage into the skin after bathing or showering.*
Three drops each of the above oils may be used in a bath.

FLUID RETENTION
15 drops rosemary oil
15 drops geranium oil
¼ cup (60 ml) vegetable oil
TO MAKE: *Mix together in a small bottle*
TO USE: *Massage into the skin after bathing or showering. Five drops each of the above essential oils may be used in a bath.*

Herbal treatment

- ✤ Drinking dandelion leaf tea will help to disperse excess fluid.
- ✤ Drink chamomile tea for its calming effect in place of regular tea or coffee.

❧ Chaste tree tea or tablets (available from health-food stores) as directed.

❧ 500-1000 mg skullcap, passionflower or valerian at night.

HOMEOPATHIC TREATMENT

All 30^c, take twice daily from day 21 onwards:

❀ Breast tenderness—Calc. carb.

❀ Depression and irritability—Lycopodium.

❀ Increase in weight—Graphites.

❀ Indifference—Sepia.

Pot-pourris

Pot-pourris are attractive mixtures of dried flowers, leaves, cones, seeds, fruit stones, coarse sawdust, and any other eye-pleasing materials.

Dried plants often lose much of their scent and the addition of essential oils and a fixative will enhance and preserve the aroma. To dry the leaves and flowers see Herbs, Drying herbs in the microwave. Health-food and variety stores often sell dried-plant materials suitable for making pot-pourris. (See also Sachets, Air fresheners and Colognes & Perfumes.)

TO MAKE: *Mix your chosen material in a large sealed container or polythene bag.*

For each 60 g of plant material add 2 teaspoons powdered or crushed fixative and 2 teaspoons of salt. Mix well. Add essential oils, a drop at a time, until the perfume is as strong as you want.

Leave for 2 or more weeks for the mixture to blend, stir every few days.

TO USE: *Fill small lidded containers or sachets. Remove the lid occasionally to release the perfume—if the pot-pourri is left uncovered the oils will evaporate very quickly.*

Refresh with essential oils when the scent becomes faint.

FIXATIVES

Choose from the following: gum mastic, myrrh, oak moss, orris root, sandalwood, sweet flag root.

PLANT MATERIALS

It's interesting to choose either a colour combination or a theme.

POT-POURRI	MATERIAL
FLOWER GARDEN	A delicate mixture of flowers such as calendula, carnations, chamomile flowers, geranium leaves, jasmine, lavender, lemon and orange flowers, rose petals, violet flowers
CITRUS	Lemon verbena (the perfume lasts for years), lemon-scented geranium, lemon balm, dried citrus peel, peppermint leaves
FOREST	Pine needles, tiny cones, scented gum leaves, coarse wood shavings
SPICE	Whole nutmeg, vanilla pod, cinnamon sticks, cloves, whole coriander and cumin seeds

ESSENTIAL OILS

Try to match the oils to the blend to enhance the overall effect. Be imaginative—for instance, Spice could have a little citrus oil with clove and cinnamon oils to enliven the whole scent.

Poultices

Used to apply heat or cold to the skin to soothe sprains, draw pus or foreign bodies from a wound, relieve chest congestion, draw boils to a head and blood to the area.

TO MAKE: *Mash or blend fresh herbs into a paste with either boiling or iced water/tea/decoction depending on the complaint. A few drops of essential oil or tincture may be added for strength. If bread, slippery elm powder or mashed potato is added to the mixture it keeps it hot/cold for longer.*

TO USE: *Spread the mixture on a piece of cloth, fold the cloth to enclose and test the heat on the inside of your wrist. Place the poultice on the injury, cover with plastic wrap and a thick towel to retain the heat. The same mixture may be used 3–4 times and reheated between two plates over a pan of boiling water. Use frequently for the first 2–3 hours.*

Pregnancy ❦ See also Aromatherapy & Essential oils and Babies

Many women are led to believe that during pregnancy they will blossom as never before, become Madonna-like and tranquilly await the birth of their baby. This myth may plunge some women into even greater gloom than their overworked hormones are already creating—they feel a failure of not living up to the story-book image.

There are steps you can take to ease you through the difficulties that you may experience during pregnancy. You will need plenty of rest and fun; a balanced diet with lots of fresh fruit, vegetables, wholegrain bread, fish and chicken and very little high-fat food; herbs and essential oils to ease nausea, backache and depression.

DAILY SUPPLEMENTS

* Vitamin B6 plus a vitamin B complex tablet.
* Zinc.
* Iron.

See Vitamins and Minerals for foods containing these vitamins.

MORNING SICKNESS
INTERNAL TREATMENT

* Morning sickness has been associated with low blood sugar. A ginger capsule or a cup of ginger tea and a couple of dry water biscuits before raising the head from the pillow in the morning (eat on your side not your back to prevent choking) may help to avoid nausea.
* Avoid greasy and fatty food and eat plenty of fruit, vegetables and wholegrains.

- Eat 6–8 small meals a day rather than 3 large ones.
- Many people have experienced complete relief from morning sickness and nausea after one or two visits to an acupuncturist.
- If sickness is prolonged or frequent and causing distress consult a health professional as the vomiting may be indicative of a more serious problem.

ESSENTIAL OIL TREATMENT

Keep a bottle of spearmint or ginger oil next to the bed and sniff the aroma on waking.

HERBAL TREATMENT

Ginger or spearmint tea (no more than 2 small cups a day) or crystallised ginger taken whenever there is nausea.

HOMEOPATHIC TREATMENT

All 6–12^c, take as required to control nausea. Check with a practitioner if symptoms persist.

- Nausea with coated tongue—Nux vomica.
- Continual nausea with vomiting—Ipecac.
- Empty, nauseous feeling better after eating—Petroleum.

STRETCHMARKS

ANTI-STRETCHMARK MASSAGE OIL

6 tablespoons (120 ml) almond oil

2 tablespoons (40 ml) wheatgerm oil

2 tablespoons (40 ml) olive oil

40 drops mandarin oil

20 drops chamomile oil

20 drops lavender oil

TO MAKE: *Mix together in a bottle, shake well. Leave for 1–2 days to blend.*

TO USE: *Massage onto the thighs, abdomen and breasts once or twice daily from the fifth month of pregnancy.*

PERINEUM MASSAGE

Massage the perineum (the area between the vaginal opening and the anus) for 5 minutes daily with a mixture of olive and wheatgerm for the last two months before the birth. This has been shown to lessen the risk of tearing.

LOWER BACK PAIN

BACK MASSAGE OIL

For use after four months of pregnancy where there is no history of miscarriage.

2 tablespoons (40 ml) vegetable oil

2 drops chamomile oil

1 drop lavender oil

1 drop ylang-ylang or mandarin oil

TO MAKE: *Mix together well.*

TO USE: *Massage during pregnancy should be very soft and gentle. Use the oil to help to relieve lower back pain.*

BATHS

Baths (see Baths) can be wonderfully soothing to an expectant mum especially during the last few months when your body feels heavy. Don't have the water very hot and never use more than 4–5 drops of essential oil mixed with 1 teaspoon (5 ml) vegetable oil. A good blend would be:

1 teaspoon (5 ml) vegetable oil

2 drops mandarin oil

2 drops grapefruit oil

1 drop sandalwood or ylang-ylang

BREASTS

BREAST FEEDING

It's beyond the scope of this book to talk in depth about this subject but I would urge you, even if you have decided not to breast feed, to consider feeding for the first vital days when the baby will receive

colostrum. This is a thin creamy coloured fluid, which contains
constituents vital for the baby's immunity to disease.

BREAST CARE
If nipples are massaged for a few weeks prior to the birth there is less
chance of getting sore and cracked nipples (horribly painful) once the
baby has started feeding. Make the following oil or ointment and
begin to use it several weeks before the baby is due. If you prefer,
Calendula ointment is also available in health-food stores.

NIPPLE OINTMENT
A
2 tablespoons coconut oil
1 tablespoon finely grated cocoa butter
2 teaspoons honey
2 tablespoons (40 ml) calendula infused oil (see Aromatherapy &
Essential oils, Extraction of essential oils)
B
2 tablespoons (40 ml) distilled water
C
10 drops borage (starflower) oil or evening primrose oil
2 × 500 iu capsules vitamin E
TO MAKE: *Melt the ingredients for A very gently in a small pan (a*
double boiler is even better). Melt but don't overheat.

Warm the ingredients for B until a little hotter than hand heat, add
and stir until no water droplets can be seen.

Add the ingredients for C squeezing the oil capsules into the
ointment. Mix until all is well incorporated. Pot.
TO USE: *See the instructions following Nipple oil.*

NIPPLE OIL
2 tablespoons (40 ml) almond oil
1 teaspoon (5 ml) wheatgerm oil
1 teaspoon (5 ml) calendula infused oil (see Aromatherapy &

Essential oil, Extraction of essential oils), this oil can be bought from health-food stores if you can't make your own
TO MAKE: *Mix all in a little bottle. Shake well. Keep refrigerated.*
TO USE: *Massage the ointment or oil into the nipples and surrounding area with the thumb and first two fingers using a firm, rolling movement. Use the treatment as often as possible before the birth and between feeds after the birth. Be sure to wash the nipple clean of cream or oil before feeding the baby.*

LABOUR

Labour is, as the word suggests, very hard work. The needs and desires of the mother-to-be are paramount and will vary with individuals. Some mothers need constant reassurance that they are doing well and that it will be over soon, others (like me!) don't want to be talked to or even touched very much, other than have a hand to hold when things get busy.

At the beginning of labour enjoy a warm bath to which you have added 6 drops of lavender oil. The first stages of labour, when there is some time between contractions, can really drag on and the mother can become agitated anticipating the next contraction. It makes it easier if you find something to do between contractions—reading, walking, watching television—anything rather than sitting or lying down waiting. Physical activity (I used to vacuum carpets and bake cakes) can also help to speed things along. Add a few drops of lavender or geranium to an oil burner to diffuse into the air.

A few comforting things may be soft music, a hot water bottle for a sore lower back, lip salve for dry lips (see Lips, Lemon lips), diluted apple juice to keep the blood sugar up and ice cubes to suck if the mouth is dry. Homeopathic arnica and hypericum can be used for pain during labour and for after-birth pains. Rescue Remedy will prove very useful if the mother-to-be is nervous or if labour is lengthy.

The main thing is that the atmosphere in the delivery room should be as calm and tranquil as possible, and essential or herb oils can help enormously. They can be used to scent the air and also be used in blends to massage the feet and lower back as few women in labour can tolerate massage on the abdomen. The mother should guide the person conducting the massage as to the movements that are most comfortable and helpful.

The best oils to use during labour are the following but the choice is obviously dictated by the mother-to-be: lavender for its analgesic, antiseptic, anti-inflammatory, anti-viral, anti-shock and calming properties and its soft and gentle fragrance and very affordable price; jasmine for its antidepressant, anti-inflammatory, antiseptic, pain-relieving and contraction-strengthening properties (some people find the perfume of jasmine overpowering); clary sage for antibacterial, antidepressant, antispasmodic, muscle-relaxant, mildly analgesic and birth-facilitating properties; geranium to help uterine contractions and for its calming and antidepressant effect.

BIRTHING MASSAGE OIL

1 tablespoon (20 ml) almond oil

6 drops lavender oil

2 drops jasmine or geranium oil

2 drops clary sage oil

AFTER THE BIRTH
ESSENTIAL OIL TREATMENT

The perineum may be sore after the birth but can be eased by massaging with the Perineum oil (above) to which 2 drops of lavender have been added to each teaspoon (5 ml).

A sitz bath is very soothing for a sore perineum. Choose a bowl large enough to sit in (or run enough water into the bath to cover the lower hips), add warm water, 2 tablespoons salt and 2 drops each of lavender and tea-tree oils in 1 tablespoon of vegetable oil or full-cream milk, or an extra-strong tea of lavender and calendula. Agitate the water thoroughly before sitting in the bath. Soak for 10 minutes.

Herbal treatment

To help the uterus to contract use any of the following herbs either singly or in combination: raspberry, squaw vine, black cohosh taken as a tea (1 cup 3 times daily); a tincture (15 drops in 2 tablespoons water 3 times daily) or as capsules (as directed).

Homeopathic treatment

All 30ᶜ:

* To help uterus to contract—Caulophylum, take every hour for four hours then 4 times daily.
* Bruising—Arnica, take 4 times daily.
* Soreness—Calendula, take 4 times daily.

Post-natal depression

Some people have difficulty understanding or sympathising with post-natal depression. This is unfortunate as the new mother feels guilty enough about it without the added burden of disapproval. The hormonal changes that take place after the birth are as great or greater than those that occur during the first months of pregnancy. The depression can range from mild (experienced by most women on the second or third day after the birth) to very severe. First-time mothers have the additional burden of being afraid that they won't 'cope' or that the baby will get sick. Have plenty of rest. Once a day, while your baby is asleep, pamper yourself with a bath, snooze, good book or whatever makes you feel relaxed. You will have more energy and enthusiasm to cope with the baby and household chores.

I have heard two wonderful tips from a midwife:

* If you have a short stay in hospital or have a home birth, *stay in your nightie during the day for up to 10 days*. Visitors who see you fully dressed assume that you are once more in charge of the household and will wait to be offered hospitality. Visitors who find you in your nightie spring into 'caring' mode and rush around making cups of tea, washing dishes, etc.
* If friends phone or if you phone friends to announce the birth the conversation should go like this 'Would you like to come

around to see the baby on Tuesday evening (morning) and Teresa (or whatever your midwife's name is) says would you bring dinner (lunch)?' This apparently provokes a delighted response of 'Yes, I'd love to'.

Use the following oils to lift your spirits and give confidence.

BYE-BYE BABY BLUES BLEND

30 drops bergamot oil

30 drops lavender oil

20 drops geranium or clary sage oil

20 drops grapefruit or mandarin oil

TO MAKE: *Mix together in a little bottle.*

TO USE: *Add 10 drops to 1 teaspoon (5 ml) vegetable oil for a bath, agitate the water well to disperse the oils.*

Sprinkle 2–3 drops on a wet flannel and use as a final rub after showering.

Use a few drops in an oil burner to perfume the air.

Add 15 drops to 1 tablespoon (20 ml) vegetable oil for a massage.

Caution: *There are a few oils that are not safe to use during pregnancy. Check the lists below before using any essential oils. (See also Aromatherapy & Essential oils, Pregnancy.)*

OILS TO USE DURING THE FIRST FOUR MONTHS OF PREGNANCY

Use 1 per cent dilution only in oil blends and 4–5 drops in the bath: ginger (to sniff if nauseous), grapefruit, mandarin, neroli, spearmint, ylang-ylang.

OILS TO USE DURING THE LAST SIX MONTHS OF PREGNANCY

Use 1 per cent only in blends and 4–5 drops only in the bath: chamomile, grapefruit, geranium and rose geranium, lavender, mandarin, orange, petitgrain, spearmint, ylang-ylang.

Preservatives

Without the addition of preservatives, most home-made preparations that contain moist ingredients (herb teas and decoctions in particular) will last for only a few days, even with refrigeration. In order to keep these preparations mould and bacteria free it's necessary to use some form of preservative which either kills or inhibits the growth of bacteria and acts as an antioxidant to slow down oxidisation.

I have been using the preservative Phenoxitol (Phenoxyethanol) for about 12 years now and in that time haven't received a single report of any adverse skin reactions. When I have included this preservative in formulations in my other books, some people have experienced problems buying it so I have added (in brackets) the chemical name for this product.

The suppliers listed at the back of this book may have other preservatives such as grapefruit seed extract that you may wish to consider. **Caution:** *Strict attention must always be paid to the percentage of preservative used and this must never be exceeded. Phenoxitol is used at a concentration of 1 per cent (that is 1 g to every 99 g of other ingredients).*

Prostate problems

The suggestions in this section must only be followed after an examination by a doctor has ruled out anything more serious.

The prostate gland is situated behind the base of the penis and at the base of the bladder. The prostate surrounds the urethra and bacteria can travel through the urethra, and settle in the prostate causing acute or chronic infection. This infection can cause pain and tenderness in the area of the prostate, pelvic area and lower back.

In older men there may be a benign swelling of the prostate which causes pressure on the urinary passage, this in turn leads to problems with urination; difficulty 'getting started', slow weak stream, stopping and starting of urine flow, frequency of desire to urinate and some dribbling.

It is often useful to try the 'Kegel exercise' following which has the effect of massaging the prostate gland.

KEGEL EXERCISE

Between urinating, firmly tighten the muscles that you use to stop the flow of urine. Repeat 10–15 times. Do this five times a day.

INTERNAL TREATMENT

- Drink lots of filtered or bottled water to help to increase the flow of urine. Replace tea and coffee with dandelion coffee. Avoid alcohol.
- Eat plenty of fruit, vegetables, wholegrain bread and cereals, nuts, legumes and a handful of pumpkin seeds every day.

DAILY SUPPLEMENTS

There are formulae available in health-food stores and through naturopaths that contain all the most important supplements needed to treat problems of the prostate gland. The formula should ideally contain zinc (picolinate) and EFAs (essential fatty acids) among the other ingredients. Some formulae also contain saw palmetto, if not this can be purchased separately and taken as directed.

- Panax ginseng as directed.
- 3000 mg borage (starflower) oil or evening primrose oil.
- 2 × 10 000 mg cranberry capsules or unsweetened cranberry juice.

ESSENTIAL OIL TREATMENT

Not appropriate.

HERBAL TREATMENT

As Daily supplements above.

HOMEOPATHIC TREATMENT

Consult a homeopathic practitioner.

Psoriasis

Psoriasis is a skin condition characterised by thick, scaly, pink patches of cells with overlapping silvery scales. It usually appears on the scalp, back of the wrists, elbows, knees and ankles.

Psoriasis often runs in families and seems to be caused by cells that begin to grow too quickly and so can't be shed as fast as they need to. The condition is very difficult to treat and all the suggestions below may have to be tried over a long period. The reason the condition happens isn't easy to ascertain and varies with the individual.

Stress is often a factor with the immune system becoming compromised and the body failing to regulate its own cell production. If you feel that this could be your problem join a meditation group, take a holiday, and if possible change your job—look at every aspect of your life that may need a change. Read the Stress section for more suggestions.

An under-functioning liver is another possible cause with the over consumption of fats, refined carbohydrates and/or alcohol often being the reason.

I once spent time with a person who suffered badly from psoriasis. He would come home from work and eat a 2 litre tub of ice cream washed down with a large can of fruit in heavy syrup. This man was not a glutton but he hated his job and this food was his subconscious 'security blanket'. He had (also subconsciously) chosen the food that would possibly 'feed' his psoriasis. He changed his job and dietary habits, spent more time 'smelling the flowers' and is now free from the skin complaint.

Many people find that their skin improves after exposure to sunlight, and recent reports indicate that sufferers may have a faulty vitamin D metabolism. Taking a walk in the sunshine either in the early morning or late in the afternoon can often prove beneficial.

INTERNAL TREATMENT

- Cut down on animal protein (particularly offal), sugar, fats and alcohol. Eat more fruit, vegetables, wholemeal bread and cereals, pulses and legumes and other fibre foods.
- Eat liberally of the foods containing the omega-3 acids such as sardines, mackerel, salmon and tuna. Or take 1–2 tablespoons fresh linseed (flax) oil daily.

❧ Try excluding milk and milk products from the diet for a month to see if there is any improvement.

DAILY SUPPLEMENTS

❧ 5000–10 000 iu beta-carotene.
❧ 1 multi-vitamin tablet.
❧ 1 vitamin B complex tablet.
❧ 500 iu vitamin E (d-alpha tocopherol).
❧ 100 mg vitamin B6.
❧ 25 mg zinc.
❧ 1000 mg vitamin C with bioflavonoids twice daily.
❧ 100 mg milk thistle.

ESSENTIAL OIL TREATMENT

MASSAGE OIL BLEND
½ cup (125 ml) vegetable oil
30 drops lavender oil
30 drops bergamot oil
10 drops rosemary oil
10 drops tea-tree oil
TO MAKE: *Mix together in a small bottle.*
TO USE: *Massage over the entire body after showering or bathing.*

HERBAL TREATMENT

❧ Drink 3 cups of dandelion coffee instead of regular tea or coffee.
❧ Massage affected areas with calendula ointment (see Ointments).
❧ Drink decoctions of yellow dock and burdock root 3 times daily.
❧ Use burdock root decoction as a wash for affected skin.

HOMEOPATHIC TREATMENT

All 6–30ᶜ, take 3 times daily:
❧ In tidy, intelligent people—Arsen. alb.
❧ Cautious 'dithery' people—Graphites.
❧ Oversensitive people—Hepar. sulph.

Psyllium seed (*Plantago ovata*)

HERB PARTS USED

Seed husks.

HERB ACTIONS

Mucilaginous soluble fibre.

USE TO TREAT

High blood cholesterol, constipation.

Pulsatilla (*Pusatilla nigricans*) ✲ Homeopathic

Suited to people with fair hair and complexions and blue eyes; and to those who are emotional, gentle, affectionate and shy, tending to be overweight and emotionally moody and changeable.

USE TO TREAT

Acne, arthritis, catarrh, cystitis, depression, diarrhoea, fainting, flatulence, headache, incontinence, menstrual pain, menopausal hot flushes, PMS, prostate problems, tinnitus, varicose veins.

Raynaud's disease

Raynaud's disease is characterised by sudden episodes of blueness, followed by pallor and coldness of fingers and toes. This may be accompanied by an uncomfortable feeling of fullness. The episode may last for one or several hours. It is caused by a sudden constriction of small arteries but there is no definite trigger established. There are theories that smokers may suffer more episodes than non-smokers, and that sudden anger or fear or exposure to cold may trigger an attack.

Red clover (*Trifolium pratense*)

HERB PART USED

Flowers.

HERB ACTIONS

Alterative, antispasmodic, diuretic, expectorant.

USE TO TREAT

Psoriasis and childhood eczema. Coughs, bronchitis, whooping cough. Stimulates liver and gallbladder function; use for constipation, rheumatism, and gout.

ESSENTIAL OIL ACTION

None.

Relaxation & Meditation

RELAXATION

To know what relaxation feels like we need to recognise the difference between tension and relaxation. Learning to progressively relax is very simple.

* Lie down on a mattress. Breathe easily in through your nose and out through your mouth.

* As you inhale tighten the muscles in your feet by curling the toes tightly. Hold for 2–3 seconds and as you breathe out, uncurl and relax your feet. Feel the difference. Repeat once more, making the feet even more relaxed than before.

* Move the attention to the ankles and calves, gently inhale, tighten the ankles and calves. Hold for 2–3 seconds and as you exhale let the stress run like oil from your legs.

* Use the same breathing ... tensing ... relaxing technique on the thighs, then the buttocks, the stomach, the waist. From the waist down your body should feel heavy as lead, as though it might sink through the mattress.

* Continue in the same way for your upper body, hands and arms. When you get to your head, pay special attention to the shoulders and neck—areas that hold a lot of tension. Also the little muscles around the eyes. Are you clenching your jaws? Do you clench your jaws and hold your shoulders tight when driving a car?

* Let your attention wander all over your body to see if any areas have become tense once more. If so, do the breathing and tensing in this area again. Enjoy the feeling that you now have of complete relaxation.

You may have to practise relaxation for a while before you have mastered it but once you recognise the difference between tension and a state of relaxation you will be able to use this technique any time you feel stressed. This can have a profound effect on the lowering of stress and its attendant problems of high blood pressure, depression, stomach ulcers and much more.

MEDITATION

Meditation can create very deep relaxation and healing of both mind and body and from there can take us slowly to get in touch with our higher consciousness. It is arguable that relaxation, meditation and visualisation are the three most profoundly beneficial processes to aid your health and wellbeing. They reduce stress and all its attendant health problems and lower blood pressure

Put simplistically, meditation is the art of doing one thing at a time. You are meditating when your attention and awareness is immersed and directed at only one function, object or idea to the exclusion of everything else. Meditation happens when you dance, cycle, swim, juggle or run until, after a while, the thought process stops and you become the dancing, not the dancer; the swimming, not the swimmer; the running, not the runner. It happens when you sit silently on a beach watching the sun setting: alone, mindlessly watching flames dancing in a fire; not analysing, just 'being there'.

To begin meditating is like starting on an adventure—a journey with an unknown destination—the only thing to expect is the unexpected! Your mind is tricky, it will resent meditation and will fight to fill with the endless chatter in which it has always been allowed to indulge.

At first you will need to resist the urge to 'feel a failure' because the chatter of your mind seems to be more powerful than your desire for silence. You have expectations that the habits of a lifetime can be undone in one session, whereas if you were learning to speak a foreign language or to play a musical instrument you would be content to take it slowly and be very proud of each small step.

The morning is probably the best time for most people to meditate. You will find that you are fresh, the house is quietest then and you will begin your day feeling more positive and ready to face what that day has to offer.

To begin, you need a quiet place where you won't be disturbed. After some time you will be able to meditate anywhere—washing dishes, driving to work, playing with your children—remember, it's the art of doing one thing at a time. Leave the phone off the hook, sit on a straight-backed chair, put warm socks on (feet get very cold during meditation) and, if you like, play some soft, gentle music. If your household is very noisy, you might like to use your car for meditating! It's quiet, maybe equipped with a cassette player and has a comfortable seat.

Don't fight the thoughts that will intrude, it's impossible to get rid of them. If you make a conscious decision 'not to think' you will fail and become tense and frustrated. Trying to 'force' the mind is impossible, you need to gently move the thoughts to one side and return to the meditation. This is easier if you have chosen something on which to focus such as breathing, a word or an object. The mind will continue to interrupt like a naughty child but don't get upset, just move back to your chosen focus.

All right—you are ready.

Here are a few meditation techniques. If one doesn't suit you, then move to another, it's no good continuing with something that you don't like. At first do the meditation for as long as you are comfortable with it, this may be only 5–10 minutes but that's alright. Extend the time slowly for up to half or even an hour, whatever feels good.

Sit in the chair, or on a cushion on the floor with your back against a wall, and fidget around until you are comfortable and then begin to sit silently, doing nothing.

Begin to breathe a little more slowly and deeply than usual, be conscious of your body and any tension being held in it. Each time you breathe out let the tension drain away from tense areas. Enjoy the feeling of peace that begins to come as you relax.

Listen to noises far away, not analysing them, just hearing them. Leave them and find a noise quite close to you, be aware of it without judgement, leave it and enter your own space.

Feel where the body touches the surface it rests on.
Feel the spaces where the body doesn't touch.
Feel the clothes touching the body.
Feel the heart beating, sending nourishing blood around the body.
Feel the breath easily and lightly entering and leaving the body.

ONE
*With each outgoing breath, say 'one' in your mind and see the
number on the mind's 'screen'.*

   As the breath goes out, say and see 'one'.
   Breathe in gently, don't say anything.
   Breathe out, saying and seeing 'one'.
   Feel that you are at one with the exercise.

BREATH WATCHING
Breathe gently and easily in and out through the nostrils.

   *Find the point where you can most easily feel the air entering
your body.*
   *It may be the opening to your nostrils, it my be the point where
your nostrils meet the back of your throat.*
   Notice the difference between the in-breath and the out-breath.
   *If thoughts intrude, put them gently aside and return to the
watching.*

MANTRAS
*Mantras are incantations that are repeated over and over in the mind,
they have been used for centuries as a gate to meditation. Be
constantly aware of the significance, beauty and power of your
chosen mantra—watch that it doesn't become a word that you repeat
parrot-fashion otherwise you might just as well say 'soft drink
bottles'.*

   *Single-word mantras may be said out loud if you like. Phrases or
two-syllable mantras are spoken in the mind.*
   *The words 'love', 'peace', 'shanti' (peace) or short phrases like 'I
am love', 'peace and light', 'every day, in every way, I am getting*

better and better' can be used as a mantra. You can choose a mantra that has special and meaningful significance to you.

SO-HAM

This ancient mantra means 'I am the One'.

As you breathe in, say and see in your mind, 'so'...

As you breathe out, say and see in your mind, 'ham'...

Sitting quietly, breathing easily, 'so ... ham ... so ... ham' ...

Over and over ... over and over ... feel the words in your heart, don't just repeat them.

Repetitive Strain Injury

This is a term used to describe a whole range of conditions that can include bursitis, tendonitis and possibly Carpal Tunnel Syndrome which are created by using the same movements over and over again. This overuse can cause other damage to tissue, bone and cartilage.

The condition can cause great pain or discomfort and, if neglected, can lead to permanent damage. It's important to identify the cause of the problem and to rectify it by changing working position, improving work posture, taking breaks during repetitive actions, doing simple stretching exercises to lessen stress on the sets of muscles involved and frequently massaging the most used muscles.

See Tendonitis and Carpal Tunnel Syndrome for suitable treatments.

Restless legs

Those who haven't suffered this complaint can realise how distressing it is. The symptoms may not occur for up to one hour after going to bed, so if you can get to sleep before the symptoms appear you will have a good night's sleep as I have rarely heard of restless legs actually waking people up. Insomnia is a common problem of restless leg sufferers and it is frustrating and upsetting as nobody else can appreciate the reasons behind your lack of sleep. The symptoms may include one or more of the following: involuntarily jerking leg muscles, an irresistible urge to move the legs, muscle contractions, aching legs or pins and needles.

Daily exercise such as walking, swimming or cycling and particularly a walk before bed is often effective as it improves the circulation to the legs.

Try pulling a sleeping bag up as far as your waist at night or lay a hot water bottle on the worst affected part to keep the legs warmer.

INTERNAL TREATMENT

- Heavy smokers or heavy tea and coffee drinkers should either cut down or stop their habit as caffeine and nicotine constrict blood vessels and either contribute to or aggravate the condition.
- Eat plenty of foods containing iron, calcium or folic acid (see Vitamins and Minerals) as a deficiency can sometimes be a cause of the problem.
- Eat bananas daily to provide potassium for the muscles.

DAILY SUPPLEMENTS

- 400 iu vitamin E (d-alpha tocopherol).
- 50 mg folic acid daily if a deficiency is suspected.
- 1 vitamin B complex tablet.
- Vitamin B6 as directed.
- 1000 mg calcium citrate half an hour before bed, as a muscle relaxant.
- 1 teaspoon fluid extract ginkgo biloba 3 times daily to improve peripheral circulation.

ESSENTIAL OIL TREATMENT

'RESTFUL LEGS' MASSAGE BLEND

4 tablespoons (40 ml) vegetable oil
20 drops rosemary oil
20 drops marjoram oil
20 drops lavender oil
10 drops black pepper oil

TO MAKE: *Mix all in a small bottle. Leave for 48 hours to blend.*
TO USE: *Heat a teaspoon and pour some oil blend into the hot spoon and then into a tiny bowl. Use the warmed oil last thing at night after showering or bathing to massage the legs using firm, upward strokes. Deep massage and shiatsu often provide relief and, in some cases, effect a cure.*

HERBAL TREATMENT

Take one of the following or a blend of all to relax muscles and to help you sleep: passionflower, valerian, skullcap and chamomile.

None of these remedies result in sluggishness or a 'hung-over' feeling the following day. There are blends of these herbs to be found in either liquid or tablet form in health-food shops.

HOMEOPATHIC TREATMENT

30^c, take 4 times daily: Arnica and Rhus. tox.

Rheumatism

Rheumatism is a general term used medically to cover any inflammatory disorder that involves pain and inflammation in the joints and muscles. Refer to Arthritis and gout for treatment of rheumatism in the joints. The treatment delineated below deals with muscular rheumatism.

It's important to detoxify the system by increasing exercise and making the dietary changes outlined below.

INTERNAL TREATMENT

* Reduce intake of sugar, junk foods, tea and coffee.
* Eat less red meat and more fish, tofu and tempeh.
* Eat lots of fresh fruit, vegetables, wholegrain bread and cereals.
* Drink 6–8 glasses of filtered or bottled water daily.

DAILY SUPPLEMENTS

As for Arthritis, Rheumatoid.

ESSENTIAL OIL TREATMENT

OIL BLEND FOR COMPRESSES & FOMENTATIONS

1 teaspoon (5 ml) rosemary oil

50 drops lavender oil

50 drops marjoram oil

TO MAKE: *Mix together in a tiny bottle.*

TO USE: *Apply a compress (see Compresses) or fomentation (see Fomentations) using 5–8 drops of the mixed essential oils. Try both the hot and cold treatment to see which one gives the greatest relief. Treat as often as needed.*

OIL BLEND FOR BATH

6 drops juniper oil

2 drops cypress oil

2 drops rosemary oil

TO MAKE: *Mix the oils with 1 teaspoon (5 ml) vegetable oil.*

TO USE: *Pour into the bath after it has been drawn, agitate water to disperse the oils. Massage the sore muscles with the little 'blobs' of oil that will be floating on the water.*

HERBAL TREATMENT

- Dandelion coffee, 1 cup twice daily alternated with wild yam decoction.
- Ginger root decoction twice a day.
- Meadowsweet as directed.
- Add 2 handfuls of Epsom salts to the bath while it's running. Stir to dissolve. Soak in the bath massaging the aching areas of the body.

HOMEOPATHIC TREATMENT

All 6–30c, take 4 times daily:

- Back and neck—Actaea rac.
- Back and limbs—Apis mel.
- Fear of being touched—Arnica.

* Aggravated by movement—Bryonia.
* Pain improves after gentle movement—Rhus tox.
* Pain in muscles—Ruta grav.

Rheumatoid arthritis   See Arthritis

Rhus tox. (*Rhus toxicodendron*)   Homeopathic

Restlessness and anxiety characterise these people who often feel the cold and have a triangular red tip at the end of the tongue.

USE TO TREAT

Arthritis, bruises, chickenpox, cold sores, eczema, fibrositis, gout, herpes, lumbago, rheumatism, sciatica, shingles, sprains and strains, tickling cough.

Ringworm

A general term to describe a highly contagious fungal skin condition. It is an itchy rash that appears in the shape of a red ring, it often affects the scalp and can cause hair to fall out. Very strict hygiene needs to be observed in order to prevent the spread of the problem.

DAILY SUPPLEMENTS

* 1000 mg garlic oil capsules three times a day or 2–3 teaspoons 'Long-life juice' 3 times daily.
* ½ teaspoon (2.5 ml) echinacea liquid extract 3 times a day.
* 500 mg vitamin C with bioflavonoids.

ESSENTIAL OIL TREATMENT

Dab the ringworm alternately with neat tea-tree and lavender oil several times daily for a few days. When the moist stage has passed, massage the areas with equal parts of tea-tree, lavender and olive oil. The olive oil will help to prevent excessive drying out of the skin.

HERBAL TREATMENT

In the early stages, drip calendula tincture alternately with myrrh tincture (see Tinctures) directly onto the ringworm. Leave the tincture to dry on the skin. As the infection dries out use either calendula or golden seal ointment (see Ointments).

HOMEOPATHIC TREATMENT

All 6–30ᶜ, take 4 times daily until symptoms disappear:
* Itching turns to burning after scratching—Sepia.
* If the lesions ooze sticky liquid—Graphites.

Rose (*Rosa damascena, R. centifolia* & species)

HERB PART USED

Petals and hips (fruit).

HERB ACTIONS

Aperient, astringent, stomachic.

USE TO TREAT

Headaches, dizziness, mouth sores and to ease uterine cramps. The petals of the rose may be sugared as decorations for cakes and desserts or made into jam. Long-lasting rose beads are time consuming but easy to make, and are lovely to wear—the warmth of your body releases the scent. Cosmetically the petals may be made into a delicately scented flower water (see Colognes) for use as a toilet water or skin freshener. The hips of the wild rose have been used to make rose-hip syrup—a valuable source of vitamin C.

ESSENTIAL OIL ACTION

Antibacterial, antidepressant, anti-inflammatory, antiseptic, aphrodisiac, astringent, detoxifying.

USE TO TREAT

Disorders of the reproductive system such as PMS, heavy or painful periods, labour pains and menopausal problems; and in this area has proved more important than most oils. It is also very powerful on the mental and emotional plane where it has a reputation for helping to overcome frigidity, ease depression (particularly post-natal) and re-vitalise the nervous system. Rose has long been considered an aphrodisiac for both men and women. Rose oil, one of the oldest, most famous and expensive oils, is known affectionately as the 'Queen of Oils'.

Rose-water is a gentle antiseptic and soothing treatment for dry, sensitive, irritated and mature skin. It may be mixed with other ingredients or used alone. Use also to treat eczema, scars and thread veins.

Rosemary (*Rosmarinus officinalis*)

HERB PART USED

Leaves, flowering tips.

HERB ACTIONS

Antispasmodic, antiseptic, analgesic, cholagogue, detoxifying, emmenagogue, stimulant, stomachic, antiviral, antibacterial.

USE TO TREAT

Poor circulation, headaches, bacterial and viral diseases, poor liver function, stimulates the production of bile, inhibits the formation of kidney and gall stones, strengthens fragile blood vessels. Use in ointments to help to heal eczema, bruises and wounds. Use in baths and massage oils to treat aching muscles, arthritis, gout, rheumatism, sports injuries such as sprains and strains.

Caution: *Excessive use of rosemary is dangerous. Drink no more than 1 cup of tea daily for no longer than 1 week.*

ESSENTIAL OIL ACTION

Properties the same as the herb. Central nervous-system stimulant, (brain stimulant), analgesic, antiseptic. Use to treat fatigue, increase circulation, assist digestion; in massage oils to ease the pain of rheumatism, muscular pain, arthritis; and in inhalations for respiratory problems.

Caution: *Not to be used during pregnancy or by those suffering from epilepsy. Not to be used for extended periods.*

Rose-water

A scented water made from rose petals or rose oil. Triple rose-water (which may be bought from pharmacies) is prepared by distillation of fresh blooms of *Rosa damascena*. To use, add one part rose-water to two parts distilled water. The resulting rose-water can be used in cleansers, creams, lotions, tonics and as toilet water.

Rosewood (*Aniba rosaeodora*)

HERB PART USED

Heartwood chips from the tree.

HERB ACTIONS

Logging (unfortunately) for making furniture etc.

ESSENTIAL OIL ACTION

Antiseptic, anticonvulsant, antidepressant, antimicrobial, bactericidal, cellular stimulant, deodorant. Immune system stimulant, mildly analgesic, tissue regenerator, tonic.

USE TO TREAT

Acne, dermatitis, scars and wounds. A very useful skin oil for all skin types but the very oily. For colds, coughs, fever, chronic infections where the immune system is compromised. (Aromatherapists are using rose-wood oil in massage blends for use with AIDS patients. It may also be useful for chronic fatigue.) Headaches, nervous tension and stress related conditions. Use in deodorant blends.

Ross River Virus

A mosquito-borne virus that causes epidemic polyarthritis (known as Ross River Virus and also Barmah Forest Virus). The viruses are passed back and forth between animals and mosquitoes and are caught by humans after they are bitten by an infected mosquito.

Symptoms usually appear within 7–14 days of being bitten, but only about 1 in 3 people will develop symptoms after being bitten.

The range of symptoms is wide, varying from person to person. They can include swollen (rare) and/or painful joints, painful muscles, fever, skin rashes, profound fatigue, sore eyes and/or throat, headaches and swollen glands. Pain can be sudden and severe, coming and going in different areas at different times.

The symptoms can easily be confused with Chronic Fatigue Syndrome or some rheumatic diseases but can be diagnosed by a blood test.

A good support system is needed for sufferers of this disease as they can become profoundly depressed and emotionally distressed. One of the reasons for depression is the uncertainty attached to this condition. The pain may leave for some time and suddenly recur; the patient may get little sympathy, as there are frequently no obvious symptoms; and there can be no prognosis as to how long the disease will last. Rarely, the person recovers in a few weeks. Most people will still be unwell after 3 months, about half will still have symptoms after 6 months and many will have symptoms for 1–2 years. People with Ross River virus are rarely sick all the time—they may have quite lengthy periods of feeling quite well and these periods tend to lengthen with time. The danger of relapse seems to occur when, because there is feeling of 'wellness', the person gets buoyed up and over-exerts him/herself. Depression is a natural outcome of this situation, as the feeling of hopelessness of ever being well becomes profound. Always try to keep in mind that you *will get well*.

Gentle exercise such as walking or swimming in a heated pool is beneficial when the patient feels well enough. Stress management (see Relaxation) and pain management are important (see Pain).

Follow the treatment programme outlined in Chronic Fatigue Syndrome.

The only way to avoid contracting this disease is to avoid being bitten by mosquitoes. Wear loose clothing with long sleeves and long legs (mosquitoes can bite through cloth as thick as denim). Stay indoors at sunset and sunrise when mosquitoes are most active. Use mosquito nets over beds if you live in a danger area. Always apply mosquito repellent when going out of doors. The following recipe doesn't contain any harmful chemicals but if mosquitoes are especially attracted to you it may not be strong enough. This recipe is also quite effective in detering sandflies.

MOSQUITOES & SANDFLY REPELLENT

This is probably the only time that I would recommend using paraffin oil on the skin, the reason being that it isn't easily absorbed and remains effective, holding the essential oils on the skin, for a longer time than vegetable oils which absorb more quickly.

40 drops lavender oil

20 drops citronella oil

20 drops peppermint oil

¼ cup (60 ml) cider vinegar or distilled witch-hazel

¼ cup (60 ml) paraffin oil

TO MAKE: *Mix all together in a bottle.*

TO USE: *Shake well before use. Rub on all exposed areas of the body. Reapply every 2–3 hours.*

Rubefacients

Produce localised redness and warmth when applied to the skin by increasing the flow of blood to the area.

HERBS

Horseradish, cayenne, thyme.

ESSENTIAL OILS

Black pepper, eucalyptus, ginger, juniper, marjoram, rosemary, thyme.

Rubella (German Measles)

A highly infectious viral disease. The symptoms are fairly mild in children but women who plan to become pregnant should be tested for rubella antibodies—if German measles is caught during pregnancy it can seriously damage or threaten the life of the unborn baby.

Symptoms include a slight fever, a rash and swollen glands, all lasting only for a few days. Follow the treatment for chickenpox (see Chickenpox).

HOMEOPATHIC TREATMENT

30ᶜ take 8 times daily in early stages, then 4 times daily during recuperation:

✻ Belladonna and pulsatilla.

Ruta Grav. (*Ruta graveolens*) ✻ Homeopathic

USE TO TREAT

Torn and strained tendons and ligaments after the initial swelling and pain has decreased. Useful to treat repetitive-strain injuries.

Sachets

Sachets are fragrant mixtures of herbs, spices and essential oils enclosed in cloth. They are used to perfume rooms, drawers, wardrobes or anywhere that a faint herbal perfume would be appreciated. Sachets may be made from little hand-made bags or pretty handkerchiefs folded up around the contents and tied with a matching ribbon. Small crocheted doilies make lovely sachets but the herbal contents need to be tied first in a piece of muslin.

Small pillows may be made by using pillow filling and adding 2–3 sachets per pillow.

Sachets can be used on car dashboards and on radiators where the heat will release the perfume, under pillows and in drawers and cupboards. (See also Air fresheners, Colognes & Perfumes, Deodorants and Pot-pourris.)

BASIC MIXTURE

2 teaspoons dried, ground orris root

1 teaspoon (5 ml) mixed essential oils

50 g dried herbs, crumbled

2 teaspoons salt

If you have insufficient herb material you may substitute some or all with sawdust. Many sawdusts have their own lovely scent and blend wonderfully with tree essential oils such as cedar, pine, eucalyptus and the citrus oils—lemon, mandarin and grapefruit.

If you don't have access to either dried-plant material or sawdust you can drip essential oils onto small cosmetic sponges, leave overnight to absorb surplus oil, and enclose them in sachet covers. Drip more oils on as needed.

Some lovely blends of herbs are:

- lavender, thyme and mint.
- lavender, lemon verbena, ground cloves, mixed spice.
- rosemary, lemon verbena, dried ground lemon and orange peel, crumbled dried lemon leaves.

Sage (Salvia officinalis)

HERB PART USED

Leaves.

HERB ACTIONS

Antioxidant, antibacterial, antispasmodic, astringent.

USE TO TREAT

Excessive sweating (particularly night sweats), nervous conditions such as depression and vertigo. Use as a douche for vaginal discharges (see Douches). Use as a gargle for sore throats, laryngitis and tonsillitis (see Gargles). It is an excellent remedy as a mouthwash for mouth ulcers or other inflammations in the mouth.

Caution: *Extended use is not recommended. Avoid during pregnancy.*

ESSENTIAL OIL ACTION

Not recommended due to the high percentage (50 per cent) of thujone, a toxic ketone.

St John's wort (Hypericum perforatum)

HERB PART USED

Flowers.

HERB ACTIONS

Analgesic, anti-inflammatory, antiseptic, antiviral, antibacterial.

USE TO TREAT

Herpes simplex, influenza, depression, menstrual cramps, sciatica, rheumatism, arthritis. Healing and soothing to wounds, minor burns, sunburn and bruises. Helps to reduce inflammation and eases the pain of fibrositis, sciatica, arthritis, rheumatism, gout, neuralgia.

ESSENTIAL OIL ACTION

No essential oil. The infused oil (see Aromatherapy & Essential oils, Extraction of essential oils) is exceptionally healing.

USE TO TREAT

Inflammations, sprains, wounds, burns, bruises, varicose veins and pain.

Sandalwood (*Santalum album*)

HERB PART USED

The essential oil is extracted from the heartwood of trees that are at least 25 years old.

HERB ACTIONS

The heartwood is used for incense, building and furniture making.

ESSENTIAL OIL ACTION

Antiseptic (particularly urinary tract), antispasmodic, aphrodisiac, pulmonary antiseptic, digestive.

USE TO TREAT

Bronchitis, catarrh, coughs, sore throat, cystitis and to ease colic and nausea. Inflamed skin conditions such as acne, eczema, dry skin and dehydrated skin. One of the most spiritual and uplifting oils, used in temples for centuries and now in our homes to help us to move deeper into meditation.

Saw palmetto (*Serenoa repens*)

HERB PARTS USED

Berries.

HERB ACTIONS

Diuretic, expectorant, tonic, urinary antiseptic.

USE TO TREAT

Enlarged prostate gland; to strengthen the male reproductive system; for catarrh, colds, asthma and urinary tract infections.

ESSENTIAL OIL ACTION

None.

Scabies

A very contagious skin condition caused by a tiny insect that burrows beneath the skin and lays its eggs. When the eggs hatch, the movement of insects causes intense and distressing itching. Scratching causes a secondary problem, as it often leads to infection. This condition is difficult to treat and medical help may be needed.

All clothing, towels and bedding and indeed anything washable that has been in contact with the infected person must be washed in very hot water with eucalyptus oil added to the washing and rinsing water. Hang the washing out in the sun to dry. Mattresses and pillows should be put out in the sun and wiped over with a mixture of tea-tree, clove and lavender oils. In severe cases which resist treatment it may be necessary to burn articles such as mattresses.

DAILY SUPPLEMENTS

⚹ 1000 mg garlic oil capsules 3 times daily or 2–3 teaspoons 'Long-life juice' 3 times daily.

⚘ ½ teaspoon (2.5 ml) echinacea fluid extract three times daily may be useful.

ESSENTIAL OIL TREATMENT

SCABIES OINTMENT

This ointment has a much higher proportion of essential oil than usual. Apply very frequently but use only on the affected areas.

3 tablespoons finely grated, firmly packed beeswax

40 g anhydrous lanolin (available from pharmacies)

2 tablespoons (40 ml) olive oil or, even better, infused calendula oil
(see Aromatherapy & Essential oils, Extraction of essential oils)

½ teaspoon (2.5 ml) tincture of calendula

30 drops bergamot oil

60 drops lavender oil

20 drops peppermint oil

10 drops lemon oil

10 drops clove oil

TO MAKE: *Melt the beeswax over a very low flame, taking care not to overheat.*

Add the lanolin, stir until melted.

Slowly add the olive or calendula infused oil, don't re-harden the wax. Take off heat, cool slightly.

Mix together the tincture and essential oils and add slowly while stirring thoroughly to incorporate until the mixture is just beginning to thicken. Pour into jars.

Scalds ❦ See Burns & Scalds

Sciatica

A neuralgic pain stemming from the lower back and running down the back of the legs to the feet. Chiropractic treatment should be considered as a way to correct the problem.

For treatment also see Neuralgia.

HOMEOPATHIC TREATMENT

All 6–30ᶜ, take 4 times daily:

* ❦ Worse on cold, damp weather and at night—Rhus tox.
* ❦ Phytolacca.

Sedatives

Reduce stress in the body, calm the nervous system.

HERBS

Chamomile, hops, lavender, passionflower, St John's wort, skullcap, valerian.

ESSENTIAL OILS

Benzoin, bergamot, chamomile, clary sage, frankincense, jasmine, lavender, mandarin, marjoram, melissa, neroli, rose, ylang-ylang.

Sepia (*Sepia*) ❦ Homeopathic

Suited to people who are depressed, sluggish and apathetic and who have many imaginary fears; they can be emotionally cold, easily angered and sad.

USE TO TREAT

Dandruff, fear of being alone, impotence, menopausal hot flushes, morning sickness, PMS.

Shingles (*Herpes zoster*)

A skin eruption caused by the reactivation of the chickenpox virus, which lives on in the nerve cells in a dormant state after the initial infection has cleared. The virus travels along a nerve and appears on the skin at the nerve ending, the blisters look similar to chickenpox but are usually bigger. There can be, and usually is, severe pain as nerve endings are involved.

Get plenty of sleep and relaxation. Get professional help if the blisters are on or near the eyes.

Painkillers and calamine lotion are the only treatments offered by allopathic medicine unless the shingles are on the eyes when the treatment is with antiviral agents. Natural treatments are much more effective overall.

INTERNAL TREATMENT

* Eat plenty of fresh fruits, vegetables and grains.
* Drink 6–8 glasses of bottled or filtered water or diluted fruit or vegetable juices daily.

DAILY SUPPLEMENTS

* 1 vitamin B complex tablet.
* 1000 mg vitamin C with bioflavonoids 3 times a day for 2 weeks.

ESSENTIAL OIL TREATMENT

* Use a mixture of neat tea-tree and lavender oil on the blisters.
* A compress (see Compresses) on the blisters using lavender and/or chamomile oil is often very soothing.
* When the blisters have gone, follow the recommendations for Neuralgia.

HERBAL TREATMENT

Follow the recommendations for Neuralgia.

HOMEOPATHIC TREATMENT

All 6–30ᶜ, take 3–4 times daily:
* Burning blisters, there is relief in warmth, discomfort from cold—Arsen. alb.
* Intense itching and pain—Rhus tox.
* Skin sensitive to touch, can't even bear clothing—Hepar sulph.

Shoulder, frozen

Also known as capsulitis. An extremely painful condition caused by inflammation of the muscle or joint-capsule fibres. The condition is found mainly in middle-aged women but the reason for this is not known. In some cases deposits of calcium worsen the condition. Acupuncture, massage and physiotherapy are suitable treatments.

ESSENTIAL OIL TREATMENT

MASSAGE OIL

3 tablespoons (60 ml) vegetable oil

10 drops chamomile oil

10 drops rosemary oil

10 drops marjoram oil

5 drops peppermint oil

5 drops clove oil

TO MAKE: *Mix together in a small bottle, shake to blend. Shake well before use.*

TO USE: *Deep massage after cabbage treatment (see below). Alternate hot and cold compresses (see below) followed by deep massage using the massage oil.*

HERBAL TREATMENT

- ✤ Willow bark tincture, capsules or tablets for pain; take as directed.
- ✤ Alternate hot fomentations and cold compresses using very strong teas of chamomile and lavender. Follow with a deep massage (see above).
- ✤ Heat a cabbage leaf in the oven until hot and soft (or you can iron it), apply to the shoulder and slip on a shirt or blouse to hold it in place. Leave until cold. Follow with a massage (see above).

HOMEOPATHIC TREATMENT

All 6–30ᶜ, take 4 times daily:

- ✷ Aggravated by movement, improves with gentle movement— Rhus tox.
- ✷ Pain in tendons and muscles—Ruta grav.

Silica (*Silicea*) 🦋 Homeopathic

Although Silica people dislike responsibility and find mental effort difficult they are usually excellent and reliable workers. They are unassertive and timid but can be stubborn and irritable if asked to do something they don't want to. They are often fair-complexioned with fine, pale skin and feel the cold intensely.

USE TO TREAT

Abscess, acne, athlete's foot, boils, bunions, constipation, hayfever, migraine, sinus problems.

Sinusitis

The sinuses are cavities in the bones above the eyes and behind and below the eyes. They are lined with mucous membranes and normally are full of air but, during an allergic reaction or a cold, the membranes may swell and produce excessive mucus. The openings from the nose into the sinuses are very narrow and quickly become blocked by the build-up of mucus. This and the pressure of the air in the now constricted space can cause moderate to severe pain. This is called 'sinus congestion'.

If, however, there is a bacterial infection the face feels tender to touch; a coloured, thick nasal discharge is produced; there is fever, sometimes a frontal headache and the person can become very sick. In the case of bacterial infection it's best to seek professional help as well as using the following treatments.

INTERNAL TREATMENT

- 🦋 Drink plenty of fluid such as diluted fruit and vegetable juices and herb teas.
- 🦋 Cut out all dairy products to reduce mucus production.

DAILY SUPPLEMENTS

- 🦋 500 mg vitamin C with bioflavonoids every 4 hours.
- 🦋 5000–10 000 iu beta-carotene.

- ❧ Suck a zinc lozenge every 2 hours (for no longer than 1 week).
- ❧ 500 mg golden seal 3 times daily or as directed.
- ❧ ½ teaspoon (2.5 ml) liquid extract of echinacea 3 times daily.
- ❧ 1000 mg garlic oil capsules 3 times daily or 2 teaspoons 'Long-Life juice' 3 times daily.

ESSENTIAL OIL TREATMENT

- ❀ Fomentations (see Fomentations) and compresses (see Compresses) using eucalyptus oil every 2–3 hours.
- ❀ Inhalations (see Inhalations) using tea-tree, eucalyptus and peppermint oils every 2–3 hours.

HERBAL TREATMENT

Drink elderflower and peppermint tea 3 times daily.

HOMEOPATHIC TREATMENT

All 6–30^c, take 4 times daily:
- ❀ Stringy, tough discharge—Kali. bich. (first choice).
- ❀ Worse at night or in a warm room—Pulsatilla.
- ❀ Pain improves with pressure—Silicea.

Skin brushing (Dry-brush massage)

Dry-brush massaging is an excellent treatment for your skin, liver, kidneys, lungs and bowels. The skin, if in optimum condition with pores not clogged with dead skin flakes, is responsible for a third of our excretion thus taking much of the load off the other excretory organs. Dry-brush massaging not only gets rid of these dead cells but also stimulates the circulation leaving the skin glowing, fresh and feeling very clean.

Long-handled bristle brushes are available from some health-food stores and pharmacies. Use the brush before bathing or showering and brush firmly but gently in a circular movement all over the body paying special attention to the areas such as the armpits, groin and below the throat. Be gentle on the breasts and around the genital area.

Skin care

In our continual search for line-free, youthful skin we literally 'buy-in' to the myth that only the young are beautiful. Don't be fooled by the extravagant promises of the cosmetic companies, and don't forget that they aren't charitable institutions—they exist to make as much money as they can from *you*! Nothing short of plastic surgery or muscle-numbing injections is going to get rid of the lines you already have, but the use of cleansers, moisturisers and sun screens can help to delay the appearance of more lines, and to give a clear glowing colour and an improved texture. It doesn't take many minutes a day to give your skin some attention, and the rewards in the form of softened lines and improved colour and texture will be apparent in as little as one to two weeks.

Do yourself and your skin a favour and make your own skin-care items. The skin-care preparations that you can make in your own kitchen will contain *much* better ingredients and will cost a mere fraction of the price of the brand-name cosmetics. It doesn't take long to make your own cosmetics, the ingredients are easy to find (see suppliers), and the resulting creams and lotions are lovely to use.

No amount of external care will improve our skin if the internals aren't being cared for. The enemies of skin are stress and insufficient sleep, too much sun and wind on unprotected skin, poor diet, insufficient moisturising, insufficient fluid intake, poor cleansing habits, ill health and smoking. All these things have a bad effect on your skin.

Eat plenty of fruit and vegetables; good, tasty multigrain bread and cereals; nuts, legumes and pulses. Drink 6–8 glasses of bottled or filtered water every day. Keep your consumption of 'junk' food (that includes chocolate and sweets) to the absolute minimum. Get plenty of sleep, go for a walk or swim (or whatever) for 30 minutes at least 3 times a week. Find ways of reducing unnecessary stress and neutralising on-going stress (see Relaxation and Stress). Stay out of the sun if possible after 10.00 a.m. and before 4.00 p.m. If this can't be done, use the best sun-screen cream that you can find, cover your arms and legs and wear a hat.

CLEANSERS

Dry, sensitive and delicate skins benefit the most from cream cleansers. The use of soap on these types of skin will leave them feeling parched, 'tight' and uncomfortable. Normal, oily and combination-skinned people may feel perfectly happy with soap as their choice of cleanser.

Soap doesn't always do a good job of cleaning off cosmetics such as mascara. A cream may also be needed if you wear heavy cosmetics, as soap and water don't penetrate far enough into the pores to float the cosmetics out.

ALMOND CLEANSING CREAM (DRY/NORMAL SKIN)

2½ level tablespoons firmly packed, finely grated beeswax

2 tablespoons (40 ml) almond or olive oil

2 tablespoons (40 ml) rose-water

8 drops essential oil (choose from ingredients for Steams, masks & scrubs, following)

TO MAKE: *Melt the beeswax in a small bowl or jar standing in a pan of simmering water, don't overheat. Have another small bowl containing the rose-water in the same pan of water. When the beeswax is melted, add the oil slowly taking care not to re-harden the beeswax. Take off the heat.*

Very slowly *add the warm rose-water to the wax and oil beating all the time. As soon as the rose-water has been incorporated stop beating. Allow to cool a little and when the outside of the bowl is just above hand heat (about 39°C), add the essential oil, mix well and pot.*

STEAMS, MASKS & SCRUBS

Ingredients for steams, masks and scrubs follow:

DRY & NORMAL SKINS

Good things *include almond meal, arrowroot, buttermilk, cider vinegar, cream, full-cream dried-milk powder, egg yolk, glycerine, honey, oatmeal and rose-water.*

Essential oils *include benzoin, chamomile, carrot, evening primrose, frankincense, geranium, jasmine, lavender, myrrh, neroli, palmarosa,* *patchouli, rose, rosewood, sandalwood and ylang-ylang.*

Herbs *include aloe vera gel, burdock root, calendula flowers, chamomile flowers, clover flowers, comfrey leaf and root, elderflowers, lemongrass leaf, mallow root, orange blossom, orange peel, rose petals, rosemary leaf, violet leaves and flowers, yarrow leaves and flowers.*

Vegetable and fruit pulps *include apple, apricot, avocado, banana, celery, orange juice and strawberries.*

Oils *include almond, apricot, avocado, canola, castor, cocoa butter, olive, palm, peanut and wheatgerm (10 per cent only).*

OILY SKINS

Good things *include almond oil, almond milk, arrowroot, bran, brewer's yeast, buttermilk, cider vinegar, dried skimmed-milk powder, egg white, fuller's earth, glycerine, honey, kaolin, oatmeal and yoghurt.*

Essential oils *include benzoin, bergamot, cedarwood, cypress, geranium, grapefruit, juniper, lavender, lemon, neroli, palmarosa, petitgrain, rosewood, sandalwood and ylang-ylang.*

Herbs *include aniseed, calendula flowers, chamomile flowers, clary-sage leaf, comfrey leaves and root, lavender flowers, lemongrass leaves, lemon peel, mallow root and marjoram leaves.*

Vegetable and fruit pulps *include apple, apricots, asparagus, avocado, carrot pulp, cucumber, fig pulp, lemon juice, pineapple pulp, strawberries, tomatoes, cooked turnip and watermelon.*

Oils *include almond, linseed, soya bean, walnut and wheatgerm (10 per cent only).*

FACIAL STEAMING

Facial steaming softens the skin and makes it perspire. This in turn loosens deep-seated grime, dead skin cells and blackheads, making them easier to remove. The heat and moisture from the steam increases the blood supply and rehydrates the skin leaving it looking and feeling softer and more youthful.

If you have 'thread veins' (broken capillaries) in your skin you need to protect those areas from anything such as steam, masks or packs and exfolients that will stimulate the blood supply and cause further damage to the veins or create more. Apply a thick layer of moisture/night cream over the veins and holding the face about 40 cm away from the bowl of water.

STEAMING INSTRUCTIONS USING HERBS

Cleanse the face in your preferred fashion.

Put ¹/₃ teacup finely chopped herbs (see ingredients for Steams, masks & scrubs above) in a saucepan. Cover with 2 litres cold water and a lid. Bring to the boil and simmer gently for 3–5 minutes.

Put the pan on a table on a heatproof, non-slip mat; sit at the table and form a tent over the pan and your head with a large towel.

Remove the lid from the pan, keep the face about 20 cm away from the pan and enjoy for 5 minutes. By this time the steam and herbs will have done their work.

Splash the face with cool (not cold) water then with skin tonic and finish with moisture cream.

STEAMING INSTRUCTIONS USING ESSENTIAL OILS

Cleanse your face in your preferred fashion.

Place a bowl on a heatproof, non-slip mat on a table. Add 2 litres boiling water, sit at the table and form a tent over the bowl and your head with a large towel.

Add 2–4 drops essential oil suitable for your skin type (see ingredients for Steams, masks & scrubs above). Keep the face about 20 cm away from the bowl and enjoy for 5 minutes. By this time the steam and essential oils will have done their work.

Splash the face with cool (not cold) water then with skin tonic and finish with moisture cream.

MASKS

Masks cleanse, moisturise, refine, tone and heal the skin. They also have a definite 'feel-good' factor, are fun to use and leave you feeling relaxed and pampered.

Use a shower cap or head band to keep your hair off your face and wear clothing that won't be ruined if you drip mask onto it. Cleanse your face in your usual manner before applying the mask. The mask should be of a consistency that will stay mainly on your face and not drip all over the place but also not be so stiff that when dried out, it becomes like a clay-pan. Don't apply face masks on broken veins or on the delicate skin around the eyes.

Green clay (available from health-food stores) is a useful base as it is rich in minerals and has antiseptic properties. One teaspoon of the clay can be mixed with 1 teaspoon yoghurt, runny honey or water and three drops of essential oil of your choice. For a basic mask, choose the ingredients to suit your skin type from those given for Steams, masks & scrubs.

MASK BASE

TO MAKE: *To 1 teacup of fuller's earth or kaolin (available from pharmacies) add ¼ teacup ground arrowroot or cornflour. Add 1 tablespoon finely ground rolled oats or fine cornmeal or ground almond meal or wholemeal flour and/or powdered herbs. Mix together and store in a tightly covered jar.*

TO USE: *Mix 1 tablespoon of the mask base with 1 teaspoon skimmed dried milk and any of the suitable ingredients for your skin type. Use 2 drops only of essential oil.*

Combine to make a soft paste.

Apply the mask and then lie down! The mask will work better if you are relaxed and also will stay on your face and not the carpet. Leave the mask on for 10–15 minutes, wash off with warm (not hot) water and finish with a cool (not cold) splash.

SCRUBS

These are used to exfoliate (peel) the outer, dead layer of skin. This can leave your skin looking cleaner, brighter and younger but shouldn't be done too often. Avoid using scrubs on the areas around the eyes.

BASIC SCRUB MIXTURE

1 teacup fine ground rice

¹/₄ teacup fine cornmeal

¹/₂ teacup finely ground herbs

2 tablespoons kaolin

2 tablespoons raw sugar

TO MAKE: *Mix together and store in an airtight container.*

TO USE: *Put 2 teaspoons of basic mix in a small bowl. Add any of the following ingredients (or choose from ingredients for Steams, masks & scrubs) to the mixture until a soft paste is formed: honey, yoghurt, glycerine, egg yolk. Add two drops of essential oil. Mix very well.*

Wet your face, spread the scrub onto your skin (an area at a time) and, using circular motions, massage gently into the skin. Splash off with cool (not cold) water and pat the skin dry.

TONERS & ASTRINGENTS

Toners remove some of the excess skin oil and restore the acid mantle to the skin, leaving the skin feeling clean and fresh. Astringents contain more of the oil-removing ingredients but those that contain a large amount of alcohol do more harm than good as they remove *all* the oil. The skin then produces a lot *more* oil to counteract the effect and you are worse off than before.

TONER FOR DRY SKIN

³/₄ cup (185 ml) rose-water (available from pharmacies and health-food stores)

¹/₄ cup (60 ml) distilled witch-hazel

¹/₂ teaspoon (2.5 ml) glycerine

2 drops palmarosa oil

TO MAKE: *Mix together in a bottle. Shake well. Leave for 2–3 days to blend.*

TO USE: *See below.*

ASTRINGENT FOR OILY SKIN

1 cup (250 ml) rose-water

¼ cup (60 ml) vodka

¼ cup (60 ml) distilled witch-hazel

10 drops geranium oil

10 drops rosemary oil

10 drops lavender oil

TO MAKE: *Mix together in a bottle. Shake well. Leave for 2–3 days to blend.*

TO USE: *See below.*

Did you know that home-made mayonnaise is an excellent treatment for hair and skin. It contains proteins, oils and acids all of which will moisturise, soften and help to give clear, glowing skin and bouncy, shiny hair.

HERBAL ASTRINGENT/AFTERSHAVE

1 cup calendula petals or elderflowers

½ cup peppermint leaves

2 cups (500 ml) boiling water

¼ cup (60 ml) distilled witch-hazel

1 teaspoon (5 ml) tincture of benzoin

4 drops peppermint oil

TO MAKE: *Put the herbs in a heatproof container, pour the boiling water over them. Cover closely and leave in a warm place for 24 hours. Drain through a sieve, squeeze thoroughly. Strain through coffee-filter paper. Add the distilled witch-hazel, benzoin and peppermint oil and mix well. Bottle and store in the refrigerator.*

TO USE: *See below.*

TO USE: *Try one of the following methods.*

🦎 *Wet a piece of cotton wool with water and squeeze dry. Sprinkle with a few drops of lotion and wipe the throat and face using an upward motion. (Wetting the cotton wool and squeezing dry before adding the lotion will prevent wasting of the lotion.)*

🦎 *Wet a piece of cotton wool with water, squeeze dry, flatten and fold in half. Pour on a little lotion, hold a corner of the cotton wool and slap your face briskly. This will bring the blood flow to your face and leave it feeling fresh and stimulated.*

MOISTURISERS

Moisturisers used regularly will help to keep the skin soft, supple and smooth. What moisturisers *won't do* (despite the extravagant claims of the manufacturers) is to 'turn back the clock'. They won't remove or totally prevent wrinkles but can soften and help to retard the appearance of fine lines. *Everybody* needs to moisturise their skin — particularly the exposed skin such as the face or hands.

The following recipes use emulsifying wax and preservative. If you have trouble getting these (or other ingredients) at your local pharmacy they may be obtained by post from the suppliers listed at the end of this book.

CALENDULA MOISTURE CREAM

The following two recipes are for very sophisticated 'vanishing' moisturising preparations for dry, normal and combination skins. They feel luxurious on the skin and leave no oily residue.

A

1 cup (250 ml) calendula tea (see Teas)

1 tablespoon (20 ml) glycerine

80 drops phenoxitol (if another preservative is used, follow the amounts and directions on the container)

B

25 g cetomacrogol emulsifying wax (if another emulsifier is used, follow the amounts and directions on the container)

5 teaspoons (25 ml) calendula-infused oil (available from health-food stores or see Aromatherapy & Essential oils, Extraction of essential oils)

3 teaspoons (15 ml) almond oil

C

1 dropper palmarosa or rosewood oil

1 teaspoon (5 ml) tincture of benzoin (optional, see Benzoin)

TO MAKE: *Put ingredients A in a heatproof jug or bowl.*

Put ingredients B in another heatproof jug or bowl (large enough to hold all the ingredients for this recipe).

Put both containers in the same pan of hot water (a baking dish is ideal) on a low heat on the stove.

Heat until both mixtures are 65–70°C. Pour A onto B (the order is very important) in a slow steady stream, stirring constantly in a figure-of-eight movement. Continue stirring until the mixture is 45°C. Add ingredients C and stir until well incorporated. Pour into jars and cap immediately.

COOL CUCUMBER LOTION

This lotion is for normal, combination and oily skin. To make cucumber juice, finely chop unpeeled cucumber, liquidise and strain first through a sieve and then through coffee-filter paper.

A

1 cup (250 ml) cucumber juice (see above)

2 teaspoons (10 ml) glycerine

70 drops phenoxitol (if another preservative is used, follow the amounts and directions on the container)

B

20 g cetomacrogol emulsifying wax (if another emulsifier is used, follow the amounts and directions on the container)

2 tablespoons (40 ml) almond oil

2 tablespoons (40 ml) soya oil

C

2 teaspoons (10 ml) distilled witch-hazel

½ dropper bergamot oil

½ dropper sandalwood or palmarosa oil

½ dropper tincture of benzoin (optional)

TO MAKE: *Put ingredients A in a heatproof jug or bowl. Put ingredients B in another heatproof jug or bowl (large enough to hold all the recipe ingredients).*

Put both containers in the same pan of hot water (a baking dish is ideal) on a low heat on the stove. Heat until both mixtures are 65–70°C. Pour A onto B (the order is very important) in a slow steady stream, stirring constantly in a figure-of-eight movement. Continue stirring until the

Have you heard that a slice of garlic rubbed on a pimple will help to get rid of it?

mixture is 45°C. Add ingredients C and stir until well incorporated.
Pour into bottles and cap immediately.

APRICOT SILK MOISTURE LOTION

This moisture lotion suits most skin types and is simpler to make
than the previous recipes. It doesn't sink into the skin as easily or
quickly but is ideal for those who want a totally natural product with
no preservative or emulsifying wax.

A

4 firmly packed, level tablespoons finely grated beeswax

1 level teaspoon anhydrous lanolin

½ cup (125 ml) grapeseed oil

¼ cup (60 ml) apricot oil

B

1¼ cups (310 ml) distilled water

1 teaspoon borax

C

20 drops palmarosa or rosewood oil

20 drops geranium oil

TO MAKE: *Put ingredients A in a heatproof jug or bowl.*

*Put ingredients B in another heatproof jug or bowl (large enough
to hold all the recipe's ingredients).*

*Put both containers in the same pan of hot water (a baking dish is
ideal) on a low heat on the stove. Heat until mixture A is melted and
both mixtures are the same temperature. Don't overheat.*

*Pour B onto A (the order is very important) in a slow steady stream,
stirring constantly. Reheat slightly if the mixture begins to solidify.*

*Continue stirring until the mixture is 45–50°C and no water
droplets can be seen. Add ingredients C and stir until well
incorporated. Pour or spoon into containers and cap immediately.*

Skullcap (*Scutellaria laterifolia*)

HERB PART USED

All parts above the ground.

HERB ACTIONS

Antispasmodic, diuretic, sedative, tonic.

USE TO TREAT

Nervous conditions and convulsions, epilepsy, exhaustion, depression, insomnia, excitability, hysteria, PMS, restlessness. Acts as a tonic for the nervous system, reducing stress and tension.

ESSENTIAL OIL ACTION

None.

Slippery elm (*Ulmus fulva*)

HERB PART USED

Inner bark.

HERB ACTIONS

Demulcent, diuretic, emollient, nutritive.

USE TO TREAT

Gastritis, gastric and duodenal ulcers, diarrhoea, colitis. Soothing to inflammations both internal and external but particularly of the digestive system. Externally use as a poultice for abscesses, boils and ulcers.

ESSENTIAL OIL ACTION

None.

Soap

MICROWAVE METHOD

By recycling soap scraps you can produce a fine soap into which you can blend moisturising ingredients, essential oils, softening agents or herbs. The addition of ingredients such as ground oats or fine polenta both soften and gently exfoliate the skin.

Grate or grind the left-over scraps of soap as finely as possible—
to a powder is best. To each cup of grated soap add:

1 tablespoon (20 ml) honey

1 tablespoon (20 ml) glycerine

*1–3 tablespoons (20–60 ml) water or rose-water (amount depends on
the dryness of the soap)*

¼ cup rolled oats (optional)

20 drops essential oil of your choice

TO MAKE: *Microwave soap, honey, glycerine and water on medium
power (50 per cent) for 1 minute or until the mixture begins to rise
and froth. Stir and repeat.*

*Stir in the rolled oats and mix well. If too thick, add more hot
water and reheat.*

Cool a little but don't allow to set. Add essential oils, mix well.

Shape into balls or press into moulds.

*Leave in an airy place for as long as possible to harden. The
harder the soap is the longer it will last. When set, the soaps may be
polished by moistening the hands with water or rosewater and
buffing the soap.*

STOVE-TOP METHOD

The ingredients are the same as for the microwave method of making
soap.

Place the ingredients in a double boiler or in a heatproof bowl over
a pan of simmering water. Stir often as the soap begins to melt. When
it looks as though the soap has amalgamated with the water, take off
the heat and beat well. Mix the oatmeal and oils in quickly, stir well
to incorporate.

Continue as for microwave soap.

Spearmint (Mentha spicata)

HERB PART USED

Leaves.

Herb actions

As for peppermint but milder.

Essential oil action

As for peppermint but so much milder that it may be used in moderation for children and during pregnancy.

Sprains

Essential oil treatment

Arnica oil or ointment (provided the skin isn't broken) massaged in gently twice a day.

Herbal treatment

❧ Very cold crushed comfrey poultice or very cold compresses of comfrey tea.

❧ After 24 hours gently massage comfrey ointment onto the sprain.

Homeopathic treatment

All 6–30^c, take frequently until initial symptoms subside, then 4 times a day until healed:

✳ Accompanied by bruising and swelling—Arnica.

✳ Sprains after lifting something heavy—Rhus tox.

✳ For sprained tendons or ligaments after swelling has receded—Ruta grav.

Stimulants

Produce energy and activity in the body, mind or a specific organ.

Herbs

Cayenne, feverfew, ginger, hyssop, peppermint and spearmint, rosemary, thyme.

ESSENTIAL OIL

Basil, black pepper, eucalyptus, geranium, ginger, hyssop, peppermint and spearmint, pine, rosemary, thyme.

Stomach (acid)

HERBAL TREATMENT

Drink 1 cup peppermint or chamomile tea 4 times daily *or 1 drop only* peppermint oil in ½ glass warm water twice daily.

Stress ❦ See Emotional & Nervous problems

In a stressful situation there are many chemical changes that happen in the body to enable us to cope with the situation. If the situation is satisfactorily resolved, the body reverses the process and returns the body chemistry to its normal state. If the situation is ongoing and unresolved the chemicals such as adrenalin, hormones, sugar, lactic acid, and urine are retained instead of being dispersed and they continue to keep the body in a 'fight or flight' condition that is very unhealthy. Some of the problems that may occur are cancer, colitis, high blood pressure, angina, depressed immune system leading to frequent infections, coronary thrombosis, excess cholesterol, stomach ulcers, migraine, back problems, atherosclerosis, severe depression and nervous breakdown.

There are two types of stress, namely:

❦ **Eustress**, which is healthy stress that we need in order to function in everyday life. It is exhilarating and can add sparkle to our lives and stimulate our alertness and capabilites. Most of us have experienced the thrill of competition, the sweating palms and dry mouth before making a speech or asking for a raise. These stresses are healthy—they have a beginning and a satisfactory conclusion during which the stress-induced chemical changes in the body are reversed and the body returns to normal.

❦ **Dystress** is unhealthy, unresolved stress that is both physically and emotionally draining and damaging. There are many stresses that continue day after day and don't have an obvious solution, or have a solution that is so unpleasant that we choose to live with the situation. Some of the stresses may be: loss or possible loss of a job; loss of a loved one; too heavy a workload or a job that you hate, with no end in sight; chronic shortage of money; friction with neighbours or workmates; and loneliness. Dystress can also be 'chemical stress' caused by an overload exposure to chemicals, synthetics, antibiotics, artificial fertilisers and pesticides, traffic fumes, television, computers, and additives in processed foods.

The warning signs of stress include:

- disturbed sleep or insomnia.
- frequent infections.
- persistent indigestion.
- backache.
- diarrhoea.
- irritability.
- poor concentration.
- problems with family and/or workmates.
- restlessness.
- sadness and/or tearfulness.
- tense, sore muscles.
- withdrawal.
- constant worry.
- substance abuse.

To help bodies to cope with dystress, we need to learn to like ourselves, find ways of defusing stressful situations, make sure that we make time for fun and time to share with those we love, get lots of hugs, eat well, get enough rest and sleep and learn to meditate.

Don't attempt to cope with severe dystress on your own. There are counsellors trained to help you to solve many of your problems, and even the simple act of talking things through with another person can often give clarity to a previously cloudy situation. Learn to be flexible. You may be over-rigid in your opinions—things don't always have to be done your way; people are entitled to have different opinions to yours. Bend a little—you might begin to enjoy the experience!

There are assertiveness-training courses available for those of you who 'give in' in a confrontation and find it difficult to have the courage to say what you want or feel. These courses are also for those who react (or over react) with anger or aggression in these same situations.

See also Relaxation and Breathing.

Sudorifics

Increase perspiration.

HERBS

Elderflower, peppermint, yarrow.

ESSENTIAL OILS

Basil, chamomile, dill, fennel, hyssop, juniper, peppermint, rosemary, tea-tree.

Did you know that used tea-bags contain tannin and will soothe the pain of sunburn and if laid on tired eyes they will soothe eye strain and under-eye puffiness?

Sunburn

The skin manufactures vitamin D when exposed to sun. We only need 10 minutes in the sun in the early morning or late afternoon to achieve this. Reduction in the earth's ozone layer has resulted in an increased incidence of skin cancers and premature ageing of the skin. Remember that having a tan means that you have cooked your skin.

INTERNAL TREATMENT

Drink copious quantities of filtered or bottled water to combat dehydration.

DAILY SUPPLEMENTS

1000 mg vitamin C with bioflavonoids for 3 days.

Essential oil treatment

* Run a lukewarm bath deep enough to submerge the body up to the neck. Add 10 drops of either chamomile or lavender oil to 1 tablespoon (20 ml) vegetable oil and disperse into the water. Stay in the bath for 15–30 minutes. Pat dry.
* If the face and head are burnt, apply cool compresses (see Compresses) using the same oils.
* Apply neat lavender oil to any blistered areas.

Herbal treatment

Bathe using a triple-strength tea of lavender and/or chamomile flowers. After patting dry, apply aloe vera gel to soothe the pain.

Homeopathic treatment

All 6–30^c unless otherwise indicated, take 3–4 times daily:
* For healing and also to help to prevent sunburn—Arnica.
* For pain of burns—Cantharis.
* Redness and burning—Belladonna.
* Stinging—Urtica urens.

Sunstroke

This condition can be life-threatening and must be treated as an emergency. The patient has a fast, heavy pulse and the skin is red and hot. There may be mental confusion, stupor or even unconsciousness. If conscious the patient may experience severe headache, nausea or blurred vision.

Reducing the temperature is the primary concern but professional help is needed as quickly as possible if the temperature doesn't drop to normal levels. The patient must be cooled quickly. Remove clothing and immerse the patient in a bath of cool water with very wet cold compresses on the entire head. If this is not possible, soak towels, sheets or other cloth in very cold water and wrap around the body. Change the cloths frequently or spray with fresh cold water. Fan the patient and rub the arms and legs to restore circulation.

INTERNAL TREATMENT

There is likely to be dehydration, so if the patient is conscious give
plenty of cool fluids—either water or diluted fruit juices.

HOMEOPATHIC TREATMENT

All 6–30ᶜ, take every 15–20 minutes until worst symptoms subside
then every 2–3 hours:

❋ General heat stroke—Belladonna, Arnica and Rescue Remedy.

Synergy

Occurs when the combination of more than one element becomes
more powerful than the single parts. By combining more than one
element, one creates a different chemical compound that has a greater
potency. Essential oils are often blended synergistically when 2, 3 or
4 oils having the same therapeutic uses are blended to enhance the
action.

Teas (infusions)

These are very simple herbal preparations, probably the oldest and most widely used but very rarely properly made. The making of a herbal tea can be a meditative ritual or a rushed, unthinking splashing of boiling water over the fresh or dried leaves. The first method takes no longer than the second but I'm convinced that from a therapeutic point of view the first has got to be better (my Taurean convictions regarding the power of the elemental blends). Use this method for chopped petals and leaves, crushed seeds and ground root or bark.

Use a non-metal teapot reserved exclusively for herbs as the tannin in tea could adulterate the delicate flavour of some herbs.

Teas can be used as a drink or, if made two or three times stronger, can be used in baths, compresses, fomentations, poultices, and face and hair rinses.

TO MAKE: *Pour 1 cup (250 ml) boiling water over 2 teaspoons fresh (1 teaspoon dried) plant material. Cover immediately. Stand 5–10 minutes. The longer the tea steeps, the more bitter it becomes in the same way as black tea so brew it until it's to your taste but obviously, the longer it steeps, the more constituents will be extracted.*

Sweeten with honey if liked.

To make a stronger tea to use externally in shampoos, skin tonics, creams etc. use double or triple the amount of herb to 1 cup (250 ml) boiling water and make as above.

DOSAGE

ADULTS	½–1 teacup three times daily between meals
CHILDREN	10–15 years: ½ teacup 3 times daily between meals
	6–10 years: ¼ teacup 3 times daily between meals
	2–6 years: 2 tablespoons (40 ml) 3 times daily between meals
BABIES	1 teaspoon 3 times daily

Babies should only be given teas that are safe for their age. These include chamomile, catnep, lemon balm and those mentioned in the Colic blend (see Colic).

Tea-tree (Melaleuca alternifolia)

HERB PART USED

Leaves.

HERB ACTIONS

A tea or infused oil is used for the same purposes as the essential oil. It is and was used particularly by Australian Aboriginal tribes and early settlers as a general 'cure-all' for infections and wounds.

ESSENTIAL OIL ACTION

This oil is a first-aid kit in a bottle. Antiviral, antifungal, antibacterial, antiseptic, disinfectant, immuno-stimulant.

USE TO TREAT

Urinary tract infections, trichomonas, candida, thrush. May help to heal genital herpes. Abscesses, ringworm, athlete's foot, corns, warts.

Coughs, bronchitis, colds. Cold sores, mouth ulcers, gingivitis, bad breath, tonsillitis. Acne, boils, burns, sunburn. ME and other auto-immune problems.

Caution: *In general, tea-tree oil is non-irritant and may be used undiluted over small areas of the body. However, there have been cases of allergic reaction to this oil so if you have a sensitive skin it may be advisable to do a patch-test (see Allergens). If you experience a reaction try substituting manuka (see Manuka) or rosewood oil (see Rosewood).*

Teeth

There are precautions that one can take to help to ensure strong healthy teeth, amongst these are having regular dental check-ups, brushing with a medium-bristle brush after eating, flossing, eating foods such as fruit and raw vegetables which give teeth and jaws good exercise (see also Toothache and Babies).

Did you know that if you can't clean your teeth after a meal you can eat a piece of cheddar cheese instead? It will neutralise the mouth acids that cause tooth decay.

MINT & LEMON TOOTHPOWDER

Make a separate jar for each member of the family to use to prevent the spread of mouth infections.

¹/₂ teacup bicarbonate of soda

¹/₄ teacup finely ground sea salt

1 tablespoon dried lemon peel (yellow only), finely ground to a powder

1 tablespoon dried peppermint leaves, finely ground to a powder

3 drops lemon oil

2 drops peppermint oil

TO MAKE: *Mix all except the essential oils. Pass through a fine sieve. Add the oils a drop at a time stirring constantly. Store in small airtight jars.*

Tendonitis

An inflammatory condition, often very painful, of the connective tissue (tendon) that connects muscle to bone. Achilles tendonitis is one form of such inflammation and occurs in the tendon behind the ankle. Another similar condition called bursitis (see Bursitis) can develop in joints such as the shoulder, knees and elbows. These conditions are usually caused by overuse of the joint.

❦ Rest to avoid further injury.

❦ Apply ice packs over a piece of cloth to the tendon for 30 minutes to decrease swelling.

❦ Repeat every 30 minutes for 3 hours, then decrease to 4 packs for 2 days.

❦ Follow with essential oil or herbal treatment described below.

❦ Where appropriate (such as Achilles tendonitis behind the ankle) use an elastic bandage to limit swelling, elevate foot above the level of the heart.

See also Repetitive Strain Injury and Carpal Tunnel Syndrome.

DAILY SUPPLEMENTS

Take 2 multi-vitamin capsules daily for 4 days, then 1 daily until condition improves.

ESSENTIAL OIL TREATMENT

After 3 days of the above treatment, massage twice daily with the following oil.

MASSAGE OIL

8 drops chamomile oil

6 drops lavender oil

1 tablespoon (20 ml) vegetable oil

TO MAKE: Mix together and use for gentle massage.

HERBAL TREATMENT

❧ After 2–3 days of ice-pack treatment use the following poultice.

❧ Pour boiling water over a cabbage leaf and leave for a few minutes until hot and wilted. Apply to the injured area while still hot but cool enough to bear. Bind in place. Renew poultice when cool.

HOMEOPATHIC TREATMENT

Take 4 times daily or as required for pain:

❧ First-aid—Arnica 30ᶜ; when arnica has done all that it can— Rhus. tox.

Throat, sore

Sore throats are sometimes the result of irritants such as talking too much or having to shout for some time, hayfever, open-mouth breathing, dust, cigarette smoke, air-borne chemical fumes or air conditioning. Other sore throats are largely bacterial or viral in origin.

Sore throats respond very well to natural therapies. If there is a high fever or there is no improvement after a few days you should seek professional help as the cause may be a streptococcal infection that can lead to complications.

Gargling (see Gargles) is indicated in cases where irritants cause the sore throat. See also Laryngitis & Hoarseness.

INTERNAL TREATMENT

Drink lots of fluids to keep the throat lubricated.

DAILY SUPPLEMENTS

❧ 500 mg vitamin C with bioflavonoids every 4 hours.
❧ 5000–10 000 iu beta-carotene.
❧ Suck zinc lozenges as directed for 1 week only.
❧ ½ teaspoon (2.5 ml) liquid extract of echinacea 3 times a day.
❧ Golden seal as directed.
❧ 1000 mg garlic oil capsules or 2–3 teaspoons 'Long-life juice' 3 times daily.

ESSENTIAL OIL TREATMENT

Inhalation (see Inhalations) using benzoin and/or thyme oil.

HERBAL TREATMENT

Gargle (see Gargles) every 2 hours with alternately a strong tea of sage, add 1 tablespoon (20 ml) cider vinegar and 1 teaspoon honey (5 ml) *or* ¼ teaspoon salt in 1 cup (250 ml) warm water.

HOMEOPATHIC TREATMENT

All 6–30^c unless otherwise indicated, take at least every hour until symptoms subside, then 4–5 times a day:

- Sore throat—Gelsemium.
- Sore throat with excessive saliva—Merc. sol.
- Sudden onset with fever—Belladonna.
- Dry and burning throat—Arsen. alb.
- Red, swollen throat with difficulty swallowing—Apis mel.

Thrush ❧ See Candida

Thuja (*Thuja occidentalis*) ❧ Homeopathic

Suited to dark-haired people who are strong minded and sometimes inflexible.

USE TO TREAT

Warts, styes, morning headaches, poor appetite in the morning.

Thyme (*Thymus vulgaris*)

HERB PART USED

Leaves.

HERB ACTIONS

Antispasmodic, antibacterial, antiseptic, carminative, expectorant, rubefacient, sedative, tonic.

USE TO TREAT

Respiratory and throat problems, catarrhal congestion, coughs, sore throat and laryngitis. Nerve and gastrointestinal tonic, eases flatulence, colic, stomach cramps, menstrual cramps and diarrhoea. The herb is used widely in cooking but note the caution against overuse.

Caution: *Excessive internal use is not recommended.*

ESSENTIAL OIL ACTION

Antispasmodic, antiseptic (thyme is the strongest antiseptic oil), carminative, diaphoretic, expectorant, sedative, stimulates the immune system.

USE TO TREAT

Respiratory problems such as asthma, bronchitis, catarrh, coughs, croup, emphysema, whooping cough. Use in ointments, washes and massage oils for boils, wounds, sores, thrush, leucorrhoea, low blood pressure, flatulence, arthritis.

Caution: *Not to be used in pregnancy or by those with high blood pressure. A very powerful oil use only at $\frac{1}{2}$–1 per cent dilution.*

Tinctures

Tinctures are an extract of the properties of herbs into alcohol or glycerine. Tinctures are much stronger than teas or decoctions — 1 teaspoon (5 ml) tincture is approximately equal to 1 cup of tea or decoction. Tinctures will last for many years if well made and stored.

The strength and keeping quality of a tincture is largely dependent on the strength of alcohol used in the preparation. You may find a pharmacist who will sell you some 95 per cent *ethanol* alcohol that will need to be diluted to 60–70 per cent with distilled water before use. The other option is to visit your local wine merchant to buy the highest proof vodka, gin or brandy in stock.

Glycerine-based tinctures don't contain as much resinous or oily material as the alcohol extract but are still good tinctures for those who either can't tolerate alcohol or who, for other reasons, don't want to use alcohol.

To make a tincture using alcohol

LEAVES, PETALS & FLOWERS (FRESH OR DRIED)

TO MAKE: *Fill a jar with finely chopped fresh plant material or half fill with dried material.*

Fill the jar with alcohol and close the jar with a non-metallic lid.

ROOTS, BARK & SEEDS

TO MAKE: *Chop the material as finely as possible.*

Cover approximately 30 g material with 1 cup (250 ml) alcohol.

Close the jar with a non-metallic lid.

TO USE: *The jars need to be labelled with the common and Latin name of the contents and a date two weeks hence when the tincture will be ready.*

Twice a day, place a folded cloth on a firm surface and tap the base of the jar gently but firmly on the cloth for at least one minute. This procedure is known as 'succussion' and releases the properties of the plant into the alcohol.

After two weeks, strain the tincture through a sieve and then through a coffee-filter paper into a dark coloured glass bottle. If you wish add 1 teaspoon (5 ml) glycerine to every 1 cup (250 ml) tincture to increase the keeping properties. Label the tincture with the name, Latin name and the date. Store in a dark, cool place.

To make a tincture using glycerine

Follow the instructions above but substitute the alcohol for a mixture of half-glycerine, half-water. If using fresh herbs use 75 per cent glycerine to 25 per cent water.

Uses & dosages of tinctures

INTERNAL: *5–15 drops depending on age (not to be given to children under the age of 5 years) in 2 tablespoons (40 ml) milk or water 3 times a day between meals.*

5 drops may be added to a tea or decoction to strengthen the action

EXTERNAL: *Add to poultices, fomentations, compresses, ointments,*

wound washes or herbal ice cubes. Use tinctures such as calendula neat on cuts to stop bleeding and prevent infection.
USEFUL TINCTURES: *calendula, cayenne, myrrh, willow bark, distilled witch-hazel.*

Tinea ❦ See Foot care

Tonics
Strengthen the whole body or a specific organ.

HERBS

Alfalfa, angelica, basil, ginger, marjoram, peppermint, spearmint, oregano, rue, thyme, wormwood.

ESSENTIAL OILS

Angelica, basil, black pepper, clove, geranium, ginger, lavender, lemon, marjoram, myrrh, rosemary, thyme.

Tonsillitis
Tonsillitis is most likely to occur in children and young adults but sometimes afflicts older people. It was once fashionable to remove the tonsils at the first sign of infection but it has now been recognised that they do a valuable job of defending the body from invading organisms.

INTERNAL TREATMENT

- Avoid dairy products until the infection is over.
- Drink at least 8–10 glasses of filtered or bottled water or diluted fruit juices.

DAILY SUPPLEMENTS

- 4000 mg vitamin C with bioflavonoids amount divided into 2 or 3 doses.
- See directions on container for dosages for children.

- ¼–½ teaspoon (1.25–2.5 ml) (depending on age) echinacea liquid extract 3 times daily.
- 1000 mg garlic oil capsules (not for young children) three times daily or 2–3 teaspoons 'Long-life juice' 3 times daily.

ESSENTIAL OIL TREATMENT

Inhalations (see Inhalations) using eucalyptus, myrrh, tea-tree or thyme oil.

HERBAL TREATMENT

- Gargle (see Gargles) using tincture of myrrh (see Tinctures) or strong teas of sage or thyme.
- Another effective gargle is ¼ teaspoon salt in a glass of lukewarm water.

HOMEOPATHIC TREATMENT

All 6–30ᶜ unless otherwise indicated, take frequently until worst symptoms subside:
- Sore throat, fever and thirst—Aconite.
- Severe sore throat with pus on the tonsils—Mercurius 12ᶜ.
- Tonsils swollen and discharging pus, pain on swallowing—Hepar. sulph.

Toothache

Obviously a visit to the dentist is indicated for toothache which often strikes at inappropriate times like the middle of the night. Pressing hard on the root of the aching tooth from the outside of the face often eases the pain. An ice cube held in the same area is also often useful. See also Teeth and Babies.

ESSENTIAL OIL TREATMENT

- Using a cotton bud apply 1 drop clove oil onto the aching tooth and use the residue on the bud to gently massage the gum surrounding the offending tooth.

* Gently massage the cheek over the aching tooth and along the jaw with 3 drops chamomile oil in 1 teaspoon (5 ml) warm vegetable oil.

HERBAL TREATMENT

A strong tea made of ground cloves held in the mouth and then spat out will often ease toothache. Whether you use the tea warm or cold depends on what eases your particular toothache best.

HOMEOPATHIC TREATMENT

All 6–30ᶜ, take whenever needed:
* Chamomilla, Mag. phos., Plantago.

Travel

Suggestions for a suitable travelling first-aid box can be found under First-aid.

TRAVEL SICKNESS/NAUSEA

To relieve car, boat or plane sickness, sprinkle a drop or two of peppermint or ginger oil on a handkerchief or tissue and sniff often.

Put drops of peppermint and lavender oil on cotton wool balls and place on the back and front window ledges when travelling by car. These will help to prevent nausea and also act as a calmative.

Half to one hour before setting off on a trip take 2 ginger tablets or capsules (available from pharmacies and health-food stores) or chew crystallised or glacé ginger.

ANTI-NAUSEA TEA

TO MAKE: *Mix up a bottle of either strong peppermint or ginger tea sweetened with honey.*

TO USE: *Take the following doses before leaving home and again as needed during the journey:*

Children aged 2–5 years: 2 teaspoons (10 ml)

Children aged 5–12 years: 2 tablespoons (40 ml)

Over 12 years: ½–1 cup (125–250 ml)

ANTI-BUG HAND WIPES

Colds, gastro-enteritis, hepatitis, influenza and scabies are just a few of the diseases that can be transmitted by handling door knobs, money, handrails, flush-buttons in toilets and many other places. The following tip can help to avoid the more obvious dangers.

TO MAKE: *Cut pieces of nappy liners to fit a small tin or cosmetic bag. Tissues or kitchen paper towels can be used but tend to fall to bits when damp. Mist lightly with water until damp, sprinkle with a mixture of tea-tree and lavender oils. Use to wipe the hands especially before eating or after using 'away-from-home' toilets. The cloths may be laundered and re-used. See also Epidemics.*

STOMACH UPSETS

Stomach upsets like Bali/Bombay/Delhi Belly, etc. are often a result of consuming different food and water and not necessarily because of some dreaded disease. If you have diarrhoea and/or vomiting it may be just the body's way of adapting to a new environment—the ginger or peppermint treatment above is useful for simple stomach upsets.

Dehydration is a serious consequence of diarrhoea and vomiting, particularly in small children. It's vital to drink lots of filtered water to replace the fluid loss.

The following precautions are advisable when travelling to tropical countries and/or third world countries.

✷ Drink only bottled water.

✷ Clean your teeth with bottled water.

✷ Use hand wipes (above) before eating.

✷ Avoid eating food from roadside stalls.

✷ Keep your eating as simple as possible for the first few days and avoid salads and other raw vegetables.

✷ Only eat fruit than can be peeled, and wash the fruit before peeling.

✷ Take acidophilus tablets as directed.

HOMEOPATHIC TREATMENT

Take frequently until crisis is past:

❦ To settle digestive juices—Nat. phos. 12^c and/or Nat. sulph. 12^c.

❦ Severe nausea, great thirst but inability to drink much—Arsen. album 30^c.

❦ Smell of food makes nausea worse—Cocculus 30^c.

FLYING

Even though it has been demonstrated statistically to be one of the safest forms of travel some people are very afraid of flying. Air travel can be very tiring, sitting for long periods of time in a pressurised cabin with nothing to do but eat or drink isn't exactly stimulating to either our brains or bodies.

❧ Drink lots of filtered or bottled water or diluted fruit juice (no alcohol) to counteract the dryness of the air.

❧ Walk around the aisles every half-hour if possible to help to prevent the swelling of legs and feet.

❧ Make up the following essential oil blend, which will both refresh you and calm your nerves.

PLANE NERVES & EXHAUSTION

This blend may be used for adults and children over the age of two.

6 drops lavender oil
6 drops geranium oil
4 drops chamomile oil
1 teaspoon (5 ml) vodka

TO MAKE: *Mix together in a small spray bottle. Shake well before use.*

TO USE: *Spray on a tissue and sniff as often as liked.*

❧ Carry a damp flannel in a plastic bag, spray lightly with the blend and use to wipe over hands and face. If you are stressed or nervous, wring the flannel out in very hot water, spray as above and use as directed. Holding the hot flannel on the back of the neck is also soothing and relaxing. The spray must be *very light* if used for children—only one quick squirt.

HOMEOPATHIC TREATMENT

All 6–30^c, take frequently as long as symptoms persist:

❀ Fear of flying and jet lag—Rescue Remedy.

❀ Travel sickness and jet lag—Arnica, Kali. phos.

JET LAG

Flying can get us from one side of the globe to the other in the space of a few hours. A few simple tactics can be helpful to overcome the problems our bodies often experience adjusting to this time change.

❧ On arrival have a shower or bath using the following blend. If this isn't possible wring a flannel out in cool water, sprinkle with 2 drops of the following blend and use to wipe over the face, neck and arms. Repeat over as much of your body as possible. Have a fresh change of clothes.

❧ Don't go to sleep until local bedtime.

❧ Drink lots of filtered or bottled water, not alcohol.

JET-LAG 'LET-GO'

1 teaspoon (5 ml) grapefruit oil

1 teaspoon (5 ml) lavender oil

½ teaspoon (2.5 ml) rosemary oil

TO MAKE: *Mix together in a little bottle. Shake well.*

TO USE: *See the first suggestion under Jet lag.*

u

Ulcers

MOUTH ULCERS

This is the best method I have found for treating mouth ulcers: dissolve 1 teaspoon Epsom salts in 1 glass of warm water. Take a mouthful of the mixture and 'swoosh' around the mouth as vigorously as possible, spit out. Repeat with all the mixture. Continue the treatment as long as needed.

HOMEOPATHIC TREATMENT

Merc. sol. — 2 tablets for adults, 1 tablet for children, 1 crushed tablet for babies.

STOMACH ULCERS

An ulcer is a sore or hole in the lining of the stomach or duodenum (the first part of the small intestine). It is characterised by a gnawing or burning pain in the upper abdomen between the breastbone and the navel and occurs about an hour after eating or during the night. The pain may last for minutes or hours and is often relieved by eating, antacids or vomiting. Sometimes ulcers bleed (the blood is sometimes vomited or may be passed as dark red blood along with bowel motions) which, if continuing for a long time, can lead to anaemia. An X-ray is usually needed for a definite diagnosis. The term 'peptic ulcer' is used to describe any one of several types of ulcers in the upper gastrointestinal tract.

It was once thought that all peptic ulcers were caused by stress, excess stomach acid or over indulgence in spicy foods. It has now been discovered that nine out of ten cases of ulcers are caused by a bacterium called *Helicobacter pylori* that lives on the lining of the stomach. The presence of *H. pylori* can be detected by a blood or breath test. The use of appropriate antibiotics will rid the body of the bacterium.

Medical attention is vital for sufferers of peptic ulcers as life-threatening complications such as haemorrhage, obstruction and perforation can occur.

The following treatments have been found most effective for those who have peptic ulcers in the absence of *H. pylori*: Use after consultation with your doctor. For identification and reduction of stress (see Relaxation).

- ❦ 300 ml cabbage juice twice daily.
- ❦ Golden seal tablets, take as directed.
- ❦ Slippery elm powder or tablets, take as directed.

Consult a homeopathic practitioner for an appropriate remedy.

TROPICAL ULCERS

Grind dried comfrey root to a powder or blend fresh root to a pulp, mix to a paste with water or calendula tea and pack gently into the ulcers. Bandage the area. Change once or twice a day, washing the area with warm, boiled water to which you have added a few drops of tea-tree oil.

Urethritis

Urethritis is inflammation of the lining of the urethra (the bladder outlet tube). For treatment see Cystitis.

Urticaria ❦ See Hives

Uterines

Tone and strengthen the uterus.

Herbs

Blue cohosh, cramp bark, dong quai, false unicorn root.

Essential oils

Clary sage, frankincense, jasmine, melissa, myrrh, rose.

Valerian (*Valeriana officinalis*)

HERB PART USED

Leaf (vulnerary) and root.

HERB ACTIONS

Antispasmodic, calmative, carminative, nervine, stomachic, tranquilliser.

USE TO TREAT

Headaches, hysteria, hyperactive children, fatigue (acts as a stimulant), stress, insomnia, nervous tension, migraine. Decreases muscle spasms: use for stomach and menstrual cramps, irritable bowel syndrome, nervous indigestion. Use the leaf in healing ointments.
Caution: *Can cause headaches, depression and palpitations if overused. Take only in recommended doses.*

ESSENTIAL OIL ACTION

Anodyne, antidandruff, antispasmodic, bactericidal, carminative, diuretic, hypnotic, hypotensive, sedative, stomachic.

USE TO TREAT

Boils, ringworm, scabies, wounds. arthritis, gout, muscular aches and pains, rheumatism, sciatica. Bronchitis, catarrh. Cystitis, urethritis. Neuralgia.

Varicose veins

There is now evidence that shows that varicose veins are likely to be a genetically inherited complaint. If one or more of your family suffer from this complaint take extra care of your legs. Avoid standing for long periods of time, constipation, being overweight, smoking, very hot baths, sitting with your knees crossed. Take frequent walks. In the evening rest with the legs elevated.

INTERNAL TREATMENT

Eat a diet rich in fibre. When cooking use the spices that stimulate the circulatory system such as ginger and cayenne. Eat buckwheat porridge every morning for the rutin content.

DAILY SUPPLEMENTS

- 1 vitamin B complex tablet.
- 1,000 mg vitamin C with bioflavonoids.
- 500 iu vitamin E.
- 15–30 mg zinc.
- Horse chestnut (*Aesculus hippocastanum*) as directed.
- Gotu kola (*Centella asiatica*) as directed.
- 500–750 mg bromelain 3 times daily between meals.

ESSENTIAL OIL TREATMENT

COMPRESS BLEND

10 drops cypress oil

5 drops geranium oil

5 drops juniper

2 tablespoons (40 ml) ice cold distilled witch-hazel

TO USE: *Use as a compress 2–3 times daily.*

HERBAL TREATMENT

- Ice-cold compresses of distilled witch-hazel 2–3 times daily.
- Teas of gotu kola leaves twice daily, 6 days a week.

HOMEOPATHIC TREATMENT

Take 4 times daily:

✻ Varicose veins—Hamamelis 12^c, Pulsatilla 30^c and Calc. fluor. 12^c.

Vasoconstrictors

Cause small blood vessels to contract.

ESSENTIAL OILS

Chamomile, cypress, geranium, peppermint, rose.

Vinegars, bath ❦ See Bath vinegars

Visualisation

This powerful technique of 'seeing' pictures or scenes in your mind can be used to make changes to your physical and mental health and your self-esteem. It can be a useful tool in pain management.

Visualisation done regularly can change your life. It can get you that job you want, improve your athletic performance and/or win that race (many sportspeople use visualisation as a training tool before a big event). It can also cure the physical problem from which you are suffering.

Visualisation involves 'seeing' an image in your mind. Many people insist that they can't visualise but in fact we visualise unconsciously for most of the day. Think about shopping and visualise the vegetable counters with their piles of coloured fruits and vegetables, see yourself choosing some fruit and putting it in a bag. Think about your office, look at the items on your desk; open the top drawer and see what's inside. Play around with visualisations of familiar objects, places or people (for some reason, people are often very hard to visualise) until you feel comfortable with the knowledge that you can, and already do, visualise.

One illustration of the powers of visualisation: when my youngest daughter was 16 years old she fell off a horse and fractured a vertebra in her spine. She was hospitalised but after three days I discharged her as I was very unhappy with the treatment that she was receiving.

A special bed was prepared in a room next to the kitchen where she could still feel part of the family. I suggested to her that she should find some visualisation that would benefit the vertebra. At first she was adamant that she couldn't think of anything and asked if I would suggest something—I was equally adamant that 'this is not how it works'. I left her with some peaceful music playing and after 20 minutes or so was called back into the room. Her visualisation was the Seven Dwarves! They went to work carrying small tools and pieces of clean, new bone. Some of the dwarves would sit fashioning pieces of bone while the others painstakingly removed, bit by bit, the damaged vertebra; the dwarves then changed places and the fitting of the new bone segments would begin.

The process continued daily—probably for 15–20 minutes, 3–4 times each day. After about 6 weeks she announced that the dwarves has finished and her vertebra was now OK. Her spine was X-rayed once more and to the disbelief of the doctor there was absolutely no trace of a fracture having ever occurred.

Find a visualisation that is positive and powerful. For example, ulcers may be visualised as Daleks pouring acid onto your membranes; the conquerors may be huge white polar bears with syringes that squirt healing, cool liquid that counteracts the acid and destroys the Daleks. It's most important that the images be your own, coming from your own heart and mind.

Try to do the visualisation several times a day even if only for a few moments—this is more powerful than doing an hour once or twice a week.

Vitamins

Preferably vitamins and minerals are obtained by eating a diet rich in the necessary nutrients but sometimes this isn't possible. Ill-health, stress, difficulty in obtaining fresh fruits and vegetables, falling food intake and poor food absorption in the aged mean that our bodies become depleted. It mustn't be thought, however, that vitamin supplements are a substitute for food, in fact the vitamins cannot be assimilated without eating food.

The following list shows the foods and herbs richest in each vitamins and minerals. If possible, increase your intake of the foods needed for your particular complaint but if the complaint is long-standing or severe, supplements may be taken until the problem eases.

Supermarkets are not usually the best place to buy supplements. Buy your vitamins and minerals from a reputable source where the assistant is helpful and knowledgeable, and ask for natural, not synthetic, vitamins. Synthetic vitamins often cost less but can cause allergic reactions in chemically susceptible people and can often cause gastrointestinal upsets. They can also cause toxic reactions that don't occur with natural vitamins.

All herbs contain some vitamins and minerals in varying amounts. The herbs suggested are those that are the best source.

Please take note of the warnings that may accompany some supplements.

Vitamin and mineral supplements are best divided into three doses, each to be taken after a meal. If there is only one dose it's best taken after the largest meal of the day. Descriptions of the main vitamins follow:

VITAMIN A (RETINOL & BETA-CAROTENE)

What it can do: counteract night blindness, burning and itching eyes, inflamed eyelids and weak eyesight. Boost the immune system. Shorten the duration of infections. Build resistance to respiratory infections. Keep skin tissue healthy. Help to treat acne, boils, impetigo and ulcers if applied externally. May be useful in the treatment of emphysema and hyperthyroidism.

Main sources: *Retinol*: fish-liver oil, kidneys and liver, eggs, milk and dairy foods; *beta-carotene*: carrots, pumpkin, sweet potato, green (particularly dark green) leafy vegetables, yellow vegetables, yellow fruits.

Herbal sources: alfalfa, dandelion greens, nettle, cress (both landcress and watercress).

Destroyed by: heat and light.

Caution: *Large doses of vitamin A will cause toxicity. Abide by the recommended dosage, take for 6 days and rest for one day. Don't continue for more than one month. If headaches or skin dryness and flaking occur discontinue immediately. Avoid supplementation if either pregnant or planning pregnancy. Supplementation from beta-carotene is safer.*

VITAMIN B1 (THIAMIN)

What it can do: ease fatigue, benefit the nervous system and mental attitude. Aid digestion, help to ease travel sickness and relieve dental post-operative pain.

Main sources: brewer's yeast, wholegrains, seeds, nuts, beans, lentils, brown rice, eggs and milk products, soya flour, oats, pork and liver

Herbal sources: dandelion greens, sunflower seeds, thyme

Destroyed by: alcohol, baking powder, bicarbonate of soda, oestrogen, sulphur dioxide (preservative). In cooking 30–40 per cent is leached out (keep water to a minimum and use the cooking water).

VITAMIN B2 (RIBOFLAVIN)

What it can do: help to relieve mouth ulcers, cold sores. Helps to promote healthy skin, hair and nails. Aid in growth and reproduction. May reduce eye fatigue. It's not necessary to take this vitamin separately.

Main sources: brewer's yeast, liver, wheatgerm, cheese, eggs, wheat bran, meat, soya flour, yoghurt, milk, green-leafed vegetables.

Herbal sources: dandelion greens, thyme, watercress.

Destroyed by: sensitive to light. Leaches into cooking water (see vitamin B1).

VITAMIN B3 (NIACIN)

What it can do: help to ease and prevent migraine headaches and to reduce blood pressure. May reduce cholesterol. It creates a reaction called the 'niacin flush' if doses over 100 mg are taken. The flush is the result of the dilation of blood vessels in the skin. May ease gastrointestinal problems. May be useful (taken in 100 mg doses twice a day with food) for sufferers of Raynaud's disease (see Raynaud's disease), night leg cramps and cold hands and feet.

Main sources: (see vitamin B2) chicken.

Herbal sources: anise, dandelion greens, land cress.

Destroyed by: see vitamin B2.

VITAMIN B5 (PANTOTHENIC ACID)

What it can do: help to heal wounds, prevent fatigue, aid in recovery from post-operative shock, reduce toxic effects of antibiotics, build antibodies and so fight infection.

Main sources: see vitamin B3.

Herbal sources: catnep, dandelion greens and nettle.

Destroyed by: a combination of heat and bicarbonate of soda and/or vinegar. Lost by leaching into cooking water, drying, deep freezing.

VITAMIN B6 (PYRIDOXINE)

What it can do: help to relieve symptoms of Carpal Tunnel Syndrome and other nerve-compression injuries, PMS, some types of depression and arthritis. Help to assimilate protein and fat. Alleviate morning sickness. Help to reduce night leg cramps and muscle spasms.

Main sources: brewer's yeast, wheat bran, wheatgerm, oats, pig liver, soya flour, bananas, nuts, meats, green-leafed vegetables, fatty fish, avocados.

Herbal sources: anise, dandelion greens.

Destroyed by: cooking and exposure to light.

VITAMIN B12 (CYANOCOBALAMINE)

What it can do: regenerate red blood cells, aid the nervous system and relieve irritability. Increase energy levels, improve concentration and memory. May be useful as part of overall treatment of AIDS (see AIDS).

Main sources: liver, organ meats, meat, fish, dairy produce, eggs, brewer's yeast.

Herbal sources: alfalfa.

Destroyed by: bicarbonate of soda and other alkalis.

FOLIC ACID (FOLATE)

What it can do: improve lactation, act as an analgesic for pain, give protection against internal parasites, help to prevent anaemia, act as a preventative against canker sores. Deficiency may cause brain and spinal-cord deficiency defects at birth.

Main sources: liver, green vegetables, carrots, kidneys, egg yolks, wholegrain cereals.

Herbal sources: red raspberry.

Destroyed by: some destroyed by cooking.

BIOTIN

What it can do: ease muscle pain, alleviate skin problems such as dermatitis and eczema, and help to prevent baldness.

Main sources: brewer's yeast, meats, dairy produce, and wholegrain cereals.

Herbal sources: alfalfa, dandelion greens, thyme, watercress.

Destroyed by: leaches into cooking water (use in drinks or gravy).

CHOLINE

What it can do: may prevent build-up of cholesterol on artery walls, help to improve memory, may be useful to treat Altzheimer's disease and dementia, soothe stressed nerves. Support liver function by eliminating toxins.

Main sources: liver, lecithin granules, beef heart, egg-yolk, brewer's yeast.

Herbal sources: alfalfa, dandelion greens, nettle, parsley, watercress.

Destroyed by: stable during cooking.

VITAMIN C

What it can do: act as an anti-oxidant to protect other vitamins from destruction and prevent cellular damage; essential for collagen production (vital for youthful skin, strong joints and bones); aid the swift healing of sores, burns, wounds; decrease cholesterol; strengthen the immune system (see Immune system) and aid in prevention and treatment of colds and flu and other types of viral and bacterial infections.

Main sources: most fruits and vegetables (especially broccoli and green capsicum, which are very high in vitamin C), potatoes, liver, kidney.

Herbal sources: most herbs but particularly rosehips, dandelion greens, parsley and watercress.

Destroyed by: prolonged cooking and storage.

VITAMIN D

What it can do: aids in the treatment of conjunctivitis. Essential for the absorption of calcium and phosphorus (needed for bone formation). It releases calcium from the bones into the blood.

Main sources: sunlight, fatty fish, cod-liver oil, eggs, milk, cheese, butter and other foods to which vitamin D has been added.

Herbal sources: alfalfa, land and watercress, nettle, red raspberry.

Caution: *Most toxic of all the vitamins, supplementation only to be used under professional supervision.*

VITAMIN E (TOCOPHEROL)

What it can do: act as an anti-oxidant, protect against cell damage, ensure a good supply of oxygen to the cells and protects other vitamins in the body. Bring blood to the small capillaries and also prevent blood clots. Help to lower blood pressure, prevent thrombosis, atherosclerosis, heart attacks and strokes. Excellent, applied topically, for healing scars. (There are eight tocopherols but d-alpha is the most effective to use.)

Main sources: vegetable oils, nuts, seeds, soya, peanut butter, lettuce, tomatoes, peas, green beans, celery, apples, bananas, eggs, dairy produce.

Herbal sources: alfalfa, dandelion greens, land and watercress.

Destroyed by: deep frying, some by cooking.

VITAMIN P (CITRUS BIOFLAVONOIDS, RUTIN, HESPERIDIN)

What it can do: acts as an anti-oxidant for vitamin C, strengthens the capillary walls (tiny blood vessels), helps build resistance to infection and helps to heal bleeding gums.

Main sources: white pith and segment skin of citrus fruit, apricots, and buckwheat.

Herbal sources: blackberries, rosehips.

Vulneraries

Arrest bleeding and help wounds to heal.

HERBS

Aloe, calendula, chamomile, comfrey, lavender, mallow, plantain, rosemary, sage, shepherd's purse, thyme, valerian, willow bark, yarrow.

ESSENTIAL OILS

Benzoin, bergamot, chamomile, lavender, myrrh, rosemary, tea-tree.

Warts

The best treatment for warts is to make the body pay attention to them by applying any of the following treatments. The body will then be alerted and will begin to fight the warts.

One of my daughters 'sold' her warts to her older brother. The warts disappeared in a week and appeared on the brother a few days later! Another method is to visualise white light surrounding the wart and gently melting it away, or you can find a visualisation that works for you. Do the visualisation at any time when you are alone and can spend a few quiet, uninterrupted moments getting rid of your wart!

DAILY SUPPLEMENTS

If you suffer from either recurrent or large numbers of warts your immune system may need help (see Immune system).

ESSENTIAL OIL TREATMENT

Considerable success has been achieved in the removal of warts with the use of tea-tree oil. Use a cotton bud to paint one drop of tea-tree oil directly onto the wart. Put a sticking plaster over the wart.

Repeat this treatment twice a day until the wart has gone. If the skin is very dry after the treatment is complete, massage with a little calendula infused oil or, if this is not available, prick a capsule of vitamin E and squeeze the contents onto the area massaging it in gently.

HERBAL TREATMENT

Use the white latex that oozes out when the stalk of the dandelion flower or fig is snapped. Apply one drop only onto the wart, taking care not to get any on the surrounding skin. Cover with a sticking plaster. Repeat twice daily until the wart is gone.

If the skin is dry where the wart dropped off the vitamin E treatment described above may be used. Thuja ointment is also a very effective treatment for warts.

HOMEOPATHIC TREATMENT

- Soft, fleshy wart and plantar warts—Thuja 12^c.
- Large, jagged wart that stings—Nit. ac. 12^c.
- Sore wart—Causticum 30^c.

Water

Water is an excellent growth medium for bacteria. As water is one of the main ingredients called for in many of the recipes in this book, it's advisable to use distilled or purified water to ensure that the preparations last as long as possible. This applies particularly to moisture creams, lotions, tonics and similar skin-care preparations.

Drinking 6–8 glasses of filtered or bottled water a day will help your liver, kidneys and intestines to excrete efficiently. Drinking this amount of chlorinated tap water could be very harmful.

Many vague 'unwell' feelings have been traced to the chlorine gas given off in hot water from the bath or shower water. Keep the windows and/or the door wide open and use an extractor fan when bathing or showering.

Wax

BEESWAX

Beeswax, a wax secreted by bees which forms the cell walls of the honeycomb, is an excellent hardener for ointments and creams. It is available for purchase from most of the suppliers listed in the back of this book, from pharmacies or direct from apiarists.

Beeswax is quite difficult to handle as it is hard and yet persistently sticky. Try to keep separate equipment for beeswax and woolfat as they are difficult to clean well enough for later use in cooking.

To prepare beeswax for use try one of the following methods.

🐝 Melt down an amount of wax and pour into ice cube trays making sure that the levels are pretty much the same in each compartment. Leave to set. Take 10 of the cubes, weigh and divide the weight by 10. You will now know the average weight of each cube. Pack the cubes in an airtight container, mark with the weight per cube, and store in a cool place.

🐝 Very finely grate the beeswax. Press into a metric teaspoon measure until level. Each level teaspoonful will weigh approximately 1 g and each metric tablespoonful (level) will weigh approximately 4 g.

EMULSIFYING WAX

Emulsifying wax is an agent that blends oils and water together as an homogenous mixture. There are many emulsifying agents available but the one that I have used for the past 12 years is cetomacrogol emulsifying wax. This is a mixture of 80 per cent cetostearyl alcohol and 20 per cent polyethylene glycol (cetomacrogol 1000) melted together. This emulsifying wax creates a very stable emulsion which rarely separates (in fact I have *never* had it separate) and the resulting cream or lotion is smooth and creamy in texture and sinks into the skin. If you have difficulty obtaining the wax at your pharmacy see the suppliers list at the back of this book.

Whooping Cough

This highly infectious and serious bacterial disease usually affects the very young. Professional help is always needed. The mucus is very thick and sticky causing violent and very distressing spasms of coughing and difficulty in breathing.

The suggestions below are an adjunct to professional treatment and can help to reduce the severity and discomfort of the disease.

The bedroom needs to be airy but humid. Keep a bowl of steaming water and/or an oil burner in the room at all times. A steam kettle is ideal.

INTERNAL TREATMENT

Avoid dairy foods. Give copious amounts of filtered or bottled water or fresh fruit juices.

DAILY SUPPLEMENTS

- For children over 5 years old, a supplement of 200–400 mg vitamin C with bioflavonoids may be given daily.
- Echinacea fluid extract for children as directed.

ESSENTIAL OIL TREATMENT

A
1 drop tea-tree oil
1 drop lavender oil
1 drop thyme oil
Use as an inhalation (see Inhalations) and also in oil burners, steam kettles, etc.

B
1 drop cypress
2 drops tea-tree oil
2 drops lavender oil
1 tablespoon (20 ml) vegetable oil
TO MAKE: *Mix together.*
TO USE: *Massage the chest and back.*

Caution: *Both these essential oil treatments are only to be used on children over 3 years of age.*
- From 3 to 5 drops (depending on age) of the same oils can be used in the bath.

HERBAL TREATMENT

- Very finely chop 1 onion and 1 clove garlic, put in a jar, cover with honey and the juice of 1 lemon. Leave overnight.

⚘ Take ¼–1 teaspoon (1.25–5 ml) of the mixture 3 times a day
depending on age (not to be given to children under 2 years old).

⚘ Give ½ teacup chamomile tea (see Teas) 3–6 times a day.

HOMEOPATHIC TREATMENT

Take 8 times daily until symptoms lessen:

❀ Vomiting from coughing, violent attacks of coughing—
Drosera 30ᶜ.

❀ Suffocating cough, panic attacks—Aconite, 30ᶜ.

❀ With nausea and sickness, rattling of mucus in bronchial tubes—
Ipecac. 30ᶜ.

Wild yam (*Dioscorea villosa*)

HERB PART USED

Dried roots.

HERB ACTIONS

Antispasmodic, anti-inflammatory, antirheumatic, cholagogue.

USE TO TREAT

Colitis and to soothe the pain of diverticulitis. Painful period cramps
and ovarian and uterine pain. Use to ease the inflammation in
rheumatoid arthritis and rheumatism.

Wild yam contains a plant hormone (diosgenin) which is similar to
progesterone and can be used to overcome the negative effects of
declining progesterone levels that occur with ageing.

ESSENTIAL OIL ACTION

None.

Willow bark (*Salix alba*)

HERB PARTS USED

New bark.

HERB ACTIONS

Anti-inflammatory, anodyne, analgesic, antiseptic, astringent, dia-phoretic, febrifuge. Contains aspirin-like salicylates.

USE TO TREAT

Arthritis, gout, rheumatism, pain and inflammation. Influenza and fevers. Eases internal and external bleeding. Use as a gargle to ease sore throats, laryngitis and tonsillitis. A decoction is used to wash wounds, burns, and sores.

ESSENTIAL OIL ACTION

None.

Witch-hazel (*Hamamelis virginiana*)

HERB PART USED

Young twigs and leaves.

HERB ACTIONS

Astringent, haemostatic, sedative, tonic.

USE TO TREAT

Pain and inflammation from bruises, swellings, haemorrhoids, cuts, varicose veins, insect bites. Useful as a skin astringent but distilled witch-hazel must be used as home-made teas and decoctions are too astringent to use.

ESSENTIAL OIL ACTION

None.

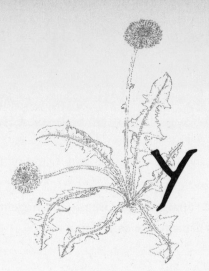

Yarrow (*Achillea millefolium*)

HERB PART USED

Flowers and leaves.

HERB ACTIONS

Anti-inflammatory, antispasmodic, astringent, carminative, chola-gogue, diaphoretic, haemostatic, tonic.

USE TO TREAT

High blood pressure, poor circulation, helps to stop bleeding. Mix with peppermint and elderflower and drink a tea three times daily to encourage sweating and reduce fever. Excessive menstrual flow. Cystitis, stomach cramps, flatulence, gastritis, gallbladder and liver complaints. Use in compresses, fomentations and ointments for wounds of all types.

ESSENTIAL OIL ACTION

None.

Ylang-ylang (*Cananga odorata*)

HERB PART USED

Flowers.

HERB ACTIONS

Antidepressant, aphrodisiac, hypotensive, sedative.

USE TO TREAT

Depression, high blood pressure, impotence and frigidity (stress induced).

ESSENTIAL OIL ACTION

As herb plus antiseptic.

USE TO TREAT

Over-excitability, shock, stress, hormone imbalance, impotence and frigidity (stress induced), rapid heartbeat, high blood pressure (stress induced), balances sebum in both oily and dry skin.

Yellow dock (*Rumex crispus*)

HERB PART USED

Roots.

HERB ACTIONS

Alterative, astringent, cholagogue, purgative.

USE TO TREAT

Chronic skin complaints such as eczema and psoriasis. Gently laxative, blood purifier, increases the flow of bile.

ESSENTIAL OIL

None.

Notes

ACNE
[1] L. Juhlin and G. Michaelsson, 'Acne' in M. Murray and J. Pizzorno, *Encyclopaedia of Natural Medicine*, Optima, London, 1994.

AIDS
[1] J. E. Groopman, 'Clinical spectrum of HTLV-111 in humans', *Cancer Research (supp.)*, 45, 1985, pp. 4649–54.
[2] V. Herbert, W. Fong, V. Gulle and T. Stopler, 'Low holotranscobalamin in patients with AIDS', in *American Journal of Hematology*, 34 (2), 1990, pp. 132–9.
[3] B. M. Dworkin, P. P. Antonecchia, F. Smith, L. Weiss, M. Davidian, D. Rubin and W. S. Rosenthal, 'Reduced cardiac selenium content in the acquired immunodeficiency syndrome', in *Parenternal Enteral Nutrition*, 13 (6), 1989, pp. 644–7.
[4] M. Murray and J. Pizzorno, p. 116.

ANGINA PECTORIS
[1] G. Orlando and C. Rusconi, 'Oral L-carnitine in the treatment of chronic cardiac ischaemia in elderly patients', in *Clinical Trials Journal*, 23, 1986, pp. 338–44 and P. Pola, L. Savi, M. Serrichio et al., 'Use of physiological substance acetyl-carnitine in the treatment of angiospastic syndromes', in *Drugs in Experimental Clinical Research*, 10, 1984, pp. 213–17.
[2] T. Kamikawa, A. Kobyashi, T. Yamashita et al., 'Effects of coenzyme Q10 on exercise tolerance in chronic stable angina pectoris', in *American Journal of Cardiology*, 56, 1985, p. 247.

AROMATHERAPY & ESSENTIAL OILS
[1] R. Tisserand and T. Balacs, *Essential Oil Safety: A Guide for Health Care Professionals*, Churchill Livingstone, New York, 1995, p. 10.

ASTHMA
[1] S. W. Simon, 'Asthma' in Murray and Pizzorno.

ASTRAGALUS
[1] D. C. Wang, 'Influence of Astragalus membranaceus polysaccharide FB on immunological function of human periphery blood lymphocyte', in *Index Medicus*, 11 (3), 1989, pp. 180–3 and D. Chu, Y. Sun, W. Wong and G. Mavligit, 'Astragalus membranaceus, potentiates lymphokine-activated killer cell cytotoxicity generated by low-dose recombitant inerleukin-2', in *Index Medicus*, 10 (1), 1990, pp. 34–6.

ATHEROSCLEROSIS
[1] D. H. Blankenhorn, 'The Angiographic evidence for lipid lowering effects in human coronary atherosclerosis regression', in *Current Opinions in Cardiology*, 6, 1991, pp. 574–80.

BLOOD PRESSURE
[1] N. M. Kaplan, 'Hypertension' in Murray and Pizzorno.
[2] R. Havlick, H. Hubert, R. Fabsitz and M. Feinleib, 'Weight and hypertension', in *Annals of Internal Medicine*, 98, 1983, pp. 855–9.

BRUISES
[1] A. Weil *Natural Health, Natural Medicine*, Warner Books, London, 1995, p. 269.

CANCER
[1] P. Davis, *Aromatherapy. An A–Z*, C. W. Daniel Company Ltd, Essex, 1995, p. 67.

DANDELION
[1] J. A. Duke, 'Anaemia', in Murray and Pizzorno.

EVENING PRIMROSE
[1] A. Weil, p. 230.

FEVERFEW
[1] E. S. Johnson, N. P. Kadam, D. M. Hylands and P. J. Hylands, 'Efficacy of feverfew as prophylactic treatment of migraine', in *British Medical Journal*, 291, 1995, pp. 569–73.

GENTIAN ROOT
[1] J. A. Duke, in Murray and Pizzorno.

HAWTHORN
[1] V. W. H. Mavers and H. Hensel, 'Angina Pectoris' in Murray and Pizzorno.

HERPES
[1] E. Mindell, *The Vitamin Bible*, Arlington Books, Horsham, UK, 1995, p. 102.

LIVER HEALTH
[1] D. B. Mowrey, *The Scientific Validation of Herbal Medicine*, Cormorant Books, Lehi, UT, 1986.

MULTIPLE SCLEROSIS
[1] B. A. Agranoff and D. Goldberg, 'Diet and the geographical distribution of multiplesclerosis', in *Lancet*, 2, 1974, pp. 1061–2.

PAIN
[1] R. Melzack and P. D. Wall, *The Challenge of Pain*, 2nd edn, Penguin, London, 1988.
[2] S. Pearce and J. Mays, 'Chronic pain assessment', in S. J. E. Lindsay and G. E. Powell (eds), *The Handbook of Clinical Adult Psychology*, 2nd edn, Routledge, London, 1994.
[3] Ibid.
[4] Ibid.

Bibliography

To the following authors I proffer my deep thanks for increasing my knowledge and also my thirst to know more. I can heartily recommend these books to you, the reader.

British Herbal Pharmacopoeia, British Herbal Medicine Association, 1983.

Cooksley, V.G. *Aromatherapy*, Prentice Hall, 1996.

Cribb, A. B & J. W. *Useful Wild Plants in Australia*, Fontana/Collins, 1982.

Culpeper, N. *Culpeper's Complete Herbal*, W. Foulsham & Co. Ltd, 1952.

Cummings, S. & Ullman, D. *Everybody's Guide to Homeopathic Medicines*, Gollancz Paperbacks, 1986.

Davies, S. & Stewart A. *Nutritional Medicine*, Pan Books Ltd, 1987.

Davis, P. *Aromatherapy: An A–Z*, C. W. Daniel, 1988.

Grieve, M. *A Modern Herbal*, Penguin, 1983.

Hoffman, D. L. *Thorsons Guide to Medical Herbalism*, HarperCollins, 1991.

Lassak, E. V. & McCarthy, T. *Australian Medicinal Plants*, Methuen, Australia, 1983.

Lawless, J. *The Encyclopaedia of Essential Oils*, Element, 1992.

Lee, John R. with Virginia Hopkins *What Your Doctor May Not Tell You About Menopause*, Warner Books, 1996.

Lust, J. *The Herb Book*, Bantam, 1987.

Martindale Pharmacopoeia, Pharmaceutical Press, 1982.

Maury, M. *Marguerite Maury's Guide to Aromatherapy*, C. W. Daniel, 1989.

Mindell, E. *The Vitamin Bible*, Arlington Books, 1995.

Mojay, G. *Aromatherapy for Healing the Spirit*, Hodder & Stoughton, 1996.

Murray, M. & Pizzorno, J. *Encyclopaedia of Natural Medicine*, Optima, 1994.

Schauenberg, P. & Paris, F. *Guide to Medicinal Plants*, Lutterworth Press, 1977.

Sellar, W. *The Directory of Essential Oils*, C.W. Daniel, 1993.

Stanton, R. *Complete Book of Food and Nutrition*, Simon & Schuster, 1989.

Tisserand, R. *Aromatherapy*, Granada Publishing, 1979.

Tisserand, R. & Balacs, T. *Essential Oil Safety*, Churchill Livingstone, 1996.

Weil, A. *Natural Health, Natural Medicine*, Warner Books, 1995.

Weil, A. *Spontaneous Healing*, Warner Books, 1995.

Worwood, V.A. *The Fragrant Pharmacy*, Macmillan, 1990.

Wren, R. C. *Potters New Cyclopaedia of Botanical Drugs and Preparations*, C. W. Daniel, 1988.

Suppliers

NEW SOUTH WALES

Essential Energies (Essential oils & candles)
16 Glebe Rd, Glebe NSW 2037
Phone (02) 9552 3538   Fax (02) 9692 9909

Essential Health (Health foods & vitamins)
328 Victoria Ave, Chatswood NSW 2067
Phone/Fax (02) 9415 2866

Nature's Sunshine Products (encapsulated herbs)
Unit 2, 360 Vardys Rd, Maryon NSW 2148
Phone (02) 9831 32233

Phyto Pharmaceuticals (Tea-tree products)
1 Liverpool St, Ingleburn NSW 2565
Phone (02) 9605 2244   Fax (02) 9618 2278

Springfields (Essential oils)
Unit 2/2 Anella Ave, Castle Hill NSW 2154
Phone (02) 9894 9933   Fax (02) 9894 0199

QUEENSLAND

Cospak Queensland Pty Ltd (Bottles & jars)
PO Box 989, Archerfield QLD 4108
Phone (07) 3274 3833   Fax (07) 3274 3112

David Craig & Co (Beeswax & pharmaceuticals)
PO Box 117, Salisbury, Brisbane QLD 4107
Phone (07) 3277 1518   Fax (07) 3277 9124

Greenridge Botanicals (Herbal extracts)
PO Box 1197, Toowoomba QLD 4350
Phone (07) 6331 203

Kewlex Pty Ltd (Essential & aromatherapy oils)
23 O'Connel Tce, Bowen Hills QLD 4006
Phone (07) 3257 3788

SOUTH AUSTRALIA

Brauer Biotherapies (Homeopathics)
1 Para Road, PO Box 234, Tanunda SA 5352
Phone (08) 8563 2932   Fax (08) 8563 3395

Cosmetic Components Pty Ltd (Containers)
17 Mengel Court, Salisbury South SA
Phone (08) 8285 7288   Fax (08) 8285 7299

VICTORIA

Auroma (Essential oils, emulsifying waxes, preservatives, dried herbs etc.)
39 Melverton Drive, Hallam VIC 3803
Phone (03) 9796 4833   Fax (03) 9796 4966

Essential Therapeutics
53–60 Easy St, Collingwood VIC 3066
Phone (03) 9419 7711

In Essence (Essential oils),
3 Abbott St, Fairfield VIC 3463
Phone (03) 9486 9688   Fax (03) 9486 9388

Southern Light Herbs (Organic dried herbs)
PO Box 227, Maldon VIC 3463
Phone (03) 5475 2763   Fax (03) 5475 1477

The Pharmaceutical Plant Company,
Unit 2, 24 London Drive, Bayswater VIC 3153
Phone (03) 9762 3777   Fax (03) 9762 9992

WESTERN AUSTRALIA

Compac (Bottles & jars)
108 Radium St, Welshpool WA 6106
Phone (08) 9350 6700   Fax (08) 9350 6699

Fitch's Pharmacy (Homeopathics and tinctures)
731 Hay Street, Perth WA 6000
Phone (08) 9321 6411   Fax (08) 9321 1920

Olfactory Sensations (Donna Arthur School of Aromatherapy, (Essential oils, raw materials, preservatives etc.)
PO Box 420, South Perth WA 6151
Phone (08) 9470 9770   Fax (08) 9470 9766

Potions Bodycare (Essential oils, creams, preservatives, raw materials etc.)
Suite G, 554 Newcastle St, Perth WA 6000
Phone (08) 9227 9722   Fax (08) 9227 9744

Silverlocks (Bottles & jars)
Lot 228, Catalano Rd., Canning Vale WA 6155
Phone (08) 9455 1366

Usher Pharmacy (Fred Kraeter), (cetomacrogol emulsifying wax and other pharmaceuticals. Fred will mail Australia wide.)
Bunbury WA 6230
Phone (08) 9795 7631